Protecting Your Financial Future

The Inside Story on Wills, Living Trusts, Probate, Estate Taxes, and Asset Protection

Third Edition

Lee & Kristy Phillips

Foreword by Theodore J. Provenza

LegaLees Corporation
556 East 1400 South, Orem, UT 84097

Protecting Your Financial Future
by Lee R. Phillips and Kristy S. Phillips

Publisher's Cataloging-in-Publication
(Provided by Quality Books, Inc.)

Phillips, Lee R.
Protecting your financial future : the inside story on wills, living trusts, probate, estate taxes, and asset protection / Lee & Kristy Phillips ; foreword by Theodore J. Provenza. -- 3rd ed.
p. cm.
Includes index
Preassigned LCCN: 98-67786
ISBN: 0-9648965-3-2

1. Estate planning--United States--Popular works. 2. Wills--United States--Popular works. 3. Living trusts--United States--Popular works. 4. Inheritance and transfer tax--Law and legislation--United States--Popular works. I. Phillips, Kristy S. II. Title

KF750.Z9P554 1999 346.7305'2
QBI98-1171

This book is dedicated to our parents who kept us from literally being homeless when the legal system attacked us.

The system can leave anyone homeless even though they do absolutely nothing wrong.
An accident, an illness, a divorce, a wayward child, a death, or even a mistake in a government computer can wipe out everything for a family.

It doesn't have to be that way.

Acknowledgments:

We have received help and encouragement from Kathy Wilde, Candy Salisbury, and Ron Speirs who read an early draft of the book and wouldn't let us stop until the book was published.

Contents

Foreword

by Theodore J. Provenza

Certified Estate Planner

A baby is God's opinion that life should go on.
Robert Frost

The millennium made it official: the future is here and the future is now. And, that future will soon belong to our children . . . they are our legacy and our destiny. Thus, it is doubly important that we give our children every opportunity to make appropriate life choices based on the wealth that we have worked so hard to achieve in our lifetime. The decisions we make today will affect the quality of life for future generations, so take action and get your estate plan in order. This is one of the best gifts you can give your loved ones.

Good News!

You do not have to read this book, especially if you don't care what happens to your estate. If you — along with 60% of the people in the United States — have not developed your own estate plan, don't sweat it. The good news is one already exists for you and your family. It has been crafted by your Federal and state government who take what they want first and then determine where the rest will go and who will get it. And, once the government and the legal system become involved, your heirs will be subject to the highest taxes imposed on the American taxpayer through estate taxes as well as probate and legal fees.

Bad News!

Imagine your children receiving less than 25% of your intended wealth because of poor planning that led to excessive estate taxes and unnecessary legal, probate and accounting fees. Think of it, the majority of everything that you have worked for in your life — and even what your parents and grandparents have worked for in their lives — slipping through your children's fingers because of improper arrangements and a lack of knowledge and planning. The awesome truth is that estate taxes can approach 55%. Taxes on leftover IRA's can exceed 72%. With additional probate and attorney fees, as well as state income taxes, your heirs may consider themselves lucky to receive 25% of your estate.

The Really Good News!

With proper planning, estate taxes can be substantially reduced and in a lot of cases, zeroed out. You can choose to create a cohesive, seamless strategy that will insure that your wealth remains with your family and goes where YOU want it to go.

Protecting Your Financial Future

This book gives you enough information about what your options are so that when you begin planning your estate, you will have an idea of what can be done, empowering you to be able to talk more intelligently with the advisors you select in helping you implement your plan. Your challenge will be to assemble a team of professional advisors which should include a Certified Public Accountant (CPA), an Estate Planning Attorney, a Registered Investment Advisor, and a Certified Estate Planner (CEP) working together while putting aside their own agenda, to maximize the net distributable assets to your heirs.

I have read this book cover-to-cover and, more importantly, I know Lee and Kristy Phillips personally. As a Certified Estate Planner in Maryland, I was impressed by the simple and complete way my colleagues explained the various options of estate planning available to every American. I was equally impressed with how they detailed the adverse and harmful effects of doing nothing, which is a choice you could choose to make.

This book is a work of love and devotion, fashioned from Lee's own real-life experiences facing death. From their shared encounters with doctors, lawyers, and bureaucrats, they created a must-read book for anyone interested in constructing the best way to transfer the maximum amount of their wealth to the next generation. This book deals with the issues of mortality and estate planning in an easily understood and practical fashion. Read this book . . . it will detail for you how your monies will be distributed if you fail to plan, or can be distributed if you choose to plan.

In my years of experience as a Certified Estate Planner, I have found that the average person will not want to read this book and not want to do anything to plan his or her own estate. Death and taxes are not sexy topics for discussion, let alone consideration. Many are not ready to face their own mortality. It is often said that nothing is more certain than death and taxes. The fact is, one is more certain than the other. Indifference falls into the three deadly sins of non-estate planning.

Deadly Sin #1: Doing Nothing

This leaves it up to the state and Federal government to probate your estate. Sadly, your heirs will find that the government quickly grabs up a large share. The final score will be: government 3, heirs 1. When your heirs receive only 25% of your total wealth, that will be a terrible waste of your hard work and sacrifices.

Deadly Sin #2: Procrastinating

By putting off thoughtful, comprehensive research into estate planning, you are waiting until your mortality becomes imminent and your options decrease. The paradox is that if you are alive and coherent enough to consider your estate planning options, you probably won't. If you are waiting for a life threatening experience to create an interest, it might be too late. You must be mentally competent to exercise your estate planning options. Unlike the author, Lee Phillips, not everyone returns from a face-to-face meeting with mortality. Even if you are lucky enough to survive, you may be too exhausted in money and energy to properly address the issues and options or not be of sound mind and body to effect a plan.

Deadly Sin #3: Taking a Sporadic Approach

This is a hit-and-run approach that involves contacting an attorney here, a CPA there, or an investment advisor somewhere else, with no overall strategy or plan. The result will be counterproductive and chaotic, with one document detailing one concern, and another document espousing yet another concern, often counteracting each other. The overall effect will be confusion, anger and a lot of wasted time, energy, and money. The negative side effect will be the additional fees and taxes paid to lawyers, courts and government offices in an attempt, by your heirs, to sort out the layers of legal papers and documents.

Take an Active Approach

Our ultimate goal is to provide you with the best possible estate planning strategy to enable your family to benefit from the wealth you have created. This requires a five-part logical approach.

1. Assess your current resources
2. Look at your needs
3. Evaluate your options and strategies for your current AND future needs
4. Develop a plan to transfer wealth with a minimum of taxes and delays
5. Provide assistance to your heirs in managing your estate when the time comes

If you have read this far, proceed on. I will help you however I can. Don't let geographical obstacles get in your way. Phone calls, e-mail, and even airfare are cheap. You can reach me at 1.800.521.7070 or visit my website at www.mycep.com.

Theodore J. Provenza
Certified Estate Planner

Introduction

Your Guarantee

Attorneys don't make a lot of guarantees, but I'll make you an unconditional guarantee. In this book you are actually going to learn how to use a living revocable trust, durable power of attorney, living will, regular testamentary will, pour-over will, and other powerful legal tools. You will also learn how to slash or eliminate estate taxes; protect your home from lawsuits; avoid probate; save on income taxes; avoid legal battles; use lawyers, not be used by lawyers; and implement lots of other money related strategies. But there is something that will someday be more important to you.

If you learn the lessons of law I will detail in this book, if you do the things I talk about, and if you actually use the tools of law you learn about in this book, I guarantee it will be worth every effort you make just for the sheer peace of mind you will obtain.

It doesn't matter whether you are male or female, married or single, rich or poor, young or old. The lessons you learn here will pay huge monetary and emotional dividends, sooner than you think. They can change your life. They can make you happy. They can make you wealthy.

Early in my legal career I prepared a will and living revocable trust for a close friend's widowed mother. It took me many days of coaxing and counseling as a friend to get her mother to the point where we actually put the will and trust in place. We detailed exactly what she wanted so that she was comfortable with the legal work. Several months after this tedious process was completed, my friend came to me and asked, "What did you talk to my mother about? What did you tell her? Why is she a totally different person?" Those questions took me by surprise. I didn't know how to answer them. I didn't understand then, but I understand now. It's called peace of mind. Peace of mind may well be the most important ingredient necessary to assure you a happy life.

My friend's mother wasn't rich. She only had a small home and some personal possessions. Even though she wasn't wealthy, she had been worried sick for ten years, ever since her husband had died, about what would happen to her property if she went into a rest home or died. She was afraid that the kids would lose money in probate. She had worried, wondering whether or not the children would fight over the property. She wanted the kids to receive everything she could possibly give them, and she didn't want the kids to fight. When we prepared the trust and will, we took our time and did everything just the way she wanted it done. She understood how the trust worked and what would happen when she became sick or died. All of the fears and worries left, and she was happy again—after ten long years since her husband had died.

Whether you will admit it to yourself or not, you worry about the same things she did, and you have the same fears. There is absolutely no need to worry or be afraid, once you understand and know the principles of law I am going to walk you through. You have to know these things for yourself because just going to a lawyer often doesn't relieve the worries and fear. In fact, when you see a lawyer, your concerns may actually be compounded, because many lawyers prey upon your fears and lack of knowledge. This is unfortunate, but true.

Yes, I am a lawyer, but don't hold that against me. Because I understand you, I am different from most lawyers. I learned law the hard way—on the street, not in a law firm. There isn't anything that you are going to learn about here that I haven't personally experienced. During one period—one long period—in my life, the legal system almost destroyed me, and there wasn't anything I could do about it, even though I was a lawyer.

Life isn't what you expect. I wasn't supposed to be the kind of lawyer that writes trusts. I was supposed to be a patent attorney.

Chapter 1

My Tragedy

Lessons To Learn

Kristy and I were high school sweethearts. We waited a long time, or at least it seemed like forever, until we got married. We waited to get married until a few days after I turned 20, so that we wouldn't both be teenagers.

I had a scholarship and our parents helped us, so I could stay in school. Yes, we were poor. We lived in basement apartments, worked odd hours, ate stuff we wouldn't think of eating now, and didn't even know we got married in the middle of a huge recession. We just knew things were tough, and we didn't have a lot of money. The baby slept in a dresser drawer, and we drove a Volkswagen. We saved our pennies so we could buy a house someday.

After five years of college, I graduated with a bachelor's degree in geology. I had worked a couple of summers for the oil companies and decided geology, although a great topic to study, wasn't a very good way to make a living. Geologists are always out in the field looking at rocks, and I wanted to be home with my wife and son. So I applied to enter a master's degree program in chemistry. Having had a total of only one undergraduate chemistry course, I was miraculously accepted into the master's program, and they even gave me a scholarship. Ultimately, I took a path that led me to a master's degree in nuclear analytical chemistry.

Halfway through the master's program, I decided that law school looked good. With all of my science training and a law degree, I could become an oil and gas attorney, practice environmental law or be a patent attorney. Even if I didn't practice law as an attorney, I could do a better job running the little analytical chemistry laboratory business I had established with one of the chemistry professors.

I took the LSAT (the get-into-law school test) on a whim, and nobody was more shocked than I was when I passed the test. Actually, I didn't just pass the test, I killed the test. I was accepted at every prestigious law school I applied to. (Yes, I only applied to one, Brigham Young University.) The only problem was, I was only half way through the master's degree program in chemistry.

When I went to the first day of law school, the dean made the students swear that they would spend all their time studying for law school, wouldn't work any outside jobs, would never see their families, would be scared to death of the law professors, and wouldn't even think of anything but the law during their first year. I said yes. I lied. I was a full-time chemistry master's student in addition to being a full-time law student.

When I went to law school, my father-in-law came unglued. He was positive that I had no intention of ever getting out of school and supporting his daughter and our then two children. The evidence definitely was in his favor.

My master's thesis was ultimately recognized as the most outstanding piece of science work in a master's program at the university that year. No, I didn't make law review. That means I *was not* in the top 10% of my law class, but I was hanging in there with the bottom 90% of the class.

Graduation day came in chemistry and then later in law. I was so happy to graduate from law school. Law school was such a miserable experience that it totally cured me of all desires I might have had to ever take another college class. So many of the law students were arrogant and deceitful. A lot of the teachers in law school didn't teach law. They played this game where you tried to guess the answer to their question. The problem is, there wasn't any one right answer to the question, and they never even told you what answer they were thinking about. Lawyers call this game "logic."

Things in science *are* logical. Science is great. You can figure out the answer by using logic. You can then prove that the answer is correct on paper or you can physically do an experiment to see if the answer is correct. In law, everything is run on what I call the "Lunch Theory of Justice." The answer to a question in law depends upon what the judge eats for lunch.

After law school I got a job as a patent attorney. It was a good job. Patent attorneys make about 1.5 times as much money as the other attorneys. I was actually making money. This was great. A year earlier we had finally saved enough money for a down payment on a house, and with our parents' help as co-signers on the loan, we bought a little house in the nice part of town. One day driving to work, I remember thinking that life was too easy after school. I thought, "OK, life can't be this easy. When is the other shoe going to drop—something has to go wrong." My patent attorney career lasted less than 90 days, and ten long hard years of college education became meaningless one winter morning.

It was mid-January 1982, and I had been sick since at least Thanksgiving. I had gotten progressively sicker for months. My back was killing me all of the time. I was sure I had blown a disk doing yard work in the fall. Every morning I would almost throw up because I was nauseated. Even though I was always sick to my stomach, I was still eating lots. I was eating everything in sight, yet losing weight. I was honestly convinced I was feeding a giant tape worm or something. I had lost 15 pounds. No, don't laugh. I had weighed 123 pounds (5'9" tall) for the prior 8 years. Not 125 or 120, the weight was 123 pounds, and I was now at 108. Simple tasks like taking out the garbage became major chores.

I would go to work, come home, and collapse on the couch. Kristy started accusing me of being lazy. I didn't know what to think. Surely it was just that I wasn't exercising enough; if I exercised I would have more energy. Maybe all I needed was more vitamins or something.

One Sunday night, I was having chest pains. Kristy called our good friends Mary and Leland. Leland was one of the local cardiologists. We lived up on a hill in town and in the two blocks around our house lived 38 medical doctors; so they called the hill "Pill Hill." Kristy explained the situation to Mary, and I was immediately invited to come over so that Leland could check things out.

Leland got me on the couch in his study, and he listened, thumped, poked, jabbed and did other scientific medical procedures. He spent over a half hour just asking me questions. He was taking a history. He told me that the history is the most valuable diagnostic tool a doctor has in his bag of tricks.

LESSON #1—ONLY USE A PROFESSIONAL THAT CARES

If your doctor, lawyer, accountant, architect, carpenter, real estate agent, or any other advisor doesn't really care what you think and doesn't ask you what you think, you had better get a new advisor.

On the way out down the big entry hall, Leland stopped me, and I remember very plainly that he said, "You know, Lee, any time someone has a serious health problem and he is hospitalized, if he can recover his health and live any type of a normal life, he is extremely blessed." I didn't think too much about the statement, because it surely didn't apply to me. I wasn't having a heart attack. Leland had just told me I wasn't having a heart attack. He told me all of my health problems were related to one source. He insisted that I not even make an appointment, but just show up at the urologists' office at 8:00 a.m. the next day, tell them there was an emergency, and I had to be seen. A year later, Mary related to Kristy that my friend Leland went into the bedroom and cried after I left their home that night.

I followed Leland's instructions and showed up in the urologists' office at 8:00 a.m. The urologists made me wait until about 11:30 a.m. before they would see me. The urology clinic had been treating me for almost a year. They said I had an infection that was very stubborn. Three of the urologists poked me, laughed at me, said I was a hypochondriac and chided me saying that if I was having chest pains, I was sure dumb to come to a urology clinic. They impatiently counseled me to rush to my cardiology friend and have him treat me.

I drove to Leland's office and his secretary got him on the phone at the hospital. I related my experiences of the morning, and he simply said, "I will reserve a bed for you at the hospital. You check yourself in before 9:00 p.m. tonight, and I will run some tests tomorrow."

The next day I was strapped on the x-ray machine. Kristy was in the control room with all of the radiologists. Five of them lived by us, and they were good friends. I noticed that they took Kristy out of the room. The tests continued. The radioactive dyes made me throw up. By 10:00 a.m. it was established that one kidney was totally nonfunctional, and the other was barely functioning. This was a urology problem.

By noon I was totally radioactive. I glowed in the dark. I had been poked from every end and in the middle. I was vomiting. Leland was at my bedside. He told me that I had a tumor around my left kidney—a huge tumor that x-rays showed to be nearly 8 inches in diameter. It was so big that it was crowding my heart, and my heart was having a hard time.

My immediate response was, "Well, can they take it out?" Leland explained that I had cancer—very advanced cancer! The cancer was everywhere. My back hurt because of the tumors on my spine. My stomach wasn't working because the cancer was making me sick. The cancer was in its final stage. There was no way to surgically remove it from my body. The consensus was that I would die, maybe within two weeks, or that I might last up to three months.

That kind of news ruins your whole day!

I was only 27 years old. Although we had never had a lot of money, my marriage was a fairy tale romance. We had three small children that would now grow up without a father. This couldn't be happening. There must be a mistake. But there was no mistake.

A year earlier, my family doctor had diagnosed a lump I had found as cancer. He had sent me to the urology specialist, because he suspected that I had testicular cancer. The family doctor had advised the urologist of his diagnosis. The urologist didn't take a history, didn't run a test, didn't do anything but make fun of me and the family doctor, because I obviously had an infection in my epididymis, not testicular cancer. All he would have had to do was give me a simple blood test, and he would have found the cancer. He did nothing. I saw him several times before I saw Leland. Each time, he laughingly told me all was well, and he did nothing.

I trusted the urologist. I blindly trusted, and as it appeared, it had obviously cost me my life.

Lesson #2—Don't Blindly Trust

You can't blindly trust your doctor, lawyer, accountant, stock broker, real estate agent, or anyone else. Check them out, and check up on what they do or do not do.

If I had only known all the urologist had to do to detect my type of cancer was poke my finger and give me a blood test, I would have said "Hey, come on, doc. Here's my finger. Let's go. Check it out!" But I had just trusted him.

I told Leland that I didn't trust the urologists any more, and I asked if he could help me. Leland saved my life. He saw to it that my treatment was conducted at a university hospital and that each research team around the nation that specialized in testicular cancer had input into my treatment. Testicular cancer was then, and probably still is, the leading cause of cancer death in males ages 20 to 40 years. It is relatively easy to treat, but not in an extremely advanced stage like mine was. My case became a national cause, as it were, in cancer treatment.

I wasn't just sick. This was a major battle—the kind of battle the doctors still talk about a decade later. There were 53 treating doctors and what seemed like hundreds of consulting doctors across the United States. The treatment was wicked. Twenty percent of the people they had tried it on died from the treatment. Chemotherapy is bad, but this wasn't your normal chemotherapy.

During the first five months of treatment, I was continuously at the university hospital. I never even knew winter and spring had come and gone. The first six weeks I was basically in a coma. At times I was blind. Between the cancer and the chemotherapy, my body had given up and pretty much totally shut down, but I wasn't ready to die. The pain associated with massive body organ failure is extreme. My daily morphine dose was almost double what the handbooks state is a lethal dose for a healthy body. Special drugs were flown across the country in the middle of the night. State-of-the-art technology was used to keep me alive. On several occasions Kristy was called to the hospital to say good-bye for the final time.

When I was released, nearly 6 months later, to the care of my home town hospital, the home town technicians at the hospital had no idea what some of the equipment poking out of my body was even supposed to do.

You have probably read about people who have such great willpower and desire that they run marathons while they are on chemotherapy. Willpower and desire may have something to do with their ability to run a marathon, but their abilities mostly depend upon the types and doses of chemotherapy they are given. When I got through with chemotherapy, I was an 80-pound pile of bones that lay motionless in the fetal position. I wasn't running anywhere. I couldn't even walk.

The complete story of my ordeal and the ordeal that my family went through is another full book or a movie. The medical experience was incredible. The personal love story with Kristy is touching. A majority of spouses faced with what she faced simply divorce. Only one conclusion can be reached. I was very blessed.

I now live a normal life, and it is a good life. But, it is a life so different from the life I had dreamed of living.

As the medical system worked on my body, the legal system worked over my financial life. I had done everything exactly right, but everything went wrong.

The IRS assessed taxes, an obscene amount of taxes, against my little chemistry company. The taxes were assessed for a period beginning a year before I had even founded the business or gone into chemistry. Living in another city where the university hospital was, Kristy naturally missed one of the ten-day notices the IRS sent to our home. One day she wrote a check at the store and the check bounced. She later discovered that the IRS had closed all of our business accounts, had closed all of our personal accounts, and had put a lien on our home. A year and a half later they finally gave everything back, simply stating that they had made a mistake. They paid interest on the money they had wrongfully taken, but because we didn't have any money to operate with, we lost our business. We couldn't fulfill our contracts, so the companies we had contracted with were suing. Kristy had been through hell, but it was OK—the IRS gave the money back. The IRS had no further responsibility.

I was a lawyer. I hadn't done anything wrong. Yet, I was at the mercy of the legal system. I learned the value of a good lawyer.

LESSON #3—GOOD LAWYERS COST LESS THAN BAD LAWYERS

A good lawyer is worth his weight in gold, and a good lawyer doesn't cost much more than a bad lawyer. In fact, the real cost of a good lawyer is always much less than the real cost of a bad lawyer.

Unless you know the basics of the law, you are at the mercy of the lawyers, because you don't know whether or not the lawyer is doing a good job for you. This is not a book about how to bash the IRS or lawyers. You are going to learn to use the law—not gray law, but nice black letter law. (That means there is no question in everybody's view that it is 100% legal.) Using the laws, you can control your income taxes, avoid estate taxes, protect against IRS seizures, avoid probate, and avoid other legal disasters of life. All you have to do is know enough law to keep your counselor in check. Use the law. The legal system is the most powerful system we have in America today.

You can't bury your head in the sand and hope that the legal system will leave you alone. The United States is graduating so many lawyers today, that in order to eat, they have to sue anything that moves. If you are dead already, you can stop reading now. If you are alive, you must be moving, and that makes you a prime target for the lawyers.

When I got through being sick and got to the point that I could work again, there was no job. I tried everything I could do to get another job, but with a statistical life expectancy of a year, I wasn't prime meat for law firms or anybody else. The social workers and psychologists who were assigned to work with me compassionately counseled me. After nearly a hundred job rejections, they told me I would have to work for myself.

I opened a little one-room law office in town. Actually, my good neighbor, who was an insurance agent, said he had an extra office, and he gave me a deal on the rent. Because there aren't a lot of people needing nuclear chemistry patents who walk in off the street, I had a problem. I had to practice some kind of law other than patent law.

One of the girls who had been in my law school class said she would help me learn how to write wills. Because everybody needs a will, lawyers make their bread and butter writing wills. But I had no idea how to write a will. They certainly don't teach you in law school, even if you take the wills and probate class, which I had done. She tried the best she could, but she didn't know how to write wills either, even though she had an impressive legal position and had taken the class. Together we went to the form books to find a will, but after doing that, I still wasn't satisfied.

My friend assured me that most lawyers just go to the form books and get what they want. As long as the form fits at least some of the client's needs, that is supposed to be good enough.

Many attorneys really don't know what the form says or why certain words are used, and it is an absolute surety that the client doesn't know. I didn't buy that philosophy. I wanted to know what the words meant and why they were there. The form books didn't tell me, and very few lawyers knew. One law professor took some time to answer some of my stupid questions. He shared with me a big picture—a picture most lawyers never see.

Chapter

2

The Big Picture

Controlling Your Wealth

In this book I'll show you the big picture and explain the little things to you. I'll answer the questions it took me years to answer. I'll show you that living revocable trusts and wills are not things to be afraid of. They are just pieces of paper, but these simple pieces of paper give you great power. They let you transfer property when you die, and they allow you to make your everyday life go smoothly. Living revocable trusts are actually easy to understand and use.

Books on living revocable trusts generally start with horror stories, usually about celebrities, where the probate system totally obliterated everything these people had worked for during their lives. The scare factor is so powerful that you immediately think your hair and teeth will fall out if you don't go to your attorney and get a living revocable trust tomorrow. The books rarely even start to give you the big picture. You need to see the big picture. I'll have to expose you to probate from every angle. If you're going to avoid probate using a living revocable trust, you have got to know what probate is and how it traps people. Probate is a trap, and you don't have to be a celebrity or be rich to get caught.

I have dozens of tragic stories about normal, everyday clients who have come through my office. These people aren't famous or super rich; they are just ordinary people. They all fit into a big picture. You fit into a big picture.

After writing wills and trusts for a year or so, I became disgusted with the legal system. People would bring me reams of papers that a lawyer had "fixed" for them. They had paid $2000, $3000, $5000, $10,000 and more for their papers, and they had no idea what the papers were. They had never saved any money on taxes. They had not avoided probate when Dad died, and all their dealings with the legal system had been disasters.

Your Estate is Never Too Small

A middle-aged man came into my office one morning. His eyes were red. He had obviously been crying. We had never met, but he said he had been assured by one of his friends that I could help him. He sat down at the desk and said, "Gramps died this morning." He then produced a bunch of papers. He waved the papers in my face, exclaiming that they were Gramps' living revocable trust. He proudly stated that Gramps' family wouldn't have to go through probate. But his voice had a question in it.

I asked if the trust were "funded." "Oh, yes," he assured me. When Gramps was dying, someone had told them that the trust had to be funded, and they had called the attorney who drafted the trust. The attorney had agreed that the trust should be funded and told them the exact wording Gramps needed to use in order to fund the trust. The man then produced for me a piece of paper with the magic words. The paper had written on it, "I hereby fund my trust with ten dollars and other good and valuable consideration," signed "Gramps." Chapter 12 is dedicated to teaching you how to properly fund your living revocable trust.

No, the story about Gramps isn't a story about a famous celebrity or a rich man. Gramps was not rich. In fact, he was relatively poor. However, Gramps had paid a lot of money, an amount of money that could be measured as a small percentage of his net worth, for the supposed trust. The trust itself was legally inadequate. The piece of paper "funding" the trust was a total joke. The family went through probate, and Gramps had wasted his money and time.

You are wasting your money if you get a bad trust or if your trust isn't properly funded. That means your trust has to be written right, and it has to **own** your bank accounts, stocks, bonds, boats, house, real estate, and all of your other property.

You Can Get a Good Trust— Many People Don't

A trust is one of the most powerful tools an attorney has in his bag of tricks. Yet they are seldom correctly used, and most attorneys really don't know much about them. *Fortune Magazine* had an article on trusts in its February 25, 1991, issue. The article made the statement that only 1% of American lawyers can properly write a living revocable trust. Whether the number is 1% or not, your chances of getting a well-written trust, if you just walk blindly into an attorney's office, aren't good.

If you walk into the attorney's office and say, "Hi, here I am. I need a living revocable trust. Set me up." What is the attorney going to do? The attorney is going to set you up! That is what you just asked him to do.

The attorney will go to the form book and pull out a form. If it isn't exactly what you want, fine. He will get some language out of another form. People bring me trusts and wills that have language in them that obviously comes from a corporation form, a limited partnership form, or some other form. I am always amazed.

Even if you have a living revocable trust, you also need a will, which must be tailored to interface with your trust. So you not only need to know how to operate a living revocable trust, but also how to use wills. Living revocable trust advocates make you feel like a fool, or worse, if you even entertain the idea of having a will. Don't be intimidated. The will is a necessary legal tool. You will learn to use it. In fact, you may not need a living revocable trust. You may only need a will.

The Law Destroys Lives and Kills

Simply planning to use your living revocable trust to pass property to your heirs after you die isn't enough. I'm sure you would agree that, from a medical standpoint, there are things worse than death. Well, the same is true legally. If a family member becomes sick or has an accident which renders him legally incompetent, i.e., he can't handle his own financial, social, and legal affairs, it is critical that you keep the legal system in check. Otherwise, the emotional and financial strain put on you will be disastrous.

It is clearly obvious that a physical accident or illness can destroy lives and kill. It is much less obvious that the legal system can destroy lives and kill. The physical effects of a lawsuit, bankruptcy, probate or custody battle are just as destructive to the lives involved as a major medical problem. The legal destruction from an auto accident may not be as immediate as the medical destruction, but over the long term, it can result in a total destruction of your life and directly result in death.

Legal Tragedies Are Preventable

Unlike medical tragedies which strike unexpectedly when there isn't really any way of preventing illness or accident, most legal tragedies can be almost totally prevented, or at least their damage can be controlled or eliminated. There is no reason to worry whether your son or daughter will receive the property you want to leave them. When a family member dies, there is no reason to lose the family fortune (big or small) to lawyers or taxes. There is no reason to let a frivolous lawsuit or business failure destroy your life, cost you your marriage, or make your children live in poverty. But, you can't blindly trust a lawyer on the street to do all of the legal planning for you, and the lawyer certainly cannot maintain your legal security. It is up to you to secure your property and your peace of mind. That is exactly what we will teach you to do in this book.

Create Wealth For Yourself

Trusts have been traditionally known as the tools of the wealthy. Only the Kennedys, Rockefellers, Hearsts, Carnegies, Gettys, and other wealthy people used trusts in the past. Laws were established to favor the wealthy families, and those laws still exist today. I work with many wealthy people. I also work with a lot of people who are just normal folks who aren't really wealthy, but who still use the legal "tools of wealth" to make their lives a whole lot easier. There is absolutely no reason you can't use these tools also. The biggest mistake you will ever make is to take the attitude that says, "I don't have enough wealth to worry about." That attitude will cause you to fail in your financial life.

Now is the time to put your financial and legal life in order. You may not have much wealth, but you can't build a financial fortune from the roof down. You have to build the foundation first. The foundation is the legal work this book teaches you to do. You can't wait until you are rich to do this work.

As I have worked with clients over the years, I have seen that when they use trusts and other tools of wealth, they are actually repositioning their lives onto a different stage. I have never met a wealthy person who doesn't understand and use the legal tools of wealth. When you understand and use the legal system to your advantage, every aspect of your life will be enlightened. If you walk into the bank to open up a new account and you ask to have a trust account, the banker is going to treat you with a little more respect. You aren't just the average Joe off the street at that point. You must have money, or at least that is the message you give the banker when you ask for a trust account, whether you have money or not.

Statistics show that more and more people are slipping into poverty in the United States. The gap between the rich and the poor is widening. The good old middle class is disappearing. They are being beaten to death by government regulations, taxes, and lawyers. The only way to fight back against government regulations, taxes and lawyers is to know and use the laws—the same laws that are being used against you.

In the big picture, living revocable trusts are used not only to transfer property at death and thereby avoid probate costs, but also to protect you against legal disasters that accompany a family member's physical or mental incompetency. They can assure your family some estate tax protection and help assure that your children inherit what you want to leave to them, when you want to leave it to them. They can even protect people from their own financial follies.

Too many people go through life falling into one legal trap after another. For example, they lose their parents' estate—the money they would have inherited—to probate. Maybe there's a divorce. Maybe there's a business investment that turns into a legal problem, not just a bad investment. If you know about the legal system, you can avoid the legal traps. It's really very easy. Once you know what the traps look like, you can just walk out and around them. If you can avoid just one or two of these traps during your lifetime, it will mean the difference between retiring and being able to do anything you want or retiring broke on Social Security.

Chapter

3

When Life Meets Death

Be Prepared

Legal planning for life is just as important as legal planning for death. Planning isn't something just paranoid or morbid people do. Your plans for living have to interface with the plans you have for your estate at death. At some point, life meets death.

Jim flew a little airplane. He had a very nice Cessna and loved to fly to Southern California to enjoy the beach life. One trip proved fatal. The plane crashed, and though Jim was badly burned, he was still alive. He had done very well financially, but when the plane hit the ground, it became painfully obvious that he had failed to fulfill a moral obligation he had to his family. He was a great trial lawyer, but he had never learned to use four powerful legal tools: (1) the living revocable trust, (2) the will, (3) the durable power of attorney, and (4) the living will.

After the plane crash, Jim's wife and children were in the hospital by his side as much as possible. However, their attentions were not totally on his medical care and emotional support.

Their attentions were drawn away by the army of lawyers that continually marched in and out of the hospital room.

These lawyers, Jim's friends, directed the family activities. The family wasn't in charge of the activities. Each family member was repeatedly dispatched from the hospital to locate files, deeds, investment papers, insurance policies, journals and other papers needed to put together the developing estate plan for Jim. Thousands and thousands of dollars in legal fees were expended in a single day. An emergency court order was sought to allow his wife to try to move assets to a living revocable trust. The secretaries at the law firm worked at a fever pitch to produce the paperwork for the court orders and living revocable trust.

The family was not able to control Jim's medical care either. Doctors directed his treatment, and they gave the lawyers and the family orders. At one point, Jim's wife objected to the medical treatment. A conference was held with some of the doctors, the lawyers, and his wife. Part of the discussion centered on the family's right to direct the doctors and to access medical records. The hospital asked for a durable power of attorney for health care. There was no such paper. Jim had never signed one. Basically, because no written orders existed, the family gave up their efforts to direct the doctors, and the hospital went ahead with their plans.

The pain Jim was suffering must have been incredible. He really wasn't "with it" most of the time. He would call for his family often. Sometimes they were there; sometimes they weren't there because unfinished business had taken precedence.

Draw yourself back from the scene in his hospital room, and view the scene from a distance. Who is supposed to be in the hospital room the last few hours? What is supposed to happen as life meets death? As Jim slipped into a coma and life left, there was no calm, tender good-bye from his family.

Legal Tools to Plan With

Sooner or later, each one of us will be a participant in the scene where life meets death. Is it worth planning now so that you can have the scene unfold quietly and peacefully? Planning for life and death is a duty you owe your family—your loved ones.

Your plan for life includes protecting yourself and your family from the legal problems associated with a catastrophic illness or accident. This is done by using a durable power of attorney, a durable power of attorney for health care, and a living will. The durable power of attorney allows someone you appoint to manage your daily affairs when you can't manage them for yourself. The durable power of attorney for health care allows someone you appoint to oversee your medical treatment. The living will is the document that expresses your desires to the doctors, telling them when to back off and let you die. Each of these documents works in conjunction with your living revocable trust and testamentary will. Note that the living will is very different from the testamentary will, which disposes of your property after your death. These three documents will be discussed in Chapters 6 and 14.

Your plan for life must also include some contingencies to preserve enough wealth to survive a lawsuit or bankruptcy, which could be totally devastating absent prior planning. "Asset protection" is the term used to describe the techniques you can use to protect your property from legal problems that will occur during your life and threaten your financial security. Throughout this book I will give you "Asset Protection Tips" which are easy to implement and could save your financial life. More complicated techniques, such as the use of 2503 trusts, family limited partnerships, corporations, and other legal tools are discussed in another book I have written. The simple techniques given in the Asset Protection Tips will teach you how to avoid a lot of grief and put up an asset protection shield.

Of course, the living revocable trust and will form the basic foundation of your plan for death. Although the children's trust and the family limited partnership can have a huge influence on what happens at a death and can play a critical part in any death planning, most families don't need to use those tools. If they are needed, you will use one or both of them in addition to the will and living revocable trust. The term "death planning" sounds morbid, but when your plan is done properly and you understand it, your life can be lived with a much greater degree of satisfaction and peace. Death planning is often called "estate planning." Actually, estate planning includes both life planning and death planning.

Because over the past twenty years life insurance salesmen have renamed themselves estate planners, most people equate estate planning with life insurance sales. In this book we will call planning for death "estate planning" and use the term "plan for life" to refer to planning done to ward off problems associated with income taxes, lawsuits, incompetencies, catastrophic health care, and legal quagmires in general.

Using Insurance Wisely

There is no question, insurance plays a major part in both your plan for life and your estate plan. Handling insurance is a fine art. Kristy and I have learned a lot of insurance lessons the hard way. We made it through the first 10 years of our marriage without carrying any life insurance. We had always carried health insurance, but it seemed like the insurance companies always weaseled out of their responsibilities to pay when we got sick.

When our son was three and had his tonsils out, we were starving students. We never thought twice about the insurance. We had purchased the policy in January, and the boy had been totally healthy all spring, all summer, and then he had his tonsils go bad in the late fall. Certainly his tonsillitis wasn't a preexisting condition.

The insurance company didn't pay. Unknown to us, the pediatrician 11 months earlier had simply written down that our son appeared to have inflamed tonsils. He had been given an antibiotic, and everything was fine. The insurance company saw the word "tonsils" in his record, and therefore, anything to do with tonsils was absolutely, unquestionably a preexisting condition.

We also got burned by our homeowner's insurance. We had spent $800 on a hand calculator. We didn't really have $800 to spend on calculators, but the calculator helped me compete in school and qualify for scholarships, so we justified the expense. More powerful calculators cost $29 today, but that was back when calculators were competing with slide rules. The calculator was stolen.

The insurance company sent an adjuster out to see us, and he casually asked how we made money to live on. I fed us and paid the rent by grading papers for professors. The insurance adjuster pointed out that a calculator like mine must make grading papers a lot easier. I agreed. It was a trap! Because "the calculator was business equipment which wasn't covered under our policy," the insurance company never paid.

When my cancer struck, we had a health insurance policy. For long-term patients like me, the hospitals billed at the end of each month. Between February 21 and March 1, I managed to run up about $11,000 in hospital bills at the local hospital. Our insurance company paid the first bill, less deductible.

When the insurance company got the next bill from the University Hospital, it was for a full month. The bill dwarfed the mortgage on our house. In today's dollars, I was running up a bill of about $3,000 per day. The insurance company refused to pay. They figured that there had to be some way they could get out of paying the bill. I had only had the insurance for about 18 months. The insurance company was sure there was something in my past that would make my cancer a preexisting condition.

The insurance company interviewed every doctor I had ever seen. But, it didn't stop there. The company literally contacted every doctor in town. They interviewed every neighbor that lived within a radius of two blocks from my house. They interviewed the professors I'd had in college. No rock was left unturned. But, my condition did not exist when I took out the policy. I had been totally healthy prior to that, and the cancer didn't show up for months after I got the policy. Finally, the insurance company paid. There is one insurance company that wished they had never met me.

Having the insurance pay literally saved our lives. Had we not been insured, the stress of having such a massive debt would certainly have had a physical effect. Stress resulting from financial or legal problems has a direct effect on one's physical health. Simply to avoid stress is one major reason why it is so important that your family has the wills, living revocable trusts, and durable powers of attorney in place and they are actually being used. It is also important that you have insurance. At least have a home owner's policy, a health policy, and life insurance.

Even though insurance companies may seem so ruthless, they are a necessary evil. Maybe insurance companies really aren't so evil. Good insurance companies that appear to be ruthless may be simply making sure that their system isn't being abused. Actually, my attitude about insurance companies has changed over the years.

One day, about a year before I got sick, I shocked Kristy. I actually called the neighbor who sold life insurance and asked him to come over and sell me a life insurance policy. We had three children. I reasoned that it was time to stop being stupid and fulfill the responsibility I had to Kristy and the kids.

Later, when my cancer struck and I was told that I would die within a matter of weeks, I made two telephone calls. First, I called Kristy. Second, I called my neighbor and asked him to make sure my life insurance was in order. He cried when he heard my condition. He really cared. Lots of insurance agents do care, and they offer you a product which is vitally important. They aren't just trying to sucker you by selling you an insurance policy.

There weren't many bright spots in the nightmare that followed my diagnosis, but I hung onto the satisfaction that my family had a life insurance policy. Leaving a life insurance policy wasn't a big consolation for dying, but it was the only consolation I had. I can't overstate the hope the life insurance policy gave me. It gave me the hope that my family could go on, when I couldn't go on with them. Money—the life insurance—would make a huge difference in fulfillment of my last hopes for the family.

As I have dealt with death as an attorney, I have learned that there are many life insurance agents that are real professionals providing a valuable service and product. They deal with an emotional issue. Their sales techniques may sometimes come across poorly, but their products and services are very valuable, and what they are offering you is very cheap security for your family.

I had $250,000 of life insurance. Looking back, I can see that even a quarter of a million dollars wouldn't have seen my family through. Life would have been hard for them. Don't underestimate how much coverage you should carry.

In my new life after being sick, I have been very involved counseling families about their financial lives. From a purely financial perspective, I can say that there are many excellent insurance products that have incredible value as pure investments, independent of the life coverage. When you throw in the life insurance coverage, some of these products become an offer you can't refuse—or at least one you shouldn't refuse.

Health insurance, casualty insurance, and life insurance are all critically important in providing security and meeting your goals in both your plans for life and your estate plan.

Chapter

4

Three Vital Goals

Focusing Your Plan

In estate planning, there are three basic goals.

1. Pass property according to your desires.
2. Avoid probate.
3. Eliminate estate taxes.

Are those good goals? Let's discuss each of them in this chapter.

People have this amazing ability to mess up their estate planning. Most people don't even have a will. Even though they don't have a will, they may have an elaborate "plan." In their mind they have taken care of the bank account, based on the advice of the 19-year-old "cute" new accounts person. The new house deed is all ready, just the way the people did it on one of the daytime soaps. They aren't worried about estate taxes, because the life insurance salesman ran some computer program to figure everything out and sold them just the right amount of life insurance to cover everything for taxes and probate. Everything is "taken care of"! However, their plans are like card houses. They are easily destroyed by their own weight.

People haven't received good advice. They are afraid that they will be "set up" if they go to the lawyer, and they are sure that a trip to the lawyer will be an intimidating and expensive experience. So they go to great lengths to avoid the legal system.

There are a number of ways people try to circumvent the lawyer and probate. The most popular method of avoiding probate is to own property jointly with the person you want the property to go to when you die. The concept of joint ownership is certainly valid, and it accomplishes the goal in many situations, but in a huge number of other situations, joint ownership leads to total disaster. Joint ownership will be discussed in detail in this chapter.

Goal #1—Pass Property According to Your Desires

The first goal is to pass things according to your desires. That means if you want your son to have the house or the stock certificate after you die, you want to make sure he actually receives the property and nobody else gets the property. That sounds simple enough, doesn't it?

Four common actions you might take will almost always assure that your property passes to someone other than the person you wanted to receive the property.

These are:

1. You Do Nothing—You or your spouse never make out a will or trust. (This is actually a failure to take any specific action.)

2. The Second Marriage—You or your spouse are in your second marriage.

3. You Put Out a Contract—You or your spouse have entered into a contract that designates what will happen to specific property when you die. For example, you have designated a beneficiary in your life insurance policy, which is a contract.

4. A Joint Affair—You or your spouse own property jointly with one or more other people. This is the big mistake. Everybody does it.

Mistake #1—You Do Nothing And Die Intestate

Many people never take the time to make even a simple will. They die "intestate." Intestate means they die without a will, not that they die out of the state. The court proceeding necessary to distribute their property after they die is called an "intestacy proceeding."

The reasons people give for not making out a will are actually funny. For example, some people falsely believe that if they don't have a will, their family will be able to avoid all of the courts and lawyers because their estate will not have to go through probate when they die. So they intentionally avoid making out a will. Dying without a will guarantees a probate if the deceased person owned anything in his or her name alone.

Another reason many people don't make out a will is simple. People don't want to face the problem. There is always a fear of something which you don't fully understand. Wills and probate are seldom fully understood, and there is a negative emotion associated with both words, so people simply choose not to think about their own will or probate. Because you don't like to think of your own death, estate planning is hard.

Even if you can face the fact that you will die and that estate planning is an essential part of life, the decisions that have to be made in the estate planning process can be hard decisions. Who will raise the children after you are gone? Which one of the children will actually receive the prized family heirloom? Cutting through all of the talk and actually putting a name down in writing can be very hard. When you learn in the following chapters what your options are and what considerations should be taken into account, your decisions will be much easier to make.

Everyone Has a Will

In reality, everyone has a will. If you choose not to write your own will, or if the will you write is rejected by the probate court for some reason, the state you live in has written a will for you.

In the state's will, the state has first claim on all of your property to assure that your debts are paid and certain people are protected. The state's will often distributes your property to people other than those you wanted to receive your property. More or less, your property passes according to state law, not according to your desires. If you have your own will, the courts will use it instead of the state intestate will.

The laws vary a little from state to state. But when your state's intestate will is written in plain English, it basically reads as follows:

YOUR LAST WILL AND TESTAMENT

Because I don't really want to take the time or go to the expense of making out my own will, or if I messed up my attempt to make a will, I want the state to make a will for me. I understand and agree to the following terms:

ARTICLE I

The Court should figure out who my spouse is and who my children are. Please don't take anyone's word if they claim to be part of my family. Make them prove their relationship to me.

ARTICLE II

I give one half (1/2) of all my property and possessions to my spouse and the remaining one half (1/2) to my children.

ARTICLE III

I appoint my spouse, or if I am divorced, I appoint my ex-spouse, as guardian to my children. I don't trust my spouse or ex-spouse; so as a safeguard, I require them to report to the Probate Court each year and render a full accounting of how, why, when, and where they have spent any money necessary for the care of my children.

ARTICLE IV

As a further safeguard, I direct the Probate Court to secure a performance bond from my spouse, or whoever is acting as guardian to my children, to guarantee that they exercise proper judgment in handling, investing and spending my children's money. Because there is money to burn in my estate, I direct that the premium for the bond be paid out of my estate funds. I realize that I could waive the requirement for the bond, but I elect not to do so.

ARTICLE V

Even with the bond and accounting to the Probate Court, my children shall have the right, when they reach the age of eighteen (18), to demand a complete accounting from my spouse of all of the financial actions that have taken place with their money since I died.

ARTICLE VI

Should my spouse remarry, the new guy or gal shall be entitled to one half (1/2) of everything my spouse possesses. Should my children need some of my possessions that go to the new guy or gal, that is basically their problem. The property that goes to the new guy or gal is his/hers to do with as he/she wishes, even to the exclusion of my children.

ARTICLE VII

Should my spouse predecease me or die while any of my children are minors, I do not wish to exercise my right to nominate the guardian of my children. Rather than nominating a guardian of my preference, I direct my relatives and friends to get together and select a guardian by mutual agreement. I direct the Probate Court to make the final selection. If the Court wishes, it may appoint a stranger acceptable to the Court.

ARTICLE VIII

Under existing tax law, there are certain legitimate avenues open to me to lower death taxes. Since I prefer to have my money used for governmental purposes rather than for the benefit of my spouse and children, I direct that no effort be made to lower taxes, and the maximum amount exacted by law shall be paid to the State and Federal governments to use in the manner they see fit.

ARTICLE IX

In the event that all of my children predecease me, and my spouse survives me and subsequently dies without a will, it is my desire that all of my property of whatsoever nature which was passed to my spouse when I died, shall pass to my spouse's relatives and none shall pass to my relatives.

ARTICLE X

Should the state be unable to locate my relatives during the statutory period, I direct the state to liquidate my estate and add the money received to the state treasury to be used for whatever purpose the state sees fit.

ARTICLE XI

I know that I can name a person or institution to administer my estate, but I elect to have the Probate Court make a selection for me. I also know that if I name a person or institution to administer my estate, I can waive the expense of a Performance Bond, but I do not desire to make this waiver.

IN WITNESS THEREOF, I have read and fully understand the foregoing, agree to the consequences described, and wish to make this document public upon my death. I adopt this, by default, as my "Will."

No Signature Required
No Witness Required

This is basically the will you have if you haven't taken the time to do a will for yourself. Is this the one you want? Do something! Almost anything is better than nothing. Read on and you will know enough to decide for yourself exactly what you need, and you will learn exactly what to do.

Mistake #2—You Forget About Ex-Spouses and Remarriages

As my law practice started to grow after my illness, I came to understand just how disastrous a second marriage could be on a family that hadn't done any estate planning or even, to a lesser degree, a family that had a good estate plan. I was amazed at the number of clients who, when they finally brought in their insurance policy and read it with me, were shocked to realize that their hated ex-spouse was still the named beneficiary on the policy. The ex-spouse would get the money when they died! Insurance policies should obviously be changed after a divorce.

Often, Mom or Dad is widowed or divorced and then remarries. The marriage may come later in life for companionship. There is absolutely nothing wrong with that. That is great. The second marriage is blissful, and the two families even get along well. Assume it was Dad that died, and Mom has married the new guy. When Dad died, Mom didn't have any probate or legal hassles because everything was held in joint tenancy. Everything had worked so well when Dad died that when Mom remarried, she and the new guy merged their property. They put the new guy's name on her house, Mom's name on his cabin, and both names on the new checking account. Since they have married, Mom and the new guy have bought a new 18 foot ski boat and one of those $100,000 monster motor homes. Of course, all of the new purchases were made in both names.

Mom dies. She never made out a will. Everything works just as well as when Dad died. The new guy doesn't have to go through probate, and there aren't any legal hassles. He owns everything outright. It is all his. It is all his! The house—everything! He walks away with everything. Even the intestate laws cannot protect you. Everything was owned as joint tenants. (The discussion of joint tenancy is later in this chapter.)

The new guy rides off into the sunset with everything Mom and Dad had worked their whole lives to leave to you and your brothers and sisters, and there isn't anything you can do about it. Even if the new guy dies in the ambulance fifteen minutes after Mom dies at the scene of the auto accident, everything has passed to him, and it then goes to his children. Even if Mom and the new guy have been married for over 30 years, unless he has legally adopted you, you get nothing. Even if he considered you one of his children, the law does not recognize you as one of his children. If he doesn't actually have children of his own, then the property would pass to his heirs, such as his brothers and sisters.

In this case, both Mom and the new guy loved both sides of the family, and each would be horrified to realize what happened. Everything happens so innocently, but it happens over and over again.

Even a simple will would have prevented this situation. Yes, there would have been a probate, and you might have lost 5% or 15% of Mom and Dad's estate to the probate fees, but you would have maybe 90% of what Mom and Dad wanted you to receive. If Mom is on her second marriage, at least have Mom and the new guy each make out a will. A living revocable trust would pass 100% of your inheritance to you, and it would be better than the will; but the will is better than nothing.

Black Widows

Black widows trap their prey, and there isn't anything innocent about what they do. Black widows are real, and they aren't spiders. People who marry older people in order to obtain the older person's estate are called "black widows." If you have a great desire to smash black widows, you are not alone. A black widow lives in a little city near my office, and every couple who has come to me from this little city wants to make sure the black widow doesn't get anything if the wife should die first. I did a full living trust plan for the couple who lives next door to the black widow. The black widow is on her 5th marriage. No, she doesn't get divorced. The husband dies. Of course she gets all of his estate. She reportedly received over $1 million from husband #2, and several of my clients have been to her home, where she displays portraits of all four dead husbands and the one living husband, who you can bet is on the way down.

Congress passed a sweeping set of new tax laws that became effective in 1982. These laws have provided us with some incredible planning strategies using living revocable trusts. Applying these laws not only can save estate taxes, but also can be used very effectively to smash black widows. The variation on a living revocable trust that lets us battle black widows is called a Qualified Terminable Interest Property Trust (QTIP for short). When it is explained, nearly all of my clients want that type of living revocable trust. Yes, there are a number of variations on the basic living revocable trust concept, and we'll discuss them. However, before you jump into a living revocable trust, you need a good estate planning background to really use the living revocable trust. Trusts are no good if you don't know how to use them.

If there is a second marriage, in order to sort out his, hers and ours, as well as to smash black widows and keep everyone happy, the couple has to do specific estate planning to protect everyone's interests. Without such planning, everything will certainly get messed up sooner or later.

Mistake #3—You Don't Control Life Insurance, IRAs, Retirement Plans, and Other Contracts

Contracts can help achieve your goals of passing property to the right person, avoiding probate and eliminating estate taxes. However, putting out a contract very often proves to be fatal for your goals.

In the situation of a second marriage, one type of contract helps in your plan for life and even in estate planning. A "prenuptial" or "ante-nuptial" agreement is simply a contract between the two marriage partners, where they decide, by contract, whose property is whose. It is common to use these agreements in the second marriage situation. They help in estate planning, and they also help protect against the effects of a divorce if the marriage doesn't work out. Go ahead and use them. They may help, but they won't solve all of your problems. Donald Trump had his wife sign five different pre-nuptial agreements, and he learned that divorce is still an emotional and financial disaster.

The effects a contract has on your estate plan are often not adequately considered when the contract is drafted or when the estate plan is made. Contracts often mess up estate plans because they can move property to someone other than the person who was "supposed" to receive the property at a death. People often don't even stop to think that they are entering into a "contract" that will affect their estate plan when they sign their name on the bottom line.

Contracts are just written agreements that are within the protection of our society's laws. Transactions we don't really consider as "contracts" are certainly contracts under the law. Notes, insurance policies, leases, and sales agreements are all contracts. Thousands of situations are covered by contracts.

The law allows you to make out certain types of contracts which designate a beneficiary for the contract after you die. Life insurance is the classic example. Technically, pension plans and IRAs are not contracts (they are actually trusts), but for purposes of this discussion you should think of them as contracts. Life insurance, pension plans, and IRAs are examples of documents you sign that have a section entitled "beneficiaries." In the beneficiaries section, you designate the person(s) who will receive the benefit of the contract after you die. The first choice is usually the spouse, and the second choice is usually the children.

Documents that name beneficiaries circumvent your will and your trust every time, and it is true, they do avoid probate. A shrewd black widow or black widower doesn't really need to have the wills redone and alert the family. By using contracts and investment documents that name beneficiaries, and by making sure everything possible is held just right in joint ownership, entire estates can be swallowed up by a single black widow.

Contracts do not take the place of a good will and a good living revocable trust, so don't even think of avoiding estate planning by using contracts. The transfer of property, other than property like life insurance policies, using a contract is something our society doesn't like; so the laws are slanted against such transfers. In fact, most contracts cannot go around a will. This is especially true for real estate contracts. However, inasmuch as there are the exceptions like life insurance, pension plans, IRAs and others where the wills and trust are circumvented, be careful.

Think of the contracts and investments that you might have. Review how they address the death of one of the parties. I'm not surprised when one of my clients digs up the life insurance policy or IRA, and the paper openly states that the ex-spouse gets it all when the client dies. Don't unintentionally disinherit your loved ones by ignoring the effects of documents you have signed in the past.

Mistake #4—You Use Joint Ownership

Joint tenancy messes up a huge number of estates, divides families, creates tax nightmares, and is something everyone—almost everyone—uses without discretion. Joint tenancy is probably the most popular probate avoidance tool in the United States. All you have to do is simply own property "jointly" with another person, and you can avoid probate. If the property is owned as "joint tenants with rights of survivorship," then at the death of one of the owners, the other owner automatically owns the total piece of property. There isn't any probate at that time.

Lawyers sometimes refer to joint tenancy as a "poor man's will" or a "layman's will." Joint tenancy moves property at your death, and sometimes it actually goes to the person you want to receive it. But it can, and often does, totally mess up one or more of your three major estate planning goals. Property ends up being owned by the wrong people. Probate is only postponed—not avoided. Disastrous gift tax, estate tax and income tax problems are created when people try to plan using joint tenancy.

Joint tenancy is so frequently used and creates so many problems that I will discuss it in detail at this point in the book. Its effects will be further explained throughout the book.

Types of Property Ownership

First, a distinction has to be made between joint tenancy and other ways you can own property.

There are many different ways you can take title to property. Please note that "property" includes everything you own, such as bank accounts, cars, stock certificates, notes and, of course, real estate. How you "own" property determines whether or not there is a probate proceeding on the property when you die, who gets it when you die, how it can be taken away from you in a lawsuit, what happens to the property if you go into the hospital or a rest home, and how it is taxed during your lifetime and at your death.

Sole Ownership

The simplest form of property ownership is "sole ownership." You own the property. It is yours. It is subject to probate and estate taxes when you die. If you are sued, go bankrupt, or need government assistance in a hospital or rest home, you will probably lose the property.

Joint Tenancy with Rights of Survivorship

Owning something as "joint tenants with rights of survivorship" means that you own the property with one or more other people. Each joint tenant, by law, simultaneously owns 100% of the property. Everybody owns the same equal share. I recognize that it is impossible for each joint tenant to own 100% of the same property. The law doesn't have to be possible, logical, reasonable or anything else. The law is the law.

A distinguishing feature of joint tenancy is its automatic transfer of the property owned jointly to the survivor(s) when one joint tenant dies. When you die, your share automatically passes to the other owner(s). There is no probate at your death. A husband and wife often own property as joint tenants, and it works well between a husband and wife.

You must recognize that, although there isn't a probate when one owner dies, there will be a probate at the death of the second owner. (If there are more than two joint tenants, the probate proceeding will be necessary when the last joint tenant dies.) Your share of the property is included in your estate for estate tax calculations. If one of the joint tenants is sued or gets divorced, his share can be taken away, and the new owner of his share can sue to require the property to be sold. However, without a lawsuit, the property or any share of the property cannot be sold unless each joint tenant agrees and signs his or her name where necessary.

If any one of the joint tenants does not pay his taxes or has IRS problems in a business or any place else, the IRS has the right to take everyone's share of the property.

Yes, the property can't be sold without every one of the joint tenants agreeing, but any one of the joint tenants alone can mortgage the property or otherwise encumber it. It is always scary to have other people in a position where they can mortgage the property you feel that you own.

In many states, if a joint tenant leases the jointly-held land, the joint tenancy relationship is destroyed, and it becomes a "tenancy in common" relationship. This means that the property held in joint tenancy will no longer avoid probate when one owner dies. If he hasn't made out a will or living revocable trust, the deceased person's interest in the property will pass according to intestacy laws.

Tenants in Common

As "tenants in common," two or more people own the property in defined shares. The shares do not have to be equal. When one of the tenants in common dies, his share passes to his heirs, not to the other tenant(s) in common. If you own property as a tenant in common with someone, this can be a major problem for you, because instead of having only one other "partner" to make decisions with, you must now deal with his heirs. Unless the deceased tenant's share is actually held by a living revocable trust, not by the individual, his share will have to go through a probate proceeding to transfer it to his heirs. The value of the share will be included in his estate for estate tax purposes.

If one of the tenants in common is sued or gets divorced, his share can, of course, be taken away from him, and a new tenant (the person who successfully sued or the ex-spouse) gets the share. The new tenant can sell the share without permission from the other tenant(s) in common. Practically speaking, a single tenant in common is going to have a hard time selling only his share of the property, because buyers always want all of the ownership of the property. If the single tenant can't sell, the tenant can sue to have the whole property sold.

The IRS can usually only get to the actual share of the individual tenant in common that the IRS is after. That is an advantage over joint tenancy. But, who wants to be any type of "tenant" with the IRS?

Tenants by the Entirety

Tenancies by the entirety look, feel, walk, talk and act just like joint tenancies. They are a creation of the law to be used specifically by married people. They exist automatically in about 40 common law jurisdictions. They are not as easily disrupted as a joint tenancy. Depending upon which state you live in, you may own property with your spouse as tenants by the entirety. For purposes of this book, think of tenants by the entirety as being the same thing as joint tenants.

Joint Tenancy Disinherits Family Members

Now that you have been introduced to some of the different ways property can be "owned," the law of joint tenancy with rights of survivorship can be exposed. Millions of Americans will be "disinherited" because their mom and dad used joint tenancy.

In the section about second marriages, you saw how joint tenancy was innocently used to deprive you of all your parents' property. Even if Mom and Dad had made out wills, you still would be out in the cold. Joint tenancy takes precedence over a will, a trust, or a contract. If two people have their names on a bank account as joint tenants with rights of survivorship and one of them dies, the survivor owns the bank account. It is entirely possible that the deceased person had a will and wanted the bank account to go to someone else. The will has no power over the joint tenancy. The signature card at the bank, not the will, controls where the bank account goes and whether or not it will be probated. The same principle applies for joint tenant names on deeds, stock contracts, car titles, certificates of deposits, and all other types of ownership documents.

There is a 40-acre tract of land near the city where I live. Thirty years ago it was an orchard. Because Mom and Dad were scared to death of probate, they brought the oldest son in and put his name on the deed to the 40-acre orchard as a third joint tenant. Later Mom and Dad went down to the lawyer and had a will made out. The will clearly said that the 40 acres were to be divided into four equal shares. They had four children, and each was to receive an equal share. Mom died, and the oldest son, Dad and the other kids got along just great. Dad died, and the oldest son and his brother and sisters were fine. They got out the will, and everybody was happy, because according to the will they would each get an equal share. But, they didn't know how to "legally" make it so they each had their equal share. They all went back to the attorney who had drafted the will and simply asked, "How do we comply with the will and make it so that we each get our 1/4 share?"

The attorney studied the situation for about thirty seconds, turned to the oldest son and said, "Son, you own this piece of property. Your name is on the deed, and you are the surviving joint tenant." The lawyer then astutely pointed out that the 40-acre tract wasn't an orchard any more. It was the local shopping mall, and the property was worth millions of dollars.

The lawyer even gave the oldest son his excuse for keeping the property. The lawyer explained that when the son gave his brother and sisters their shares, it would be a gift from him, and the gift would trigger millions of dollars in gift taxes, which he would have to pay. Today, the oldest son is a multimillionaire. His brother is a professor at a university, and his two sisters are both divorced and struggle financially. Is that what Mom and Dad wanted for their 40 acres?

Joint Tenancy Only Postpones Probate

Joint tenancy only postpones probate for your family. You and your spouse probably own your house, the contents of your safe deposit box, your bank accounts, and other property as joint tenants. When one of you dies, there won't be any problem. The bank accounts won't be closed. The safe deposit box won't be sealed, and the survivor will live in the house just like always.

The transition of full ownership to the survivor will be smooth, automatic, and instantaneous. However, when the survivor (you or your spouse) dies, everything will need to be probated. The children will not have access to the bank account or the safe deposit box without a probate order. (Probate will be fully discussed in Chapter 7, and you will understand all about probate orders.) The entire estate of both you and your spouse will be subjected to probate after you are both dead.

Yes, after one spouse dies, the surviving spouse could put another person's name on the bank account, safe deposit box and deed to the house. Putting someone else's name on the property will avoid probate at the death of the surviving spouse. Right? That is true, but if you and your spouse die together in the auto crash, there won't be time to put another person's name on the property. So, it is logical that you put the name of one of the kids on the bank account or deed right now. But then we are back to the same problem Mom and Dad had with their 40-acre orchard/mall. Some people get around that problem easily. They put all of the kids' names on the property as joint tenants and when the surviving spouse dies, there certainly isn't any probate. This is a trap! Don't do it! It is a disaster!

Keep all of your kids' names off all your property. Kids are like yogurt—you never know when they are going to go bad! Even if they don't go bad, one could go bankrupt, be sued, or have an ugly divorce, and your property would be affected. Keep everybody's name off your property. Do you understand? Can I be any more clear? It is a No-No.

If Your Attorney Didn't See Your Deed, You're In Trouble

When you had your will made out, your attorney never demanded to see the deed to your 40 acres, the signature card for the checking account, the stock certificates, the deed to the house, or anything else. As a result, right now you probably have no idea how your property will actually be distributed when you die. A joint tenancy on an ownership document that goes with your property is all controlling. The joint tenancy will transfer the property, at your death, to whomever has their name on the ownership document with you. It doesn't matter what your will or your living revocable trust says about the piece of property. The property is gone!

When you use your living revocable trust, you will have to get all the deeds, all signature cards, and all other ownership documents and change them. After reading this book, you can make the changes required with no problem.

The Surviving Joint Tenant Needs To Do Some Paperwork

The transfer of ownership may be instantaneous, and technically it is automatic, but some paperwork may still have to be done by Dad when Mom dies. To remove Mom's name from the property deed and the bank account, Dad will have to file an "Affidavit of Survivorship" at the recorder's office and bank. A sample of an affidavit of survivorship is in Scroll 4.1 (next page). Some counties and states also require Dad to sign an Affidavit of Domicile which simply verifies the city, county and state where Dad is a resident. Of course, Dad will also need to file a copy of the death certificate.

Dad should actually remove Mom's name from all of the ownership documents, such as the house deed. Otherwise, at Dad's death you may end up opening a probate proceeding not only for Dad's estate, but Mom's estate also. That could be a doubly disastrous loss of money, time and control.

Joint Tenancy Causes You To Lose Control of Your Property

When you put someone's name on a deed, stock certificate, checking account, or other property ownership document, you lose full control over the property. If your son's name is on your checking account, your son can draw all of the money out and spend it however he wishes.

I have worked with several families where one or more of the children's names were put on the deed to the family home. The children grew up in the house, and it is much more than a pile of boards, cement and nails to the children, even though they are grown now. Mom and Dad want to sell the home and move into a condominium, so they can enjoy life without worrying about yards and house maintenance. The house cannot be sold without the signature of each person who has his name on the deed. One or more of the children want the house to stay in the family, and they refuse to sign the transfer deed. Without suing their own child, Mom and Dad are powerless to sell the house. They have lost control.

AFFIDAVIT

Death of a Joint Tenant

I, John H. Doe, of legal age being first duly sworn depose and say that Mary A. Doe, the decedent, mentioned in the attached certificate of death is the same person as the Mary A. Doe named as one of the grantees in that certain warranty deed recorded in the office records of Washoe County, State of Nevada, as Entry No. 55 in Book 26 at Page 125, to wit:

(Official Legal Description of the Property)

____
John H. Doe

State of Nevada)
: ss
County of Washoe)

BEFORE ME, the undersigned, a Notary Public in and for said County and State, personally appeared John H. Doe, personally known to me or proved to me on the basis of satisfactory evidence to be the person whose name is subscribed to the within instrument and acknowledged to me that he executed the same in his authorized capacity, and that, by his signature on the instrument, the person executed the instrument.

SUBSCRIBED AND SWORN TO before me the 1st day of September, 1997.

WITNESS my hand and official seal.

____
Notary Public in and for said County and State

Scroll 4.1—Affidavit of Survivorship

The In-Laws and Out-Laws

Joint tenancy relationships with your children can cost you your home, even though that is the last thing any of your children would want.

Your son is a great kid. He only has one major problem. He chases women. In fact, he is fast and catches one of them. When he gets married, it is a joyous occasion. However, in half of such cases, your son will later get divorced.

Divorce is wicked, and it can strike the heart of your house, not just the heart of your family. If the son's name is on the deed to your house, he *owns* an interest in that house. His wife knows that his name is on the deed to your house. His interest in your house will necessarily have to be claimed as one of the assets to be divided up by the divorce court. It isn't uncommon in a divorce decree to see the divorce court give all interests in real property to the wife. Your ex-daughter-in-law, the outlaw, now owns an interest in your house.

It doesn't matter how distraught your son is, he can't do anything about the situation. The ex can walk in any day she wants with a court order demanding the sale of the house, so that she can "cash in" her interest in the property. You either sell the house or buy out her interest in your own house.

Variations on divorce and joint tenancy problems are very common and particularly disastrous for families with large pieces of agricultural property or small businesses. Beware.

The IRS and the Laws

The IRS has the capability of confiscating the entire piece of property held in joint tenancy in order to satisfy the IRS debts of any one of the joint tenants. Even though your daughter is a great girl, it happens.

Julie was the best kid ever. Being the baby of the family, she was still single. If Dad and Mom died, they wanted the house to go to her, because all of the other kids were married, had their own houses, and were doing great. Dad had Julie's name put on the deed.

Julie was the totally responsible type, and she got a job at the local elderly care home. She started as the receptionist. Before long she was in charge of the payroll and was doing all of the books. It was great, because she wanted to go into accounting anyway.

The corporation that owned the care center was owned by a couple of men who were shrewd businessmen, and they had vast fortunes. Things weren't going well financially for the care center, and the owners told Julie to go ahead and pay the payroll. They promised they would pay the payroll taxes and all of the income taxes out of their own accounts. It never happened. They bankrupted the corporation. The two fat cat owners were smart enough to distance themselves from the problems, and they were "gone" by the time the bankruptcy hit the fan. The law says that Julie was 100% personally responsible to see to it that the taxes were paid. The IRS ultimately forced the sale of Dad and Mom's house, which had Julie's name on the deed, to satisfy the care center taxes.

Do you put your kid's name on the deed to your house?

ASSET PROTECTION TIP #1

Joint ownership leads to asset protection problems. If one of the joint tenants is sued, requires extended medical care, has a business that goes bankrupt, or gets in trouble in any one of 10,000 ways, the property in which he has a joint interest will be threatened. Of course, don't use joint tenancy with any third party as an estate planning tool just to avoid probate.

Evaluate how you own property with your spouse. If your wife is an obstetrician or has started a little business that has a chance of getting sued or going bankrupt (that includes all businesses), her name probably shouldn't be on the deed to the house. Note that if only the husband's name is on the house deed and the bank account, those properties will be protected, to some degree, if the wife gets sued. But, because only the husband's name is on those properties, they will have to be probated when the husband dies. Because this probate problem is easily solved by using a living revocable trust, don't worry about the probate potential. Worry about losing the house before you die.

Common Ownership Creates Gift Tax Problems

When someone's name is put on the deed or the stock certificate, the interest that he receives in the property as a joint tenant is actually a gift to him from the person(s) whose name was already on the property ownership documents. When Mom puts the son's name on the deed after Dad dies, she is gifting the son half of the house. If the house is worth $100,000, then she has just given the son $50,000. With any gift or aggregate of gifts given in any tax year and valued over the "annual exclusion" amount, there is a serious gift tax consequence.

The gift tax exclusion amount is the magic value of property that can be gifted without having any gift tax considerations. In 1998, the magic amount is $10,000. The "Taxpayer Relief Act of 1997" is going to start raising the annual exclusion amount to match cost-of-living increases. However, increases will only be made in $1,000 jumps, so it will be at least 2001 before the incremental cost of living increases reach a total of $1000 and there is any change in the magic $10,000 number.

Until the jump in the annual exclusion amount, you can give anyone up to $10,000 in gifts during a calendar year, and there is no income tax, gift tax, or estate tax consequence to you or to the person to whom you gave the gifts. If a gift or accumulation of gifts you give to someone in a tax year is worth over the annual exclusion amount, the IRS requires a gift tax return, Form 709, to be filed.

Yes, you and your spouse can each give the same person $10,000 in a year and there won't be a gift tax. However, if a couple is giving someone over $10,000, they will have to file a gift tax return showing that $10,000 came from one spouse and the rest of the gift came from the other spouse. They have to establish that a "split gift" was given.

Otherwise, the IRS will later try to say that the entire gift came from only one spouse and assess a gift tax. So, with a split gift, a married couple can give another person $20,000 without any tax consequence.

Most people ignore gift tax considerations, even though gift tax laws are serious laws with big teeth. If Mom is like most people, she never files the return when the son's name is put on the deed, and as a result, the IRS is mad at dear sweet Mom.

If a "gift" has already been triggered by putting someone's name on the property as a joint tenant, you can't just take the person's name off of the property and call everything even for the IRS. The IRS doesn't call it even; in fact, they have it in their head that you made a gift when you put the name on the property, and then when the person took his name off the property, he was making a gift back to you. So the gift tax is assessed when the person's name goes on the property, and then another gift tax is assessed when the person takes his name off the property. Great, isn't it? Don't you just love the IRS? Bless their hearts.

In about half of the judicial districts in the United States, the courts have defended Mom in this type of situation, and the judges say that the IRS can't get away with this double gift type thing. They have held that Mom made a mistake and was just trying to avoid probate. The court says Mom was stupid, and she really wanted a trust. So they say the property was put in trust, not gifted to the son. This doesn't make sense, does it? Remember, the law doesn't have to make sense. Be happy! The judge is helping out Mom in his district. In the other half of the districts, the courts leave Mom to be chewed on by the IRS. She has broken the law when she didn't file a gift tax return.

If your family is in a gift tax trap like I have just described, there are basically two options. First, you can ignore the whole thing, take the name(s) off the deed, and hope it goes away. In a majority of cases, the IRS never figures out that the gift took place. The IRS simply doesn't have the manpower to police everything. However, the IRS is becoming very good with a computer, and in the next decade their manpower may not go up, but their effective ability to police your actions is going to get a whole lot better.

Second, you can, and probably should, seek the advice of a good accountant or lawyer to help you figure out some way to gingerly back out of the trap that you got yourself into.

In Chapter 19, we will discuss gift taxes in detail, because they mix intimately with estate taxes.

Joint Tenancy Can Be An Income Tax Tragedy

It is a little painful to talk about income taxes, but so many people get burned by income taxes when they use joint tenancy, that it is worth the pain to talk about it here. The biggest tax disasters occur with real estate, because it is usually the most valuable thing that a family has to pass on to another generation.

Assume your Dad is single, whether by death or divorce, and he puts your name on the deed to the rental unit as a joint tenant, so that it won't have to be probated when he dies. Just like the case of the 40 acres of land that is now the shopping mall, because your name is on the deed, you will totally own the rental unit when Dad dies. Dad's other children, your brothers and sisters, will not have any claim to the rental property, even if his will or trust says otherwise.

Maybe Dad really wants you to receive the rental unit. The joint tenancy arrangement will work. You will get the property, and it won't be probated. The transfer of the property will go smoothly, but the tax road will be very rocky. Remember, when Dad put your name on the deed, he "gave" you half interest in the rental unit. Not only is there a gift tax problem, but there is also an income tax problem if Dad sells the rental or you sell the rental after Dad dies.

It works like this. Assume Dad paid $50,000 for the rental unit when he bought it 20 years ago. The $50,000 is considered the "basis" of the property. Assume the unit is worth $200,000 in today's market. If Dad sells the unit, there is a profit of $150,000. (For simplicity, ignore the costs, expenses, capital gains treatment, etc.) Because your name is on the deed as half owner, half of the profit, $75,000, will have to be claimed as income on your tax return, and the other half of the profit will be claimed on Dad's tax return. It may be a disaster to you when

Dad sells the unit because he really isn't going to give you $75,000, or $100,000, which is actually your half of the sales price. He intends to use all of the proceeds to retire on and sail the Caribbean. How are you supposed to pay the income tax on the $75,000 profit the IRS is going to pin on you? That hurts!

Instead of selling the unit while Dad is alive, assume Dad dies. At his death, he owns a half interest in the rental unit, and you own the other half interest.

His half interest will be included in his estate for estate tax calculations. Basically, everything Dad "owns" will be included in his estate for estate tax calculations. Estate taxes will be discussed in detail in Chapter 19, but for now, it is enough to simply know that if Dad owns less than a specific amount, which the IRS calls the "exemption equivalent," there won't be any federal estate tax. Under the "Taxpayer Relief Act of 1997" (it should really be called the Tax Confusion Act), the exemption equivalent will gradually rise from $600,000 in 1997 to $1 million in 2006. Appendix 1 is a chart which shows the exemption equivalent scale between 1997 and 2006. As the law now stands, an estate tax return won't even have to be filed with the IRS if Dad's estate value is under the exemption equivalent.

No, an estate tax return won't even have to be filed for Dad, but technically, the IRS will tax all of Dad's property at his death. That sounds strange because nothing has to be done, and nothing will be owed in taxes. There won't be any tax to be paid because Dad's total property value was under the exemption equivalent amount. (Remember "property" is everything, not just real estate.) The IRS is really nice because it gives everyone a "credit" for the tax that should be assessed on the exemption equivalent amount of property they own. The value of the "credit" that is used to offset the tax assessed against the exemption equivalent amount is shown in Appendix 1. Note that the exemption equivalent amount and the corresponding "credit" increase each year. Because the property will be "taxed" in Dad's estate, the IRS will allow it to have a "stepped-up basis" after it is "taxed."

When the dust clears after Dad's death, Dad's half interest ($100,000) in the rental unit was included in the exemption equivalent amount he got to pass in his estate "tax free." His half interest in the rental unit took a new basis (a step-up in basis) of $100,000, because the property was "taxed" in his estate at that value when he died. That means you could sell the rental unit the day after Dad dies and the profit is not $150,000 any more. It is only $75,000 total, because the basis is now $100,000 which represents Dad's half interest after estate taxes, plus $25,000 which is your share of half the original purchase price, or the basis of your half interest.

So, the unit was sold the week after Dad died, and you only had $75,000 in profit to put on your income taxes. If Dad's half of the unit hadn't gotten a step-up in basis, your profit would have been $150,000. You saved income tax on Dad's share which got a step-up in basis, but you still had to pay income taxes on the $75,000 profit from your half share. That just cost you about $20,000-$25,000 in income taxes when all is said and done.

Consider how you could save yourself from having to claim $75,000 in income. The mistake was having Dad put your name on the deed. If Dad had "kept" the unit, he would have owned it all when he died. The full $200,000 value would have been "taxed" in his estate when he died. If his total estate was worth less than the exemption equivalent amount (see Appendix 1), then there wouldn't be any estate tax due at the time of his death. Additionally, the rental unit would have a stepped-up basis to the value of $200,000, which is the value "taxed" in Dad's estate. Now, you sell the unit for $200,000 the week after Dad dies, and you have zero profit. Nothing to report as income! What did that just save? $25,000!

If Dad's estate is over the exemption equivalent amount, it is still a bad idea to have Dad put your name on the deed. In fact, you could end up paying a gift or estate tax plus the income tax on the $75,000 profit. This will be explained fully in Chapter 19.

All you need to know is you don't want to put your kids' names on your deeds, and you don't want your name on Dad's deed. The same goes for all real estate, stock certificates, bonds, or any "property." Even if the property has to be probated at Dad's death, it's still usually cheaper than the potential tax consequences. Of course, the probate problems can be eliminated by using a living revocable trust. Because a living revocable trust can effectively double the exemption equivalent amount for a family, it will eliminate the estate tax problems for many families.

Sue, Sue, Sue—Joint Tenancy Lawsuits

Something as simple as a bad business deal or a fender bender on the street can result in a big time lawsuit that can take your house. Even a catastrophic illness which is totally unpreventable and unpredictable can take your house. If you cause the accident or get sick, you might expect your house to be lost or at least threatened.

What you don't expect is to lose your house because your son or daughter has the accident or gets sick. That is exactly what can and does happen if the child's name is on the deed as a joint owner of the house.

John was a contractor, and the housing market collapsed in his part of the country. He declared bankruptcy. The bankruptcy court sold his parents' home to help pay the debt, because his name was on the deed to his parents' home. In this case, Mom and Dad got to keep the portion of the proceeds that represented their stake in the joint tenancy relationship, but they lost their home.

ASSET PROTECTION TIP #2

Cars cause trouble. The owner of the car is always a target in any lawsuit that results from the use of the car. The owner always gets sued even if he or she wasn't in the car when the accident occurred. Never have two names on the title to a car. Have the husband own the car he drives most of the time and have the wife own the car she drives most often.

If you have to help one of your kids by throwing your financial weight behind them when they go to get a car loan, don't put your name on the title to the car. Simply sign the loan as "guarantor." Secure your interest in the car by having the child sign a note saying they will pay you back. You can get a copy of a note to use at the local office supply or stationery store. To protect your interest, you should file a security interest on the title to the car.

Solve The Incompetency Problem

The discussion of joint tenancy has centered on problems caused at the death of one of the joint tenants, but joint tenancy causes problems even before somebody dies.

You will be incompetent 90 days prior to your death. No, don't laugh. That is the statistic. It does happen. In fact, I have already had my 90 days. When I was being treated with heavy duty chemotherapy, there were weeks at a time when I was totally out of it. Kristy was faced with some major legal problems, in addition to my critical medical problems.

Legal problems, such as probate, caused by a death can be dwarfed by the legal problems caused by someone who doesn't die, but lives on as an incompetent. The cases you read about in the newspapers, where a family spends years in court trying to get permission to unplug the respirator and remove the feeding tubes, are real. The problems you will face when a family member becomes incompetent will, hopefully, not be of that magnitude, but they can be devastating.

Grandfather had an unmarried sister, and in about 1985 we went to see her at Christmas. She was well, and everything was fine. Two weeks later the family called me and said, "Lee, come quick, she's dying!" I went to the hospital and found that she had, in a matter of two weeks, deteriorated to a little pile of bones lying in a hospital bed. I looked at her, and I knew for certain that she was dying.

In order to facilitate my great aunt's affairs, five or six years earlier, she had cooked up a deal with her niece. They had gone to the bank, the insurance company, and the title office, and had the niece's name placed on all of the ownership documents as a joint tenant with our aunt. Now, the niece had been companion, daughter, everything to our aunt. The niece had paid all of the bills, filed the taxes, and taken care of all business matters for our aunt. As we looked at our aunt in the hospital bed, I turned to the niece and asked if our aunt had a will. The niece produced a will which had been written a number of years earlier by a lawyer friend of our aunt. The will said that grandfather (her brother) was to receive half of all of her property, and the niece was to receive the other half of the property and all personal items.

I then asked the second question. This is the question your attorney should ask you or should have asked you when you made out your will. "May I see the signature card for the bank account, the deed to the house, and the title to the car?" When the niece produced these ownership documents, I quietly looked at them and saw that the niece's name was on everything as a joint tenant. I handed everything back to the niece and said, "Don't tell grandfather that there is even a will." The niece immediately responded, "Grandfather needs to know, because he gets half of the property."

I explained to the niece that because her name was on everything as a joint tenant with our aunt, she owned everything at the aunt's death. There wasn't any need to tell grandfather and hurt his feelings, because he wouldn't receive any property anyway. Because our aunt didn't really have much and grandfather was self-sufficient, it wasn't a huge tragedy.

Even if we had wanted to sue the niece, which we didn't, it would have been useless, because as you know by now, the joint tenancy automatically transfers all property, independent of what the will might say.

The story of my great aunt isn't finished yet. She did not die in the hospital. In fact, she lived for almost 8 years after she left the hospital. She lived in a rest home, and she had no idea who she was. When you went to see her, she would call you by the name of one of her brothers who had been dead for at least 40 years. She lived in the world she lived in when she was 8 or 9 years old.

When we put her in the rest home, the rest home told us to "liquidate" her estate and buy her all of the tangible, personal items that she would need for the rest of her life. Basically, we were spending her money so that the government would then help pay the rest home bill. We were buying things that the government would not pay for, so that she could have the best life possible. However, you will remember that the niece was to receive half of everything when our aunt died, according to the will, and because everything was in joint tenancy, she would actually receive everything when our aunt died.

As the lawyer, I faced a very delicate situation. Without the niece's signature we couldn't sell anything. Obviously the niece would not sign any of the joint ownership documents because she wanted the property. The only way we could get the niece to sign, without her cooperation, was to sue her.

No, we didn't sue the niece, but we did go to court. The niece was more than pleased to do anything necessary to help out our aunt. However, our aunt couldn't sign. She didn't even know who she was, and her name was on all of the ownership documents. She had to sign.

A family faced with this type of situation often spends thousands of dollars and many weeks fighting the court battle to have someone appointed as "guardian" and/or "conservator."

A "guardian" is the court appointed person who has responsibility for the physical body and welfare of a minor or incompetent. A "conservator" is the court appointed person who manages the money belonging to a minor or an incompetent. The guardian and conservator are often the same person, but it is possible to have one person act as guardian while another person acts as conservator.

From the experience with my great aunt, you can see how joint tenancy ownership disinherited Grandpa. Additionally, the experience demonstrates how any joint relationship, including tenancy in common or tenancy by the entirety, causes big problems when one of the joint owners cannot legally sign for himself.

Of course, when you envision someone in the position where he can't handle his own affairs, you envision someone old and withered in a rest home, like my great aunt. Visit the rest homes. Many patients aren't old, but their bodies and minds have been spent tragically by an accident or illness.

Lawyers, even estate planning lawyers, often forget to protect their clients from the legal tragedies that come during life when a family member lives and doesn't die. It isn't easy to solve many of the legal problems that occur when someone loses his ability to manage his own legal affairs. The last thing you want to do is go to court when a family member has an accident or gets sick. Chapter 14 will walk you through exactly what needs to be done.

Question How You Own Property

You should now know more about owning property. Don't just passively let the banker or real estate agent dictate the way you own your property. How many of the kids' names do you put on the deed? NONE! Although joint ownership is certainly a valid way of owning property, ownership by a living revocable trust will bring many advantages, and some disadvantages, but everyone should have the option of owning property in his trust. Be patient, the discussion of the living revocable trust will come in due time. But, you need to understand the full picture, because the trust doesn't automatically solve all of the problems. You have to pilot the trust around all of the legal pitfalls you are learning about.

Second Goal—Avoid Probate

Joint tenancy is only one way of avoiding probate. There are lots of ways to avoid probate. The living revocable trust is the most flexible probate avoidance tool. However, it is the least used, because most people think that the trust is just something rich people use, and they rationalize that they "don't have enough to worry about." That type of rationalizing is totally wrong. There are many tactics people can use to avoid probate, but most of them end up causing a lot of grief.

Joint Tenancy Can Avoid Probate

Joint tenancy with rights of survivorship only postpones probate, and as you have seen, it can lead to many disasters. Its primary function and the reason it is used is to avoid probate, and it doesn't even do that in the long run. Yet, even with all of its problems, it is by far the most commonly used probate avoidance tool.

POD Accounts—A Way Banks Avoid Probate

"Pay on death" (POD) accounts were designed by the banking industry to get around probate. They are a special type of bank savings account. You have to make a special request at the bank to get a POD account. Probate can be a major problem and expense for a bank when one of its account holders dies. The "pay on death" account simply is a contract with the bank that says when the account holder (one party to the contract) dies, the bank (the second party to the contract) will transfer the POD account at the bank to whomever is designated in the contract. No probate! It works.

The person who is named as the person who is to receive the account (the "beneficiary") doesn't have his name "on the account." That means there isn't a "gift" when money is put in the account, and the account isn't exposed to the divorce, lawsuits, tax liabilities, or other problems of the beneficiary. This avoids some of the problems of joint tenancy. The account will be taxed in your estate if you establish a POD account.

One of the biggest problems with the POD account occurs when the beneficiary dies before the person who established the account. The account is then most often paid to the beneficiary's estate. This dumps the account into a probate proceeding. If you establish a POD account and the beneficiary dies before you do, you can simply close the account or change the named beneficiary to another person. Sometimes this is impossible (you are in the same accident as the beneficiary), and probate cannot be avoided.

Another problem occurs when the beneficiary is an incompetent or minor. Someone will have to be appointed as conservator before the bank will release the POD account.

Dresser Drawer Deeds—Don't Use Them

Your Dad and Mom announced to the family that the house won't be probated when they die. No, they didn't put any names on the deed as joint tenants. What they did was make out a deed with your name on it. The deed is signed, dated, notarized, and put in the top drawer of the dresser, so that you can get it when they die and take it down to have it recorded. Does it work? Did you avoid probate? Yes—maybe.

Note that the house didn't pass through Dad and Mom's estate. It was a "gift" to you on the date the deed was signed. They didn't file a gift tax return. You get stuck with the original basis. You pay income tax on the "profit" when it is sold. Does all of this sound familiar? It is just like the gift when they put your name on the deed as a joint tenant. However, they didn't lose control, and the house isn't exposed to your lawsuits, divorces, illness, etc., because you don't have the deed, and nobody knows it is in the dresser drawer.

But, there is another problem. Anyone who wants to can challenge the whole scheme of the dresser drawer deed. It is easy. All you need to know are the elements of a deed. A deed must be in writing. It must include the names of the grantor and grantee, a description of the consideration given, a description of the property to be conveyed, and the words of grant or transfer. The grantor has to be competent, can't be acting under "undue influence," and has to sign the deed. Additionally, a deed is not valid until the deed is delivered to the grantee. The problem is: Dad and Mom never intended to "deliver" the deed. When you went and "got" the deed out of the dresser drawer after they died, that was not delivery. The deed is invalid! Don't use "dresser drawer deeds."

Gifting—The Attorney's Fantasy

Your objective in life is to take care of yourself and your spouse (if you are married) as long as you live. The objective is not to avoid probate. Don't worry, you can take care of yourself and avoid probate. But, unless you have more money than you will ever need and it is secure, gifting is not a good idea.

Lawyers are enamored with gifting. They love to tell clients about all of the complexities of gifting. I guess they are really fantasizing about finding a client that is rich enough to actually make big gifts and pay them to establish some very expensive, legally complex, gifting scheme. The complex gifting plans can actually be tremendously valuable to a family with a huge estate, but most families don't have any need for such plans.

Coming back to reality, you need to realize that you will probably need all of your assets to assure a comfortable life, and if anything is left for your heirs, that is great. When you give something away, it is GONE! Additionally, there may be a gift tax problem. The property doesn't get a step-up in basis, and there are income tax problems. You probably shouldn't give property away, and you certainly don't want to make an "accidental" gift, like the gift that occurs when you put someone's name on property as a joint tenant.

Third Goal—Eliminate Estate Taxes

The legislators who created the estate tax laws designed them to break up wealth and redistribute it to the populace. The objective was to raise revenue for the government and keep the nation's wealth from concentrating in the hands of only a few families. You would probably agree that everyone should have a chance to become wealthy, that the government needs revenue, and that a good place to get it is from estates of the wealthy. Today, the super wealthy families have had laws passed that give them ways around the estate tax laws. They don't pay estate taxes, and their wealth passes securely from generation to generation. The upper middle class families of our nation shoulder the estate tax burden.

Lawyers call the estate tax a voluntary tax. That means if you choose to avoid estate taxes, you almost certainly can, provided you plan effectively and live long enough to implement the plan.

Unless the laws change, you really don't need to be concerned about federal estate taxes, that is, as long as you don't have over the exemption equivalent value in total assets (see Appendix 1). Be careful when you calculate your net worth. My clients are always surprised to figure out that they are worth more than the exemption equivalent. Most people are worth more dead than alive. In calculating estate taxes, everything you "own" is considered. Of course, you own your house, car, boat, bank accounts, stocks, and bonds; but you also own your little business, the real estate contract on the house you sold ten years ago, the life insurance policy, and sometimes even pension benefits. It is all there when the estate taxes are calculated.

Yes, the life insurance is included, even though your life insurance agent told you it wasn't taxable. There is a big misunderstanding. The agent meant that there isn't any **income** tax on the money collected as a death benefit, but there is an **estate** tax. Life insurance actually accounts for the IRS's major source of estate tax revenue.

The living revocable trust may eliminate estate taxes for most families because most families don't have over twice the exemption equivalent amount in their gross estate. The law simply says that a married couple that goes to the trouble of writing the trust can make it so the husband can pass the full exemption equivalent amount, and the wife can pass the full exemption equivalent amount to their heirs without an estate tax. The lawyer simply needs to write the trust the way the IRS says it needs to be written, and the couple can pass well over a million dollars tax free to their family or whomever they desire. Don't blindly trust your lawyer. This book will tell you what the IRS requires in at least some basic areas of the law. If your estate is worth over the exemption equivalent amount, your signature on that trust could save your family big bucks—hundreds of thousands of dollars in estate taxes. What is it worth to you to have a living revocable trust?

Chapter 19 explains how you can reduce and even avoid estate taxes. You might calculate how much it is worth to you to have Mom and Dad do some of the things this book tells you how to do. Remember, it isn't just estate taxes. The three estate planning goals you want to achieve are (1) pass things according to your desires; (2) avoid probate; and (3) eliminate estate taxes. Maybe we should add a fourth goal: live life well.

Chapter

5

Your Will

Making it Work For You

When someone says the words "estate planning," everyone automatically thinks "will" and then "probate." Living revocable trust advocates preach against wills. They say wills are bad and trusts are good! On the contrary, the will is actually a powerful legal tool. You have to learn how to use it. Even if you have a living revocable trust, you need to have a will. Frankly, sometimes a will is all that is needed. Whether you have a big estate or a small estate, the will should form the foundation of your estate plan.

If you have a living revocable trust, your will may be very simple. That is OK. However, the will is still an important part of your estate plan, and it shouldn't be "brushed off" as being unimportant just because you have a living revocable trust. If you have a living revocable trust and don't have a will, something is wrong.

Your will should "tie" together the living revocable trust, tax plan, and other facets of your estate plan. Specifically, if you have minor children or an incompetent family member, the will should at least name a personal representative and a guardian/ conservator. A personal representative is the person who does the leg work required by a will after you die. Remember, a guardian is the person who has legal control over a minor or an incompetent person, and a conservator is the person who controls the money and property of a minor or an incompetent.

If your will is used to direct the transfer of property after your death, there will be a probate. The purpose of a living revocable trust is to allow property to be transferred through the trust rather than through the will, thus avoiding probate.

You can get a simple will prepared by a lawyer for $50 to $5000. You can order up a will advertised on TV or in a magazine for $10 to $50. You could get a will sold by the local stationery store for $5 to $25.

Attorneys are very happy to have a client request a will. Drafting a will, the way most lawyers draft a will, is bread and butter for the lawyer. The lawyer doesn't make a lot of money up front, but once the will is written, you are psychologically "locked" into the lawyer. You will probably do other legal work with that lawyer. Nine out of ten times, when you die, your family will make a beeline to the lawyer that drafted the will. That may not be all bad, because the lawyer who drafted your will has more information on you and knows what you want better than any other lawyer. The problem is, sometimes the lawyer takes advantage of your family during the probate process.

Lawyers actually make what are called "will files." They draft lots of wills at cheap prices in order to get the probate business. It takes about 10 years to get a good will file built up, but once the lawyer gets set, his financial success is assured by the probate. Some attorneys will flat out tell you living revocable trusts don't work and shouldn't be used in 96% of the cases. I disagree. In many cases, they are simply protecting their job security.

Having written living revocable trusts for over 10 years, I can see how the probate business would be nice. I usually get a call when one of my clients dies, and the probate fees would be easy picking. I am committed to my client's goal of avoiding probate. There are some valid reasons to go through probate.

But unless there is a good reason, I have yet to have a client go through probate.

The lawyers should not try to tie you or your heirs to them. They should give you an originally signed copy of the will. You need the original will, and it needs to be kept in a place where the family can get to it if you die. Lots of people keep their will in their safe deposit box. It is OK to keep your will in the safe deposit box, but it is harder for the family to get to after you die. Just keep the will in the filing cabinet at home. If it gets stolen or burnt up, you may have to write another one. Some attorneys will keep a second originally signed copy. If you don't use an attorney to write your will, you may want to make sure a second signed copy of your will is in a safe place, so that you don't need to worry about losing the will in your filing cabinet.

When you revoke your will and make out a new one, the originally signed copy(ies) of the old will must be located and destroyed. I have seen cases where the attorney kept the only originally signed copy of the will and just gave the client a photocopy. If the family doesn't have an originally signed will, it is awkward to go back to the attorney who drafted the old will and ask for the original back, so that another attorney can amend it or draft a new will for you. It is also awkward for the family to show up at the lawyer's office and ask for the will, so that another attorney can do the probate or whatever needs to be done after you die. You should insist on having an originally signed copy of your will. It is your will, not the lawyer's! Make sure your family knows where you keep your will. The lawyer may also keep an originally signed will. That's okay. If you revoke the will, write and simply tell the lawyer to destroy his copy.

One large law firm didn't give their clients an originally signed will, and when the firm took an inventory of the wills that were being carefully kept in their vaults, they figured out that there were hundreds of wills that belonged to clients that were dead. The families didn't know that wills were being kept by the law firm. The families assumed that Dad and Mom had never made out a will and had probated their estates as intestate (no will) estates. The law firm, having its clients' interests in mind, decided not to keep clients' wills anymore.

Some lawyers write instructions into the will telling your family to contact them if you die or even just get sick. There isn't anything legally wrong with that, but it's not very professional.

Some lawyers go even further and have you name them as personal representative. Lawyers do it all the time. Don't let that happen!! Any reasonable person would see a real ethical problem with the attorney setting himself up as the personal representative. I have had lawyers openly state that they name themselves as the personal representative to avoid losing control of the estate and the probate.

The Joint Will Disaster

A husband should have his own will, and a wife should have her own will. There should be two separate pieces of paper. If you have a husband and wife will which is only one document "shared" by the two of you, that is called a joint will.

I haven't seen a joint will for a long time. Don't let someone sucker you into a joint will, because they are very awkward to work with when one of the couple dies. Joint wills were more common 30 or 40 years ago. Today, they are almost never used. If you happen to have a joint will, you better get new wills.

Pick the Right People

"Personal representative" is the modern name for the executor or executrix. The personal representative is also commonly known as the "legal representative" or the "personal administrator," in the case of an intestate estate. This is the person that will handle all of the business affairs associated with your estate after you die. The personal representative works with the courts and receives power from the courts to conduct such business. This is all part of the probate process, which will be discussed in Chapter 7.

You will probably choose a family member to act as your personal representative. The personal representative should be a person with reasonable business skills. He or she should live close to where you live, so that he or she can easily conduct the necessary business associated with your estate. More than one person should be named as a potential personal representative in your will. Scroll 5.1 is an example of how a series of individuals can be named as personal representatives. This assures that someone can act as personal representative if your first choice can't act or won't act for some reason.

Personal Representative Named

I nominate and appoint the following people in the following order of priority as Personal Representative until one such person qualifies:

1. My husband, John H. Doe
2. Son One Doe
3. Son Two Doe
4. Daughter Only Doe
5. John's Brother Doe

Scroll 5.1—Personal Representative Clause Found in Mary Doe's Will

A person can't be forced to be a personal representative. There are dozens of reasons why people can't act as personal representatives when they are needed. For example, the person chosen to act as personal representative could be dead, sick, out of the country, or incompetent.

Consider the feelings of your family members when you make out your list of personal representatives or guardians. Even though there may be one of your children that you certainly don't want to act as the personal representative, if you put that child's name at the end of the list, he will feel included. The chances of that child actually becoming the personal representative are very small, but the good feelings he will have by seeing his name on the list is well worth putting the name at the bottom of the list. Yes, be sensitive to people's feelings when you make the list of personal representatives or guardians, but make the best business decisions.

Your personal representative will be required to inventory all of your possessions; pay the bills; distribute your personal property; file your final income tax return; file an estate tax return, if necessary; collect the life insurance, pensions, social security, and veteran benefits; and do all of the other tasks required to close out your estate. Personal representatives even end up running businesses for years. Of course, as you will learn, all of the actions of the personal representative must be approved by the court. Being a personal representative is a responsibility, not an honor.

The people you list as possible personal representatives should be told that they are on the list. This gives you a chance to change the list if they don't want to be on the list, and it lets them know that they have responsibilities when you die. You may want to give the people you choose to be on the list a copy of your will and instructions telling them where the original will is located. It might be a good idea to seal the copies in envelopes, so that they can't be read until you die.

All of your estate planning should be done between you, your spouse, and your counselor. The kids probably shouldn't be consulted. It is your plan, not your kids' plan. When you start discussing your estate plans with all of the family, someone is surely going to be upset about something, and they are going to be mad at you. If someone is going to be mad, don't make him mad before you die; make him mad after you die. After you are gone, the most he can do is go out and stomp up and down on your grave. When you are the one who makes the plans, the kids can't be mad at each other, because it was your plan, and no one of the kids had any undue influence over its creation. Don't dwell, and don't let any family member dwell, over the estate planning process. Just do it, and get on with your life. You'll feel great, and life will be better.

Considerations in Choosing a Guardian

The real tragedies I see are family tragedies, not financial tragedies, and they usually involve orphaned children.

Mom and Dad were killed in an auto accident a year earlier, and Grandma and Grandpa are now sitting at my desk crying. Grandma and Grandpa wanted to raise the orphaned grandchildren. A professor uncle in town wanted to raise the grandchildren. All of the relatives wanted the children to be raised in town with the family. The family and their lawyers have just lost a yearlong court battle, and they want me to appeal the case.

Of course, Mom and Dad didn't have a will, so the judge decided who the guardian of the grandchildren would be. If you don't bother to make out a will and name the guardians to your children, the court where you lived will have to name the guardians. The judges have full power to do whatever they want. They should make the decision they feel is best for the children. Their decision is almost impossible to overturn on an appeal.

Grandma and Grandpa are sitting at my desk crying because the judge had awarded the grandchildren to a distant relative the grandchildren had never met before. He was a truck driver from Texas. He had heard of the deaths and had come to town. He got a barmaid to go into court with him, and she testified for him saying, "A number of years earlier, Mom and I had a long discussion at the bar, and Mom stated that if she ever died, she wanted the kids to be raised by the truck driver from Texas."

Why did the truck driver want the kids? He was apparently after a little life insurance policy and the social security benefits. The grandchildren are now living 1500 miles away in Texas, and there isn't anything that can be done to get them back.

If there are minor children or grandchildren in your family, see to it that the guardians are properly appointed for them. The guardianship appointment is almost always done in the parents' wills. However, it is possible in many states to appoint guardians in a document other than a will. The appointment has to be in writing, properly witnessed and/or notarized. The appointment of guardians necessitates a probate proceeding. It is a different type of probate than the one designed to handle property matters. Yes, it can be messy, long, and expensive.

The guardians must stand ready to raise your children, not only if you die, but also if you become incompetent. Guardians must be adults able to act legally on behalf of the children.

Whom do you appoint as guardians? Obviously, you appoint the people that you think will best care for and love the children. You should try to appoint guardians who feel the same way you do about religion, education, discipline, and other important aspects of life.

Get your will out, if you have one, and look at the language in the guardianship section. Most wills simply word the guardianship appointment as follows: "Mary Jones as guardian to my minor children." This isn't good enough. Mary Jones is probably a sister to you or your spouse. She is probably married, and you like her husband. What happens if she gets divorced and is living with a slime ball when your children need to have her appointed as their guardian?

Put restrictions in the language appointing your children's guardian. For example:

Mary Jones, provided she is still happily married to Jim Jones, and they are harmoniously living together.

Mary Jones, provided she raises the children in Provo, Utah.

Grandma and Grandpa, provided they have the health to take care of the children.

Grandma and Grandpa, provided they don't sell the kids.

Well, you get the idea that you need to put restrictions or conditions in the part of your will that makes the guardianship appointments.

You should name several choices as guardian. It is a good idea to put your spouse on as first choice. Actually name the spouse in your will. It may help solve some problems. For example:

The first case I handled after I was sick was a guardianship problem. A lady had lost her husband, and because the family needed the money to live, she needed to collect his life insurance. The insurance agent had named the little children as the beneficiaries, and the insurance company was dutifully going to invest the insurance money until the children were all of legal age or until a court appointed guardian/conservator was named. If the lady's husband had a will which named her as guardian/conservator, the task would be very easy. It would only take a simple filing at the court house, a little paper work, and a couple of hundred dollars.

I asked, *Did your husband have a will?*

Yes.

Well, does it name you as guardian and conservator?

Sort of!

The will read, "I hereby appoint as guardian to my minor children whomever the court shall appoint." You don't want the court to appoint your guardians. If you take the time to make out a will, one of your major purposes is to choose guardians for your children. The last thing you want is to have the court impose its choice.

You might be thinking this was one of those fill-in-the-blank wills that are good in all 50 states. But it wasn't. An attorney had drafted it, and I knew his name. He was a big time lawyer in town.

Because this was my first case, and because I was forced to practice alone (nobody wants to hire someone who has a serious health problem), I was green enough to believe that if a lawyer made a mistake or caused a problem he would clean things up for free. I didn't know that many lawyers make a living by setting up clients, just like this lady had been "set up." She now had to go to court and have the court appoint her as guardian/conservator for her own children in order to receive the money from her husband's life insurance.

I told her to go back and force the other lawyer to clean up his mess for free. She taught me a couple of lessons at that point. She said that a good lawyer was worth his fee, and she was happy to pay me if I could solve her problem. Additionally, she informed me that she had already been back to the other lawyer, and he couldn't help her now. It seems the state would no longer let him practice law, because by that time, he had been appointed as a judge.

Technically, a natural parent has the first shot at a guardianship appointment. That's OK, unless there has been a divorce. The custodial parent often doesn't want the ex to get the kids. The custodial parent should certainly make out a will and name guardians other than the ex. A short statement as to why the ex shouldn't be guardian is probably also a good idea. The custodial parent needs to "educate" the judge about the situation. Maybe the judge will see things the way the custodial parent sees them, but usually the ex can get custody of the kids after the death of the custodial parent.

The living revocable trust can be very effectively used to help solve this problem. You may not be able to prevent the court from giving the guardianship appointment to your ex, but you can use the trust and make it so that your ex doesn't get control of the money that goes to your children. I have even seen cases where the ex didn't want the kids once it was clear that the kids didn't come with any disposable assets.

Avoiding Family Fights

Taking care of the children, by naming the guardians, is one of the most important things you can do in estate planning. One of the other very important parts of estate planning is directing the distribution of the antique shot gun, the treadle sewing machine, the dollies and the doilies.

The vase has sat in Mother's front hall for years, and everyone that walks by says, "Mother, that is a beautiful vase. When you die, may I have it?" Mother says sure, and by the time Mother is dead, she has promised the vase to everyone in the family and half of the neighbors. That stupid vase starts the family fight, and the kids don't speak to each other for years.

The Smith family was rather wealthy. Mr. Smith had done everything just right. The living revocable trust and wills were in place. He had controlled the estate taxes, not only with the living revocable trust, but also with a children's trust and an insurance trust. When he and his wife died in the airplane accident, his attorneys and accountants moved the entire estate to the children in about three weeks. Millions of dollars were protected from all estate taxes and probate.

The Smiths had four married children who had always been close to each other. When Dad and Mom died, all of the money and real estate was divided evenly, and everybody was happy. However, when the children realized that there was a house full of Dad and Mom's personal property to divide up, there was a problem. Each item had a personal memory and personal meaning. The task of dividing up the "memories" was impossible for the children, and Dad and Mom hadn't made any effort to distribute their personal property—the Royal Doulton dolls, Dad's fishing gear, the kitchen knife Grandma once owned—the little things. The family was in real trouble. The house was emptied, but the four children really haven't spoken to each other for over 10 years. That was a family tragedy, not a financial tragedy.

You can never say you don't have enough property to worry about doing your estate planning! It is the little things that count.

The lawyers want you to distribute all of the little personal items through your will. That is OK. The court will make sure each item is properly distributed, but it is best to avoid the court, where possible, and avoid being locked into the attorney.

If distribution of your personal property is fully outlined in the will, then the will must be changed when you change your mind and want the property to go to another person. Because changes require a trip back to the lawyer's office, wills aren't easily changed. Any change means more costs and time.

There are easier ways of distributing the personal property than having everything written in the will. Some ways work and some don't. Putting tape on everything with a person's name on the tape is a bad idea. The first person into the house after grandpa dies simply moves the tape around the way he wants things to go, or he removes all of the tape so that nobody knows who was supposed to get what, and this starts the family war. Some families try some sort of a lottery game where the personal effects are given away by chance. This isn't very satisfactory. In many cases, only one child really wants an item, and he doesn't get it because the lottery is just a random selection.

You are the one who best knows your children and how they should be treated. Either write what is called a "personal letter," if your state law will allow one, or have your trust written so that you can add a "Schedule" which directs the distribution of the personal items through the trust. A third technique could also be used. It involves writing a holographic will which will be used to supplement your formal will. Holographic wills are explained in the next section.

The personal letter is really just a list of items and corresponding names of the people who are to receive them. It has to be referenced in your will. Scroll 5.2 is an example of language in a will which references a personal letter. The letter is not a formal part of your will until you die. Then the letter is brought in and treated just like it had been a formal part of your will all along. But, because it isn't a formal part of the will until you die, it can be changed any time you want. All you have to do is rip it up and write out a new letter. Scroll 5.3 is an example of a short personal letter.

Personal Property Letter Clause

In the event that there is in existence at the time of my death a written statement or list, in my handwriting or signed by me, disposing of my tangible personal property (other than money, evidence of indebtedness, documents of title or securities, and property used in my trade or business) which has not otherwise been specifically disposed of under the terms of this Will, each such item of personal property shall be distributed to the person whose name is set forth on the list as the intended beneficiary of that item as his or her sole and separate property.

Scroll 5.2—Language found in a will which will allow you to write a personal letter and dispose of the little personal items

Personal Letter

This is the personal letter through which I wish to designate the recipients of the personal property I am describing below. This letter is referenced in my will and is intended to become a part of my will after my death.

As part of the distribution of my estate, the following personal property shall be given to the individuals indicated.

To my son, Johnny, the antique sewing machine, in the walnut cabinet, that originally belonged to my mother

To my daughter, Jane, sawed off shotgun*, serial # Y68942

To my daughter, Joan, oak dining room table with cabriole legs and 6 oak dining room chairs with pink and blue flower needlepoint seats

____
Mary A. Doe

Dated: ______________________

Scroll 5.3—Example of a short Personal Letter
**Jane has to be given the shotgun so she can get the treadle sewing machine back from Johnny!*

Many states don't permit the use of such a letter, but some do. Check with a local attorney. Because only certain states allow such a letter and because only personal property can be distributed using the letter, the utility of personal letters is limited. Items such as business property, cash, certificates of deposit, stocks, bonds, and other items that you may wish to distribute to an individual cannot be legally disposed of through the letter. The laws simply say that a personal letter cannot be used to distribute money, evidences of indebtedness, documents of title, securities, and property used in a trade or business. Such properties must be specifically listed in the will if a specific individual is to receive them.

It is easier to distribute personal property (the little things) through your living revocable trust. If you don't already have a living revocable trust, I am sure you will consider one after reading this book. All states allow your living revocable trust to have a "Schedule" attached to it which distributes the personal items. The "schedule" which distributes the dollies and doilies is nothing more than a list or a piece of paper which is referenced in the trust as an "add on" document to the trust itself. There isn't any specific format or magic words that have to be used. It can be in your own handwriting. Trust schedules will be explained fully in Chapter 12.

Holographic or Do-it-Yourself Wills

Can you create your own will? Yes, in every state you are allowed to type your own formal or "witnessed" will. Most states require you to be at least 18 years old to have a will. You can always do any of your own legal work. Lawyers are not necessary to make wills, trusts, or any other legal document "legal." However, there are certain rules that need to be followed to make a legal document "legal." For example, your will should be all typed or all in your handwriting. Never mix writing and typing. However, you can "fill in blanks" on a pre-prepared form, but fill-in-the-blank wills often aren't detailed enough to help much.

A will doesn't need to be notarized, but all typed wills need to be witnessed. Most states require two witnesses, but some require three witnesses. If you are uncertain what your state requires, go ahead and have three witnesses because it won't hurt anything if you live in a state that only requires two witnesses. Louisiana, Maine, Massachusetts, New Hampshire, South Carolina, and Vermont are the states I am aware of that require three witnesses. The witnesses have to be over 18, competent, and not related to you; and they can't have any interest in the will. More or less, the witnesses need to be detached, independent observers. If the will is typed, signed and properly witnessed, then it is a formal will. It is probably best to have such a "formal" will.

Many wills are notarized. A will which is notarized is known as a "self-proving" will. The will still has to be witnessed even if it is notarized. Actually, the signatures of the witnesses are being notarized, not the signature of the person making out the will. When a self-proving will is taken to court, the judge will not be required to have the witnesses testify that they acted as witnesses; their notarized signatures are all that is required. This helps speed things in a probate proceeding in certain situations. In a self-proving will the witnesses usually also sign a statement which says that they feel you, the person making out the will, are competent, aware of what is being done, and old enough to write a will. This helps create a presumption that you were legally able to make your will when you did. Call the "probate clerk" at your local court house and make sure your state's laws allow self-proving wills.

Holographic wills are handwritten wills. Twenty-two states will allow you to write your will and simply sign it and date it. Making out this kind of a will probably isn't a good idea, but it is better than nothing. The following states allow holographic wills: Alaska, Arkansas, Arizona, California, Colorado, Idaho, Kentucky, Louisiana, Mississippi, Montana, Nevada, North Carolina, North Dakota, Oklahoma, Pennsylvania, South Dakota, Tennessee, Texas, Utah, Virginia, West Virginia, and Wyoming. Holographic wills cannot be witnessed. They have to be totally in your own handwriting, signed and dated. There can't be any marks on the will except your handwriting. Even using letterhead with a logo or address printed on the paper may well make the will invalid. There can't be anything except lines and your own handwriting on the will papers.

If you live in a state that recognizes holographic wills, you can use a holographic will, in addition to your formal will, to distribute your special personal items that cause the big fights. Scroll 5.4 is a sample of what you would write.

Mary Doe Will

When I die, I direct that the following property shall be given to the individuals indicated:

1. To my son, John, I give my two shot guns.

2. To my daughter, Jane, I give my Singer sewing machine, my silverware set Grandma left me, and my wedding dress.

3. To my good friend, Ann, I give my Scrabble game.

4. To my brother, Ed, I give the fishing pole Dad left me when he died.

____
Mary A. Doe

Dated: July 4, 1997

Scroll 5.4—An example of what could be written in a holographic will to distribute personal property. Note that there should be nothing on the paper except your own handwriting, and the will must be dated and signed.

By creating such a holographic will, you are actually making a second will. Most of the time you want your will to act alone and be your "last will," but when you use the holographic will to dispose of the dollies and doilies, you want both your formal will and the holographic will to be functional. There isn't any problem having two wills, as long as they don't contradict each other. When you change your mind about the distribution of your personal items, it is no big deal. Just rip up your holographic will and make a new one.

The problem is that no one of the three techniques—the personal letter, the schedule which goes along with your trust, or the holographic will—will work in every situation to effectively dispose of the little personal items. When I describe the schedule technique in Chapter 12, I will show you a technique I have come up with which should work in every case and in every state. Of course, you will have to use your living revocable trust like a master, but you can handle it easily.

Chapter

6

Living Wills

Protecting Your Right to Die

Riddle: *When is a will not a will?*
Answer: *When it's a living will.*

The living will is not a will or anything like a will. It is a directive to doctors telling them that you do not want them to use life-sustaining medical procedures in certain circumstances.

The living will addresses your "right to die." The issue of your right to die has moved from the hospitals to the courts. What should be a private, personal and family decision has been turned into a judge's decision. The issue came to the media headlines in 1975 with the case of Karen Ann Quinlan, a young woman in a "permanent vegetative state." Karen was believed by everyone to be breathing only because a respirator was being used to aid her. After years of court battles, her parents finally obtained a court order directing the doctors to "unplug" her. The respirator stopped as her parents stood by her side sadly wishing her a final farewell. The peace death could have brought Karen eluded her. She lived on in her vegetative state without the respirator. She continued to be fed through tubes. She lived several more years in her vegetative state before her "natural death."

Since the Quinlan case, all states have wrestled with your right to die. Where do your rights meet those of the medical and legal professionals? State laws addressing a citizen's right to die are very specific. The language that can be used in your living will is specifically set forth in your state's law. Many hospitals and rest homes will give you a fill-in-the-blank living will, and because it is the language required by state law, there isn't much you can change or add.

The laws distinguish "life-sustaining methods" which merely prolong the dying process from other medical treatments which could effect a cure or provide comfort. You can usually write down in your living will what procedures you do or do not want used on you. Do you want to be put on a respirator, fed intravenously, or have your heart resuscitated when you are facing certain death? The statutes allow you to decide what "life-sustaining methods" will be used when you are in a "terminal condition" which will result in death regardless of what procedures are used.

I never faced a living will type decision when I had cancer, or maybe I should say, Kristy never faced a living will type decision. The treatments given to me would not have stopped even if I would have had a living will. The treatments were intended to cure my cancer, not simply prolong my life; and in fact, some progress was always being made even though the tide of the battle would turn against me at times. I do know that there were several times when I had the power to choose between living or dying. But, I didn't want to die. I wanted to be with Kristy and my three children. Kristy was brought to the hospital several times to "help me make my decisions." When my vital signs would drop beyond medical retrieval, Kristy's presence would give me an extra will to live, even though I was basically in a coma. It is amazing what bounds love will cross. Of course, I feel I was very blessed, because the medical professionals were at the end of their ability.

Without a signed living will, the medical professionals are bound by their medical ethics and their fear of lawyers to do everything they can to prolong your life as long as possible, even if there is no chance of recovery. There are many times when life is far worse than death. You may not believe that, but it is true, even for the young.

A Medical War Lost

My heart goes out to the wife and children of my friend who was struck down by disease in his late twenties. The medical battle was very intense. After months, his life was preserved. He now lives in a rest home. He has almost no mind. He doesn't speak. He seems to recognize his wife, but he is totally helpless to move, feed himself, go to the bathroom or perform any of the normal functions of life. Had he died, his children would have known him only by his writings and the stories told to them by people who knew their father. You can bet that those stories would have been bigger than life. They now know their father, and they know he has no life.

A little star is now displayed beside his name on the rest home door. The star signifies that a court order exists which authorizes the rest home to stand aside and let him die should his life ever be threatened by "natural means." There will be no hospital battle to save his life should disease strike again. The war was lost in the first battle, even though the battle was won. His wife, although years have passed, loves him deeply, but she can tell you that some states of existence are worse than death—much worse.

I consider the living will a necessary part of every plan for life, just as a testamentary will is a necessary part of your estate planning. Consider a living will in your plans. The "right to die" or the "right to die with dignity" is an important right to preserve in life.

You can easily obtain a living will, usually free. Just go to your local hospital, and the administrator will usually give you a "fill-in-the-blank" living will which follows your state's laws. Living wills are governed so closely by state law that it is OK to use the fill-in-the-blank form. The hospital will often keep a copy of the signed form in your hospital file. If you use their form, there are fewer problems when your family tries to get the hospital to honor your wishes expressed in the living will.

Chapter

7

Understanding Probate

How the Process Works

Remember, the second major estate planning goal is to avoid probate. The problem is—a testamentary will must be probated if it is used to pass property, name guardians, or perform some other function. Probate is very misunderstood. If you only have a will, you can't avoid probate, but you can successfully and easily avoid probate if you have a living revocable trust in addition to your will. However, you have to know what probate is, so that you will know how to use the trust to maneuver around the probate problem. In reality most people who get a living revocable trust still *do not* avoid probate, because they don't know how to *use* the trust.

Everyone thinks probate is a big bad monster that eats families. Well, it isn't that bad. Oh, it can be a real nightmare for some families, but the concepts of probate are simple. If you live in a state that has passed simplified probate laws and you get the right attorney, or even do it yourself, probate can be relatively painless. You can certainly understand it. Yet some lawyers don't understand it, and many lawyers use it to take advantage of their clients.

Flying into Chicago one day, I sat next to an attorney who kept down playing living revocable trusts, because in his words, "Probate taxes just aren't that big a deal." The lawyer had no idea what he was talking about. Probate and taxes are two totally different concepts. Taxes are what you pay the government. Fees for probate are what you pay the lawyer.

On the same trip, flying out of Chicago, I sat next to a man who had been probating his mother's estate for 2 1/2 years. He had paid the lawyer over $10,000, and had spent days at the lawyer's office and going to court. His biggest worry was that he couldn't afford to take any more of his time to work through the probate process. He could afford the fees, but not the time. He knew very well what probate was.

Probate Defined

The word probate, in Old English, simply meant, "to prove." The current American judicial system uses it to mean "prove," when it refers to proving a will. Actually, the word probate in American law is now a general name or term used to include all matters over which a probate court has jurisdiction. This includes the traditional proof of wills, the disposition of estates, the appointment of guardians and conservators, and other matters. The mere fact that an entire court system for probate has been created in every state and county should tell you that probate is a problem every family faces and that it consumes a huge amount of money. The sad fact is, most of the probate system would be unnecessary if people would just learn a little and do a little planning.

An American family will be exposed to the probate court when (1) a family member dies, (2) a family member becomes incompetent, or (3) a minor child inherits property.

All societies throughout history have had some sort of "probate" process, or rules that were followed to distribute property after someone died. The English system of probate, which has existed for hundreds of years, forms the foundation of the American probate system. Our current system protects family members and creditors to assure that everyone gets his fair share of the property left behind.

All probate matters are supervised by the probate court. The court sees to it that the bills are paid, that the property is "legally" transferred to its proper new owner, that the children are placed in new homes, and that the children's financial affairs are safeguarded. All of this is good, but 85% of it is unnecessary when you do your planning ahead of time and use the living revocable trust. First, do your own planning with a living revocable trust, and then it is worth stepping in and helping Mom and Dad do their planning with a living revocable trust.

Why The Lawyer Says Your Estate is Too Small

You may have had the experience of going to a lawyer and asking for a living revocable trust. The lawyer didn't want to write a trust for you, and you were told that you "didn't have enough property to worry about." What the lawyer was saying was you didn't have enough to worry about paying estate taxes. It may be true that you won't have to worry about paying any federal estate taxes. The federal estate tax limitation, or "exemption equivalent," currently is rising from $600,000 in 1997 to $1 million in 2006 (see Appendix 1). If you have under the exemption equivalent in your estate, you don't even need to file a federal estate tax return. Estate taxes will be discussed in Chapter 19. In this chapter, probate will be explained.

I become so frustrated when a person tells me that he "doesn't have enough wealth to worry about." What he doesn't see is that probate actually hits the smaller estates harder than it does the big estates. The small estate usually loses a much higher percentage of the total estate than the big estate loses. Families with small estates need every dime. It really hurts to lose a lot on probate. Probate costs money! The value of the estate generally does not determine whether or not the assets have to be probated. Probate is a fight over ownership, not value.

I did a probate for a friend. His father had died and left him 46 shares of stock in the local bank. Because there was a question concerning ownership of the stock, the local bank wasn't going to transfer ownership of those 46 shares from the father to the son until the bank got a probate order. I probated the father's estate, even though it only had the shares of stock.

When the lawyer tells you you don't have enough wealth to worry about, he is undoubtedly careful not to tell you what you will have to pay in probate fees, or he "brushed the matter of probate under the carpet." The lawyer stands to make a lot more money from you if you don't get a trust and you have to go through probate. However, most lawyers aren't out to intentionally take advantage of you by making you go through probate. Because they simply don't know how to set up the trusts, they encourage you to go through the old will and probate system.

Living revocable trusts are easy to establish. Many lawyers have just never taken the time to learn about trusts. Law schools don't teach lawyers how to actually write the trusts, but they do a pretty good job teaching the probate system. Additionally, all the senior attorneys in the firm have always done probates, and they help the new lawyers learn how to probate. Lawyers are like everyone else; they do what they know how to do—probate.

Probate Makes It Easy For Professionals to Rob You

If you live in a state that has traditional probate laws, or if you have a lawyer that wants to milk the probate process, probate can appear to be a convoluted, protracted, expensive, frustrating nightmare. However, to a lawyer it is a relatively simple, legal process, and it can be a powerful tool that serves a useful purpose in some situations.

When a family member dies and a probate proceeding is required, this is the one time in life when you are assured the opportunity to come into contact with the legal system. Unfortunately, the legal system is way out of hand, and during the probate process, lawyers will often take advantage of their clients. The probate system makes it so easy to rob a client. My legal colleagues may disagree with me on this point, but I have seen dozens and dozens of cases where the system has failed the American family.

An older lady came into my office one day with her children and asked me to prepare a living revocable trust. She didn't want to have her children go through a probate like the one she went through when her husband died. Her husband had been dead for a number of years. She and her husband had owned a home and a couple of bank accounts. Everything had been held in joint tenancy. You know what joint tenancy means, and you know that she had full ownership of the home and bank accounts instantly upon her husband's death. But she didn't know what joint tenancy meant. Her husband's will directed her to immediately go to the lawyer after her husband died. So, she went immediately to the lawyer's office when her husband died. It was a set up! By the time she talked to me, the lawyer had "probated" all of her husband's estate. The lawyer had charged about $6,000 to perform the totally unnecessary probate process for her. Obviously, the attorney had taken this lady to the cleaners. She didn't even know that he had cheated her.

No, I didn't tell the lady that she had been cheated. The probate had been done many years earlier, and it would have been nearly impossible to recover anything from the lawyer. There was no reason to make her feel bad. I felt bad enough for both of us.

Attorneys, like all professionals, have clients at a real disadvantage, because the clients do not understand what needs to be done and do not have the ability to evaluate whether or not the professional is doing a good job for them.

Mimi's Story

Kristy and I have helped our parents and grandparents do their estate planning. Kristy's grandmother, Mimi, was a charming lady and her husband had been an extremely successful businessman before his early death. Thirty years ago, the family had a very elaborate estate plan prepared for her. When I started to work in the area of estate planning, Mimi cornered me and said that she had a wonderful will that would never have to be probated. She proudly stated that she knew that it would never be probated, because it said so right in the will. Unless you want to take on a feisty grandmother and start a war, you just say, "Yes, Ma'am. I'm sure your will won't have to be probated," and you smile to yourself. You know grandmother is wrong, because if the will passes property, it will be probated. It is a certainty.

I don't know why, but several years later, Mimi brought the will to me, and I read it. I was astounded. She was right. In about the third paragraph it stated, "This will is never to be probated." I suppose a probate judge would have accepted the will and probated it, even though it had that statement in it. A will is worthless until it is probated. Was the statement placed in the will in order to invalidate the will? Nobody knows. Needless to say, I wrote a new will and a living revocable trust for her.

I knew Mimi's will had to be probated, because a will doesn't have any "legal teeth" until it is probated. The probate court gives the will its validity and empowers the personal representative with his or her ability (legal authority) to deal with the banks, stock brokers, real estate agents, and everyone else that has an interest in the estate.

Having the court involved is bad, but when you have a will, at least the court is acting on the instructions that you have written and left behind in your will. The probate process itself is basically the same process whether you have a will or not, but if you don't have a will, the court acts on the state's instructions, not your instructions.

How Probate Works

In our society, ownership of many types of property, such as real estate, bank accounts, safe deposit boxes, cars, boats, notes, etc., is represented by written pieces of paper. Ownership of these types of property is transferred through the use of a written statement which designates a new owner and is signed by the current owner.

The current owner has to sign his name or the property cannot be transferred. If the current owner dies, he obviously cannot sign his name in order to make the transfer. Who has the right to sign the owner's name when the owner is dead? The whole purpose of probate is to determine whose name can be used to transfer the dead owner's property. Of course, if the dead owner is still the owner, then he must have taken it with him, and there isn't any probate. Well, you know what I mean.

Assume your Uncle Big Bucks wants to leave you a million bucks. He has the million bucks in a checking account with only his name on the signature card. He makes out a will which appoints you as personal representative and clearly states that you get the checking account. Then Uncle Big Bucks is a real decent chap, and he dies.

With the will and a death certificate in hand, you are going to march down to the bank and demand your million bucks. The banker will agree that the will says you get the million bucks. You have the death certificate; so it is obvious that Uncle Big Bucks is dead. The banker then forks over the money—right? No, way! The banker tells you to drop dead and go get a court order.

The banker isn't dumb. He knows that the will you have in hand might not be Uncle Big Bucks's last will. The will itself starts out, "I hereby revoke all wills and codicils I have previously made." (A codicil is just the lawyer's word for "amendment.") How does the banker know that this is the last will Uncle Big Bucks made? Big Bucks could have made out another will that invalidates the will you have, and in the other will he could have left the million bucks to his favorite niece, Denise, or his favorite nephew, Denephew.

If the banker gives you the million bucks, and someone else shows up later with another will that the probate court has approved, the banker will have to pay them another million bucks. The banker is going to cry whenever the million bucks leaves his bank, and he certainly isn't going to risk having to pay out the million bucks twice. So, whoever gets the million bucks is going to have to show up with a probate court order, directing the banker to give up the million bucks. To get the necessary court order, the full probate process must be followed.

Getting Started with Probate

When Uncle Big Bucks dies, the probate court doesn't automatically start working on his estate. People continually tell me that probate isn't a problem. They say that Dad's name was the only name on the house deed, and that Mom lived there with no problem for thirty years after Dad died. In fact, when Mom died, Daughter and her family moved in, and they have lived there for ten years with no problem. Daughter may be living in the house with no problems, but when Daughter goes to sell the house, she is going to have a rude awakening. She will probably have to "probate" Mom's estate, even though she has been dead for ten years. She may have to "probate" Dad's estate as well, even though he has been dead for forty years. Actually, because Mom and Dad have been dead for years, the legal proceeding to clear the title of the house, so that Daughter can sell it, is not a probate proceeding. It is called a "quiet title action," and it is as much or more work and can be even more expensive than a probate proceeding.

There are time limits dictating how long after a death it will be before the probate process must start. Depending upon the specific state law which governs, probates usually must be opened within a year or two after the death. Probate starts when someone files a petition for probate with the probate court. A probate filing is necessitated when the heirs can't get into the bank account, sell the house, check the orphaned children into school, or work with the public utilities and shut off the gas or water. The personal representative appointed in the will, or a family member if there isn't a will, should take the lead and get the probate filing started. After Big Bucks dies, you are going to take the lead and file with the probate court as soon as the banker tells you you can't get your hands on the million bucks.

Take Time To Love Your Family

Clients often call me, upset and crying, because a family member has just died. Clients even call in the middle of the night. They want to know what has to be done right then. Nothing has to be done. Be with your family, not the lawyer. Your family should be the most important thing in your life every day of your life. The legal aspects of life should be insignificant, but they can easily be blown out of proportion and can actually dominate life, especially when a family member dies. A living revocable trust can definitely help keep ordinary legal worries from becoming big worries when a family member dies.

When your family member dies, the world can wait for a few days. No, the world doesn't stop. When your daughter dies, everyone else in the world goes about his normal business, but for a short period, you don't have to worry about the world's business. Take time to be with your family and grieve. Make the time a sacred moment in your life and treasure your memories. Treasure the people who are still with you. Actually look at them.

In the play *Our Town* by Thornton Wilder, Emily, the young mother who died, is granted her wish of going back and reliving a few short hours of her life. She is counseled by her companions in death to pick an unimportant day, "the least important day of her life," because the tragic reality of how poorly we live, even the significant moments in life, would be too much to bear. She chooses the day of her 12th birthday, a happy day that she could remember.

As Emily stands cloaked in death, viewing the morning of her 12th birthday played out on life's stage, she sees her mother cooking breakfast and the family, including her brother Wally and herself, eating. She becomes frustrated as she watches the scene. Her mother is so "busy" cooking breakfast that she never raises her eyes to look at Emily or Wally.

Fourteen years have passed since Emily's 12th birthday. Both Wally and Emily are now dead. Knowing that death would separate her from her mother, Emily frantically tries, through the veil of death, to make her mother look up from the stove at her and Wally. She unsuccessfully pleads to have the family stop and just look at one another for even one short moment while they are together and happy. "Just look at us, Mama," she desperately screams.

After but a few moments of viewing the scene, Emily breaks down sobbing. She cries that she can't go on watching herself and her family callously disregard life and its relationships. She begs her companions to take her back up the hill to her grave in the cemetery.

As she turns from the scene, she comments that life goes so fast, people don't even have time to look at one another. We never even realize what we miss in life.

Nothing has to be done the day your loved one dies. Death is a special moment in life. Live it well. The world can wait.

The Probate Petition Process

The petition for probate is a written document or form that meets the requirements of state law. Because it has to follow the state's laws and the court's rules, a lawyer normally drafts it for you. The petition is filed along with the will that the family thinks is the real "last will and testament." There is always a filing fee at the court. The filing fee is determined by the court, and it will be $50 - $1000 give or take an arm or a leg. This is only the first of many, many fees, and the fees at the court don't include any of the lawyer, appraiser, witness, and other professional fees. All of the expenses are paid by the estate being probated. If someone challenges your claim to the million bucks, Big Bucks's estate could easily cost $50,000 to probate, and if there are complications, you could lose $200,000 or more to the probate. The probate costs will basically come out of your million bucks. You lose. Scroll 7.1 is a sample of a probate filing document.

How to Find the Will, the Relatives, and the Creditors

Just filing a will with the probate petition is not good enough. You will have to prove to the court that the will you have is the real will. Everyone who might be an heir must be notified that Uncle Big Bucks is dead, and they have to be given a copy of the will and the opportunity to claim that they have another will. Anyone can step forward and challenge the will you have for

Uncle Big Bucks. When Denise reads the will and sees that Big Bucks left you the million bucks and didn't leave it to her, she is going to make a beeline to her lawyer, because she has a letter from Big Bucks promising her that she will get the million bucks.

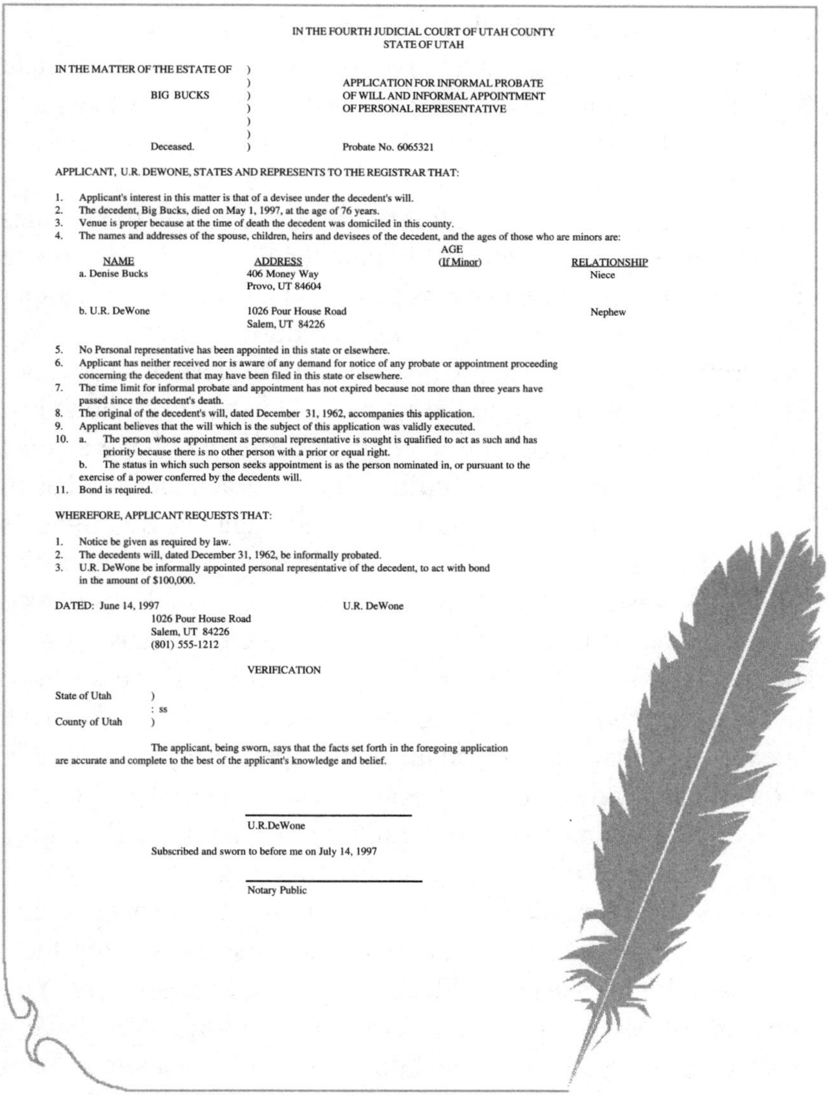

IN THE FOURTH JUDICIAL COURT OF UTAH COUNTY
STATE OF UTAH

IN THE MATTER OF THE ESTATE OF)
BIG BUCKS)
Deceased.)

APPLICATION FOR INFORMAL PROBATE OF WILL AND INFORMAL APPOINTMENT OF PERSONAL REPRESENTATIVE

Probate No. 6065321

APPLICANT, U.R. DEWONE, STATES AND REPRESENTS TO THE REGISTRAR THAT:

1. Applicant's interest in this matter is that of a devisee under the decedent's will.
2. The decedent, Big Bucks, died on May 1, 1997, at the age of 76 years.
3. Venue is proper because at the time of death the decedent was domiciled in this county.
4. The names and addresses of the spouse, children, heirs and devisees of the decedent, and the ages of those who are minors are:

NAME	ADDRESS	AGE (If Minor)	RELATIONSHIP
a. Denise Bucks	406 Money Way Provo, UT 84604		Niece
b. U.R. DeWone	1026 Pour House Road Salem, UT 84226		Nephew

5. No Personal representative has been appointed in this state or elsewhere.
6. Applicant has neither received nor is aware of any demand for notice of any probate or appointment proceeding concerning the decedent that may have been filed in this state or elsewhere.
7. The time limit for informal probate and appointment has not expired because not more than three years have passed since the decedent's death.
8. The original of the decedent's will, dated December 31, 1962, accompanies this application.
9. Applicant believes that the will which is the subject of this application was validly executed.
10. a. The person whose appointment as personal representative is sought is qualified to act as such and has priority because there is no other person with a prior or equal right.
    b. The status in which such person seeks appointment is as the person nominated in, or pursuant to the exercise of a power conferred by the decedents will.
11. Bond is required.

WHEREFORE, APPLICANT REQUESTS THAT:

1. Notice be given as required by law.
2. The decedents will, dated December 31, 1962, be informally probated.
3. U.R. DeWone be informally appointed personal representative of the decedent, to act with bond in the amount of $100,000.

DATED: June 14, 1997 U.R. DeWone
1026 Pour House Road
Salem, UT 84226
(801) 555-1212

VERIFICATION

State of Utah)
: ss
County of Utah)

The applicant, being sworn, says that the facts set forth in the foregoing application are accurate and complete to the best of the applicant's knowledge and belief.

____
U.R.DeWone

Subscribed and sworn to before me on July 14, 1997

____
Notary Public

Scroll 7.1—Probate Filing Document

Telling Denise and all of the known relatives about the will is bad enough, but just notifying all of the relatives the family knows about isn't good enough. A notice has to be published in the newspaper notifying the general public that Big Bucks is dead. You have seen such notices in the back of the newspapers. They can cost the estate hundreds of dollars. Of course, such a notice is bound to bring unknown relatives out of the woodwork. Uncle Big Bucks will end up having more long lost half brothers and sisters than Bill Clinton. Scroll 7.2 shows an example of a newspaper notice.

All of Big Bucks's creditors must also be notified. The ones that you are aware of must receive actual notice, and just to make sure all of the creditors know Big Bucks is dead, the newspaper notice is used to smoke out Bucks's creditors in addition to his half brothers. The notice process is a very important step, if not the most important step, in the probate. It needs to be done just right in order to cut off future claims people may have against Big Bucks's estate and your million bucks. Each creditor has to file a claim at the court making his claim against Big Bucks's estate. This is the only way they can legally get money out of Big Bucks's estate. Probate protects the people Big Bucks owed money to, but it is a mixed blessing for them, because it's an administrative pain for them to comply with. Each creditor must file his claim with the court within a set number of days from the date the notice is published in the newspaper. The exact number of days is set by the courts in the state where the probate petition is filed. If a claim is not submitted within the prescribed time period, the creditor cannot collect from the estate or heirs.

This whole process of notification and publishing is bad enough for Big Bucks's estate, but it becomes downright ludicrous for Mother's estate. Why publish in the newspaper? You know all of Mom's potential heirs. Mom didn't even have a credit card, and you know she didn't owe anybody a dime. Nevertheless, the probate process must be followed. When everything is in order, it is time to meet the judge.

Notice To Creditors

Estate of JOHN H. DOE, Deceased.

Probate No. ______________________

All persons having claims against the above estate are required to present them to the undersigned or to the Clerk of the Court on or before the 30th day of September, 1997, or such claims shall be forever barred.

I. M. ATTORNEY
155 Main Street
Anytown, USA

No. 9617 Published in the Herald News, June 15, 22, 29, 1997.

Scroll 7.2—Example of Probate Notices found in newspapers

Understand the Judge

The judge assigned to handle the probate of Big Bucks's estate will see the process all the way through. He is booked and overbooked; so each time you need to get in to have a hearing before him, your attorney will have to get you on the judge's calendar. The bad news is, the first opening on the court calendar could be months down the line. The good news is, in those states trying to streamline the probate process, a lot of the probate steps can be done without an actual court appearance.

Establish the Will's Proper Jurisdiction

At the first hearing, the judge will establish that his probate court has jurisdiction. The questions are: Where did Big Bucks live? Where is his property located? The court only has probate authority over the property within the state which gives the court its power, i.e., the state where the court is located.

If Big Bucks owned property in more than one state, there will have to be a probate in each state where he owned property. The "primary" probate will be in the state where Big Bucks lived. The probate proceeding in each of the other states is called an "ancillary probate." Going through probate in one state is bad. Going through probate in more than one state is a disaster. If you have to have a probate proceeding in two or three states, it could be years before you see a dime of your million bucks.

How to Prove the Will is Real

At the first court hearing, the judge will require proof that all the proper notification procedures have been followed. This protects the rights that any heir or creditor has to be heard at the court.

If more than one will surfaces, the judge will require all parties that have a will to fight it out and prove which will is the proper "last will." Howard Hughes had over 30 wills submitted to the probate court after he died in 1976. The court's efforts to prove which will was actually the "last will and testament" of Howard Hughes took years, and the court finally decided Hughes didn't have a real will. His multi-billion dollar estate was probated as an intestate estate. Actually, it is better to say his multi-billion dollar estate is *being* probated as an intestate estate. His probate will literally be the life's work for at least one generation, if not two or three generations of attorneys.

Assuming the will is proved, or only one will surfaces, the court will still have to determine that the will is a valid will. Was Big Bucks competent when he made out the will? Was it properly signed and witnessed? This is where the "self-proving will" with the notarized signatures of the witnesses can make a big difference.

If the will is a self-proving will, the judge doesn't have to call the witnesses in and have them testify. The witnesses have already given their "testimony" by affixing their signatures to the will below a signed testimony. Scroll 7.3 (next page) shows the text of a typical self-proving affidavit which is actually a part of the will. Their signatures and testimonies should be acceptable to the judge because they were validated by an agent of the state, the notary public.

Appointing the Personal Representative

If the judge finds the will to be in order, the will will be "admitted" into probate. Someone will be appointed as the personal representative (executor or executrix). The court is basically "deputizing" this person to help the court execute the instructions left in the will. Of course, the court, not the will, actually "empowers" the personal representative with power to act.

If you take the time to write a will, the court will almost always go along with your choice of a personal representative. The judge almost always appoints the first person on the list in your will as personal representative. If for some reason, your first choice for personal representative can't function as the personal representative, the second choice will be appointed, and so on through the list.

If you don't have a will, the judge will usually appoint a family member or an attorney to be the "administrator" of the estate. The administrator performs the same functions for an intestate estate as a personal representative performs for an estate with a will, i.e., a testate estate.

Self-Proving Affidavit

____

John H. Doe

We, ____________________, ____________________, and ________________________, the witnesses, being first duly sworn on this the 1st day of September, 1997, sign our names to this document and declare to the undersigned authority that John H. Doe signed and executed this document which purports to be his Last Will and Testament. We also declare that he signed it willingly as a free and voluntary act (or willingly directs another to sign for him), and each of us, in the presence and hearing of John H. Doe and of each other, hereby sign this Will as witness to John H. Doe's signing, and that to the best of our knowledge he is 18 years of age or older, of sound mind, and under no constraint or undue influence.

We declare under penalty of perjury that the foregoing is true and correct.

First Witness: ____

Address: ____

Second Witness: ______________________________________

Address: ____

Third Witness: _______________________________________

Address: ____

State of Nevada)
: ss
County of Washoe)

BEFORE ME, the undersigned, a Notary Public in and for said County and State, personally appeared John H. Doe, (Witness #1) , (Witness #2) , and (Witness #3) , personally known to me or proved to me on the basis of satisfactory evidence to be the persons whose names are subscribed to the within instrument and acknowledged to me that they executed the same in their authorized capacities, and that, by their signatures on the instrument, the persons executed the instrument.

SUBSCRIBED AND SWORN TO before me the 1st day of September, 1997.

WITNESS my hand and official seal.

____

Notary Public in and for said County and State

Scroll 7.3—Self-Proving Affidavit. Some states have a form of the affidavit dictated by law; so if your state has a specific form, use the form your state wants you to use.

The will almost always lists a number of powers that the personal representative can exercise. These powers often include the power to hire lawyers, appraisers, and maintenance people. The fees paid to anyone the personal representative hires will come directly from the estate or be reimbursed to the personal representative. The personal representative is entitled to reimbursement of all expenses he or she pays on behalf of the estate.

In addition to being reimbursed for expenses incurred by the personal representative, most personal representatives are actually paid from the estate for services rendered as the personal representative. The court will decide exactly how much compensation will be given to the personal representative. The compensation is sometimes a percentage of the value of the estate.

To insure that the personal representative acts properly and doesn't waste, misuse or misappropriate funds from the estate, the court will require the personal representative to post a bond. A bond is almost mandatory in intestate estates. If the will directs the judge to waive the bond, the bond will probably not be required. Basically, your request to have the bond waived is a testimony to the judge saying that you trust the person you have named as your personal representative.

Obtaining Power Through Letters Testamentary

The first court hearing sometimes goes smoothly, but it is amazing how often some type of snag occurs. People sometimes make frivolous contests to the will, just so that the family will pay them a few thousand dollars to get lost. It is cheaper to pay such people to get lost than it is to challenge them in court. Additionally, there can be a fight over appointment of the personal representative. The fights occur when someone doesn't "trust" the person designated by the will to become the personal representative, or when someone wants the money that will be paid to the personal representative as a "salary."

When the court is satisfied that the will is valid, that it is the "last" will, that all of the proper notices have been given, and that everybody is happy with the appointment of the designated personal representative, the court will issue a "Letters Testamentary" to the personal representative. Scroll 7.4 is an example of a Letters Testamentary issued by a court.

Letters Testamentary is a court order directing the bankers, real estate agents, and others to deal with the personal representative. The order gives the personal representative the "clout" he or she needs to clean up the estate, and it assures those dealing with the personal representative that they will be protected by the court if someone else shows up and makes a claim against them on behalf of the estate.

IN THE FOURTH JUDICIAL COURT OF UTAH COUNTY
STATE OF UTAH

IN THE MATTER OF THE ESTATE OF	)	
	)	LETTERS
BIG BUCKS	)	
	)	TESTAMENTARY
	)	
	)	
Deceased.	)	Probate No. 065321

1. U. R. DeWone was duly appointed and qualified as General Personal Representative of the estate of the above named decedent on the 10th day of July, 1997, by the Court, with all authority pertaining thereto.
2. Administration of the estate is supervised.

These letters are issued to evidence the appointment, qualification, and authority of the said personal representative.

WITNESS, my signature and the Seal of this Court, this 10th day of July, 1997.

____
Clerk of the Court

Scroll 7.4—Letters Testamentary

The banker may be crying, but he will give the million bucks to you, as personal representative of Big Bucks's estate, when you present the Letters Testamentary to the bank. The banker doesn't need to know whether you or Denise will actually get the million bucks. As personal representative you would be obligated to distribute the money to Denise, if the will accepted by the court said that she was to receive the million bucks.

The Danger of Inventories

As the personal representative, you must collect all of the assets of the estate and distribute each asset the way the will directs. Depending upon the court and the particular probate laws you are following, the court may or may not require a full inventory of everything in the estate. When an inventory is required, it is usually detailed, but it can be as brief or detailed as the judge requires. You could end up counting each piece of the silverware. If the estate is large, like Big Bucks's estate, the inventory process can take months or even years. You will be shocked when you figure out the amount of effort that is necessary to inventory even a small estate.

The inventory is usually open to public inspection. Anyone who wants to can go down and read Uncle Big Bucks's probate file, and even get a copy of the inventory. The inventory is there, the will is there, and everything else is there for full review. If you want to learn all about someone's estate, all you need to do is go to the court where the probate was filed and know the name of the person who died and the year in which he died. All kinds of people go through probate files.

Some people make a living compiling lists of estates in probate and lists of the heirs of the estates. You can actually purchase such lists to use anyway you want. When the investment scammers figure out that you are getting a million bucks, can you even imagine how many instant friends you will have? Everyone of your instant friends will have some sort of great investment. Maybe this isn't important to you, but you need to protect your family from the scammers that will certainly show up after you die. The best way to protect your family from the scammers is to appoint good trustees in your living revocable trust.

Some states have recognized that the open inventory in the probate file is an open opportunity for financial scams; so they have passed new laws which allow the judge the option of restricting access to the inventory. However, the new laws don't automatically apply. Your attorney has to ask the judge to keep the inventory private. And even when the attorney begs, the inventory is, in reality, almost always left open to the public—even in the states that have the "new laws."

Keep Good Records

Everything that the personal representative does for the estate must be reported to the court, and the court must approve the personal representative's acts. The personal representative could be held personally liable if he misuses his position. The personal representative must keep good records of all transactions, so that the court will be satisfied that he has discharged his responsibilities well.

It is important for you to keep good records of your own business affairs. When you die, how will the family find your bank accounts, stock certificates, and other property?

A man in our church group died. He had been frugal and had obviously had a bad experience during the Great Depression, because he didn't trust banks. He had reasonably large amounts of money in dozens of banks, and he had stocks in lots of companies. Actually, maybe he wasn't so dumb. The savings and loan collapses of the 80's point out again that it may be prudent to keep your money in various locations. However, you must keep records so that your family can find the property when you die or can't act for yourself. This man hadn't even told his wife where he kept his money. Finding his assets was a bigger job than his estate could afford to pay the lawyers to handle. The elders of our church group spent hundreds of hours over a year's period just trying to help his widow find "her assets."

Do You Need a Lawyer for Probate?

Everyone has the legal right to represent himself in court. You do not need a lawyer to go through a probate proceeding. However, the probate process is complicated and time consuming. You could do all of the paperwork and file it, but paperwork must be done just the way the court wants it done. I don't know of a good "do-it-yourself probate kit" on the market. Maybe that is my next book.

Most people use a lawyer to handle probate. Because judges become very impatient with unprepared people who try to do their own legal work, it is advisable to have a lawyer work for you. People working on their own always get something wrong and want the judge to "help them out." The judge has to remain "detached" from the whole process. He sits as an independent enforcer of the rights each party has in the proceeding. He cannot help any one of the parties. He cannot do your legal work for you. He cannot advise you. As a result, he will seem to be cold, and you will feel that he is against you. A confrontation almost always occurs when someone who isn't prepared tries to represent himself in court. Don't ever make the judge mad at you. In spite of the temptation to save lots of money, give the lawyers a chance.

How to Get a Good Probate Lawyer

In the first hearing with the judge, the lawyer designated by the personal representative will be recognized as the lawyer handling the probate, and the court will deal exclusively with that lawyer from that time to the end of the probate. However, the personal representative certainly has the right to fire the lawyer at any time. If the lawyer is fired, he will be entitled to his expenses and a reasonable rate for the time he can prove has been spent on behalf of the estate. It may be hard to fire an attorney, because your gut feelings always say that it is cheaper to stick it out than to change lawyers in the middle of the probate. After all, the new lawyer will have to become familiar with the estate. In spite of your feelings, it may be cheaper to get a new lawyer, if the new lawyer will shove the probate through and not just run his billing clock. At times it isn't wise to throw good money after bad and continue with a bad lawyer. Make sure the new lawyer has a reputation for getting the probate finished.

There is absolutely no obligation for a family to use the lawyer who wrote the will as the lawyer who probates the will. Most families do go back to the lawyer who drafted the will, and that is OK, but it isn't necessary. Check out the lawyer's track record. Ask for the names of estates he has probated. Don't tell the lawyer what you are going to do, but when you get the names, go down to the court and read three or four of the probate files. See if the cases were simple or complicated, and see how much time it took to do the probate. Ask the probate clerk if that amount of time is short or long for a probate in the court. In the probate file, you can probably even see what the lawyer charged. Use this technique and check out two or three lawyers. Make your own comparison. It will take some time up front to make the comparison, but it might save your skin or at least your money.

Frozen Assets Aren't the Big Problem

To assure that the personal representative has time to inventory the estate and that property doesn't "disappear," the estate assets are usually frozen during the probate process. The banker really can't give you Uncle Bucks's million bucks. In addition to running the risk of having to pay the money out twice, the banker would basically be in contempt of court if he gave you the million bucks, and the court had frozen the assets.

Horror stories about locks being slapped on buildings, safe deposit boxes being sealed, bank accounts being closed, and other property being seized are still true in some states, but in many states they don't really happen much under the "more enlightened" probate systems. Clients call me and want to know if they should stop at the bank on the way to the mortuary, so that they can clean out the safe deposit box and withdraw all of the money from the accounts.

In some states, mostly in the East, the answer is yes, clean out everything. However in the Western states, if someone can get into the safe deposit box or close accounts on the way to the mortuary, they can probably get into the safe deposit box and close the accounts two weeks later. Find out what needs to be done in your state.

The mere fact that the client can get into the bank accounts means the client must own some part of the bank accounts in some joint capacity. If the client owns them as a joint tenant with rights of survivorship, he is now the survivor, and he owns the bank accounts outright. The accounts are not subject to probate.

The court may not want to "probate" the safe deposit box, but most states will want an inventory for tax purposes. Be prepared to take an inventory when a safe deposit box is opened after the death of one of the joint owners. Of course, you need to be prepared to satisfy the IRS, courts, and heirs in every aspect of the estate administration. So, keep good records and receipts every time you transact any business with part of the estate. Have someone independent, maybe the banker, witness the inventory of the safe deposit box when it is finally opened. Having an independent witness verify what you do is always a good idea.

Appraisals Are Really Expensive

Formal probate proceedings usually require an appraisal for each piece of property to determine its value. Because professional appraisers must be used, getting a formal appraisal is very expensive. Often more than one appraiser must be employed, because estate property includes everything from real estate to ancient pieces of Ming china, and real estate appraisers don't appraise Ming china.

The really bad news is that you don't even get to choose the appraiser. The appraisers are assigned by the courts, and you get whatever turkey comes up next on the list. He can't be fired. He doesn't have a boss. There is basically no way you can put any pressure on him to lower your appraisal value, once it has been set, or even do the appraisal at all. I know one attorney who, after two years of waiting for an appraisal, visited the appraiser one night with three very large gang-related gorillas. The threat of a revisit finally produced an appraisal the next day.

Getting a Living Allowance

Although the assets of the estate are "frozen" during the probate proceeding, the court recognizes that a family needs money to live. The court will give the family a "living allowance," if the money is needed. However, obtaining a living allowance can be very awkward and just adds to the overall expense of probate.

I am going to get into trouble here with all of the avid aviators, but I will write it anyway. "Little airplanes are a disaster!" Jared was a successful businessman and flew a little airplane. The plane crashed and he was killed, along with his wife and another couple. He had a fairly large estate. The children were in their early teens when their parents were killed. Grandma and Grandpa were appointed guardians and raised the children. The court gave them just enough to support the children. The estate was in probate for well over a decade. The largest law firm in the state handled the probate. They also handled the estate's defense of the lawsuit that was filed on behalf of the other couple's children.

Of course, the probate couldn't be closed until the suit was settled, because if the lawsuit resulted in an award that was more than the insurance coverage, the estate would have to pay the difference. Jared's children grew up, were married, and had children of their own before the estate was settled. They had not had the use of their father's estate as they grew up and needed the money to buy band instruments, go to Europe with the language club, and even go to college. All of these expenses are usually above what the court deems necessary for the "living allowance."

During the entire probate, the law firm got paid, using Jared's money, every time they billed the estate. The courts almost never question an attorney's bill. The suit was finally settled for far less than the insurance coverage, but when the children finally got their parent's estate, it had dwindled, because of the legal system, from well over $1 million to just over $300,000.

You can use life insurance, IRAs and retirement plans to help assure that your family has "living money," which is not regulated by the probate court. Each of these assets goes out and around the will and probate. Designate your spouse as the primary beneficiary, then designate your living revocable trust, if you have one, as the secondary beneficiary. Or, designate the children as the secondary beneficiaries, if you do not have a living revocable trust. However, if any of the children are minors and you don't have a living revocable trust, you are guaranteeing a probate proceeding to name a conservator for the child. By the time all is said and done, the family will go through a legal nightmare if a minor ends up as a beneficiary of your life insurance.

Do not name "my estate" as the beneficiary, because that guarantees a probate. Your "estate" is not your living revocable trust; it is your probated assets. If you set up the life insurance properly, your family should be able to get to the life insurance money relatively quickly, and that will give them money to live on.

If Jared had had a living revocable trust and known how to use it, the whole living allowance and probate mess could have been avoided, and the children could have received money when they needed it. In the end, they would have received hundreds of thousands of dollars more than they finally received.

Forced Property Sales

Sometimes assets have to be sold to cover the creditor claims, probate costs, and/or estate taxes. The personal representative will sell the assets at an estate sale or auction. Estate sales are a great place to pick up antiques and other property cheap, because the personal representative has to sell the property for the going price. I have a friend who makes his living teaching classes which show people how to find probate sales and get good deals by backing the personal representative into a corner.

Closing the Estate Can Protect Assets

If you are lucky, the purpose of the second hearing with the judge will be to close the estate. However, there are often several hearings, before the estate is closed, especially if there are any disputes initiated by heirs or creditors. Each dispute must be settled by the judge, who has the final decision.

Although the judge "makes the decisions," you need to know that in 95% of the situations, the judge just rubber stamps what the probate attorney recommends. No, the probate attorney isn't your attorney. He or she is basically the court's attorney. The probate attorney works for the court and decides all of the issues surrounding your case. You may never even see the probate attorney and his or her staff of clerks and secretaries. Of course, you know how much power the clerks and secretaries have; so you can make a good guess at just how much tender loving care your case will really get from the judge or even the probate attorney.

Go to probate court some day. You will be impressed when you see the judge thoroughly review 200 cases, each of which has a three inch file folder. Oh yes, the whole process will only take two hours or so. Don't worry, your attorney will be there with the billing clock running at $200 an hour for the full two hours plus travel time, all on the estate's tab. The attorney has to be there just in case the judge wants to ask a question. Do you think your attorney has more than one file in the stack of 200? Well, you'll never know.

The judge has control over the entire probate process, and the process must be carried out to the satisfaction of the judge. The personal representative's job is to inventory everything and physically take control of all of the property, give everyone notice of the probate proceeding, present to the judge any creditor claims or challenges made against the estate, pay all of the debts and claims authorized by the court, pay the taxes, and finally, follow the instructions in the will and distribute any assets that are left. The lawyer's job is to interface between the personal representative and the court. The lawyer is basically a translator between the court and the personal representative. The law has developed a language unto itself. In fact, a lawyer goes to school for an extra three years to learn how to speak and write so that you can't understand him.

All the rules have to be followed to assure that the heirs and creditors are protected. The process also assures that the personal representative is protected, along with the banks, stock brokers and the purchasers of the real estate. Just to be sure everyone is protected, the estate is often required to publish additional notices announcing the closing of the estate.

When all the "t's" have been crossed and the "i's" have been dotted, the court will close the probate file. Hallelujah! You will finally get Big Bucks's million bucks! Or, at least what is left.

Chapter

8

The Impact of Probate

The Subtle and Not-So-Subtle Disadvantages of Probate

The expenditure of money is the not so subtle disadvantage of probate. The court fees and attorney fees add up fast. There are also personal representative fees, appraiser fees, and other fees that all eat away at the estate. Exact numbers on the total cost of probate don't really exist. I think it is safe to say that the minimum cost is around 2% of the gross value of the estate, and it is certainly possible to see 10% or more of the gross estate expended in the probate process. In some situations the attorney's fees and other probate fees may be set by statute. The attorney can ask for at least the statutory amount, and the request will almost always be granted. Additionally, the attorney can, and often does, ask for extraordinary fees, which are fees above those normally permitted. Guess what! The courts almost always grant the extraordinary fees on top of the normal fees.

If you're involved in a probate proceeding, you should always ask whether the attorney will perform the probate for a set fee or an hourly fee. Even though it's easy to run up a big bill when the lawyer is charging $150 to $200 per hour, as most attorneys do, it is often cheaper to hire the lawyer at an hourly rate. The problem is, you can't tell which will be cheaper, the set fee or hourly rate.

If the attorney is running his clock, don't ever waste the attorney's time. Get in and get out. Don't talk about the weather, sports or politics, and don't let the attorney talk away his clock and your money. Be rude if you have to; the lawyer won't think any less of you. In fact, the lawyer might compliment you on your professional lawyerly manner.

One of my friends, who is an attorney in New York, called recently and had a question about setting up living revocable trusts. He is a banking lawyer who established his own practice two years ago after working for a big law firm for many years. Although he is brilliant in banking law, he had to ask a simple question on living revocable trusts. During our conversation, he mentioned that he was handling a simple probate. One of his close friends had lost his mother and had asked him to handle the probate for her estate. He said that because the system was so awkward, he was very frustrated. Even though he was trying as hard as he could, it would take almost a year to complete the probate, and it would eat up over $85,000 of the mother's $250,000 estate. He simply commented that he could certainly understand why lawyers loved probate. The lawyer can make a ton of money just processing the probate without even trying to take advantage of the client. In fact, the lawyer's staff can process dozens of probates at the same time, and the lawyer hardly ever gets involved.

Probate Hampers Asset Management

Probate has an intangible, but very real, monetary cost in addition to the fees. Assets cannot be managed effectively because they may be "frozen," and transactions involving the assets may have to be approved by the court. There are times when the personal representative wants to sell estate assets and can't. For example, if real estate values are going down or the stocks held by the estate are going down in value, the estate can lose a lot of money, because the assets cannot be sold before the bottom falls out of the market.

The personal representative may be forced to sell assets simply to raise money for the probate costs. In addition to the probate considerations, there are many reasons that an estate might need immediate cash and be forced to sell estate assets. The personal representative may want to hold appreciating assets, but may not have the option of holding the assets until they reach their full value. Being forced to liquidate estate assets almost always costs the estate. For example, certificates of deposit may have to be cashed in early, which will result in a penalty and loss of money.

It doesn't matter whether assets need to be held or sold, probate often compounds the losses because the personal representative isn't free to conduct business without court authorizations.

Probate Takes Time—Lots of It

Time is money, and probate is going to eat up a lot of your time if you have to probate an estate. It will eat up a lot of your family's time if they have to probate your estate. Probate cuts into your business, your vacation time, and your family life. It becomes very frustrating. The courts really don't care how long the probate runs. Their major function is to assure that everyone's rights are protected and the proceeding is fair to every party. The lawyers are in no hurry to get the probate done if they are charging by the hour, or even simply charging a fixed fee. Your probate is just part of their job. It isn't anything special.

It is difficult to estimate an average length of time a probate proceeding takes. I can name many cases that have tied things up for well over ten years. In California you can almost expect the probate to last at least two years. Because California's system is supposedly streamlined, such delays are disturbing. Nobody knows the exact figure, but it is safe to say that the average probate in the United States takes at least two years. Yours could run longer or shorter.

Families Show Their Worst During Probate

Time delays also have intangible costs. The family is usually rather "humbled" when Mom dies. For a relatively short period after Mom dies, it is not uncommon to find that family love is at a high, and nobody wants to cause problems. If Mom's estate can be distributed quickly during that period, the whole process goes smoothly, and everybody is happy. As time ticks away, somebody will go into the house and "take" something. The family members talk to their friends, and the friends plant ideas in their head. Attorneys are consulted. In short, the "family love" gives way to an all out legal or even physical brawl.

Emotions Run High

Any legal process that a person is exposed to "eats" at them. If you've been through probate as a personal representative or have been sued, you know what I'm talking about. An extended probate keeps family disagreements in the forefront of everyone's thoughts. It may be hard to "accept" Mom's death. The probate will make this acceptance even harder, because the issues never die as the process winds its way to completion dragging out for months and years.

It happened in our neighborhood, not in the next town or in the next state. It was just down the street, only a few houses. One brother was extremely frustrated over the probate process. He didn't like his two brothers acting as personal representatives, and he felt he could do a better job. He didn't like the way the house was being disposed of. He called a family meeting to discuss the whole mess. The probate had eaten him up. At the family meeting, he pulled a gun and killed all of his brothers. A man I had known for years was dead. And, his brother was a fugitive mass murderer.

People Don't Think Straight When They Lose a Spouse

This is a little bit of counsel I give my clients. This advice holds whether there is a living revocable trust or a probate. If you lose your spouse, you don't think straight for at least a year, and it usually takes two years to recover your full reasoning capacity. That sounds weird, but it is true. I see it over and over again.

If you have lost your spouse or you are dealing with a person who has lost his or her spouse, you must understand that things aren't normal. I counsel the surviving spouse not to make any investments for at least a year. Take the life insurance money, the retirement death benefits, and all of the other money, and put it into a certificate of deposit or a money market account. During the first year, don't spend any more than is absolutely necessary to maintain the life-style you've always had. Don't reinvest the money that is invested when the spouse died, unless the investment will be lost if it is not reinvested. During that first year, you don't care if the investments make money. Your only goal is to protect the principal so that there is something to invest in a year or two when your life stabilizes and your brains return from your broken heart. Yes, I know that the investment advisors will tell you this counsel is garbage, but don't believe them.

When I was first diagnosed with cancer, I had about three weeks of sanity before the chemotherapy and morphine destroyed my mind. Medically, there was no question that I was going to die. During the three weeks, Kristy and I formulated a plan wherein the life insurance money would be turned over in a trust to a committee of three friends. Two of the friends were doctors, and one was a banker. We considered all three to be brilliant money managers. We knew Kristy, although very intelligent, wouldn't be thinking right for a while so we proposed to get help for her. There isn't any disgrace in admitting that you need help or that Dad needs help. As it turned out, Kristy didn't get to collect the life insurance money so we didn't need the committee to move into action, and for some reason nobody was upset, especially me.

You'll be shocked when you tally up the emotional toll that a death exacts from the family, especially the surviving spouse and children.

Probate Kills Businesses

The death of the business commander-in-chief is often a fatal blow to the business. This is especially true for a small business. The leadership, creativity, and vision often die with the owner. Even if someone steps in with the same qualities, the business will struggle.

Small business owners face a real dilemma, because the spouse shouldn't be involved in the business as an officer, director, or partner, for asset (lawsuit) protection purposes. But, the spouse is often the logical person to take over the family business. Without careful planning, if the spouse isn't intimately involved, the business may well disintegrate when the owner dies. The business will probably be drawn into the probate. In fact, most wills grant the personal representative the power to operate a business, because it isn't uncommon to have the business end up in probate. After all, it's probably the major asset the owner has when he or she dies.

ASSET PROTECTION TIP #3

Don't put all your eggs in one basket. Couples that run small businesses, the Mom and Pop shop, need to carefully insulate one spouse from the liabilities of the business. All too often, a corporation is established to "protect the family's personal assets" in the event the business is sued or fails. Corporations can protect their owners, but not in the vast majority of cases, because the corporations are almost never structured and maintained properly. The courts "pierce the corporate veil" and come after the officers' and directors' personal assets.

The mistake people make is naming both Mom and Pop as officers and directors. One is president and the other is vice president and secretary/treasurer. So, when the business goes down and the corporate shield fails, Mom and Pop are both hanging out in the wind.

Insulate one or the other spouse. Make sure he or she isn't an officer or a director. His or her name should never appear in the business records, except possibly as an employee. That way, when the business blows up, only the owner/officer/director, the one spouse, will have his or her personal assets on the line. If the insulated spouse happens to own the house and the major bank accounts as his or her sole and separate property (property owned only by one person), then when the courts come after personal assets, the assets held by the insulated spouse are protected. This asset protection technique is so simple. However, because the insulated spouse is somehow brought into the business mess, it doesn't always protect the property, but it works in a lot of cases.

When assets are held as the sole and separate property of a spouse, the assets shouldn't actually be held in the spouse's name. The assets should be placed in the spouse's trust in order to avoid any probate problems when the spouse dies. Each spouse could actually have his or her own living revocable trust, or a separate section could be "carved out" of the couple's living revocable trust so that sole and separate property can be held under separate divisions of the trust and maintain its exclusive nature.

Why The Judge is Always Against You

Doctors and lawyers are always frustrating to work with, because they usually don't communicate with you often enough, and when they do talk to you, they speak a foreign language. When you pick a lawyer for probate, or for any other reason, make sure he or she speaks your language and is willing to tell you what is going on. If the lawyer won't communicate with you, probate becomes twice as frustrating as it needs to be.

The judge's policy is to communicate only through your attorney. This policy protects the judge and you. If the judge always keeps your attorney in the loop, you always have the benefit of counsel when the judge acts. In fact, the judge will always keep your attorney and all of the other attorneys informed so that nobody can accuse the judge of favoring one side or the other. Your attorney, not the judge, represents your interests. The courts hire the judge; you don't. He receives nothing from your probate. He is totally independent and must remain unbiased.

The Uniform Probate Code—It Can Help

Efforts have been made in the last couple of decades to standardize laws in each state of the United States. The most successful example of such standardization is the Uniform Commercial Code which governs "commercial" dealings between people and businesses. More or less, when McDonald's contracts to buy buns, they are assured that the deal can be structured the same in every state.

The American Law Institute and numerous committees have put together a Uniform Probate Code that has been adopted by a handful of states, and a number of additional states have adopted laws that are based on the code. The code is supposed to streamline the probate process and make it faster and cheaper. The time for such a standardized code is long overdue, and it is definitely a good idea, but it has received a cold shoulder in many states.

The law in the United States is based on legal precedence or "tradition," and lawyers are very slow to embrace new ideas. Their resistance to the Uniform Probate Code is not only founded in tradition, but it also undoubtedly has something to do with the fact that probate is the bread and butter for thousands and thousands of lawyers and law firms. Why should they embrace something that is going to take the butter off their bread and maybe even the bread off their table?

If you live in a state that has adopted the Uniform Probate Code, probate should be easier, and your fear of the process shouldn't be as high. However, many attorneys don't seem to get the message. I practice in a state which has adopted pretty much the entire Uniform Probate Code, and a lot of the attorneys charge just as they always have.

A good friend of mine came to me recently with a probate problem. His mother-in-law had died. She owned a house, a mountain lot, and stocks and bonds. My friend had shopped extensively for a probate attorney, and the best he could do was a guy that wanted a $3000 retainer and estimated the total cost would be about $5000 and take eight to twelve months to complete. Probate isn't the way I make my money so my friend hadn't come to me at first. By the time he had done his shopping, he was totally frustrated. I gave him a sample of the petition for an informal probate (an abbreviated version of probate authorized in the Uniform Probate Code), a sample of the affidavits he had to get all of his brothers and sisters to sign, and a sample of the Letters Testamentary that the court had to sign. He changed the names in the samples to make them apply to his family, and he hauled them down to the court. When all was said and done, he reported back that everything went well.

It had taken him several weeks and over $800 in cash to clean up the estate. He had lost a lot of time that wasn't included with the $800 as the cost of his experience, and he was lucky that things fell into place for him. If an estate really is simple and is going to be probated in a Uniform Probate Code state, in theory, the new laws make probate easy enough that you can handle the probate yourself if you are sharp and are willing to hustle. The probate is still going to be a pain and there will be a significant expense in money and time.

The whole probate problem can be avoided by simply using a living revocable trust, and that is what I recommend you at least consider doing. Every once in a while, I get together with my friend the law professor and we talk about the big picture. He argues that the probate process has been so streamlined now in certain states that the need for living revocable trusts has been greatly curtailed in those states.

He is right—in theory. But the fact is, when you walk in off of the street and want Dad's estate probated, you are looking at a fair sum of money (thousands of dollars) and a fair length of time (months), even if you live in a Uniform Probate Code state and the attorney tries his best to get you in and out of the system. It is true, in order to wrap up an estate, some of the money and time will have to be spent whether the estate goes through probate or is handled by a trust. The appraiser fees, title company fees, motor vehicle division pain, real estate agent hassle, and the like are all going to be the same whether there is a trust or not. Thus, it can't be said that all time and expenses can be saved by using a living revocable trust.

The argument I make to the professor is that the chances are extremely high that your living revocable trust will save you a lot of time, money, and pain. Additionally, your chance of getting a lawyer, that will make the probate laws work to their absolute maximum benefit for you, isn't very good. The problem is lawyers make a lot of money doing probates.

Much of the problem, especially in the Uniform Probate Code states, is caused by the attorneys not the law. In the professor's words, "The problem is not a function of the law. It is a function of the way the lawyers perform the process." In Uniform Probate Code states, I agree. In the other half of the states, you had better do more than just "consider" using a living revocable trust.

Chapter

9

The Benefits of Probate

When to Use it to Your Advantage

Probate bashing is easy to do. It's like lawyer jokes. You would undoubtedly agree that there are hundreds of lawyer jokes. You are wrong. There are only three lawyer jokes. All of the rest of the stories are true.

Probate is actually a very valuable process that can solve a lot of problems. Remember, I stated that probate is a legal tool. Use probate to your advantage. In a small percentage of situations, it should be used in preference to a living revocable trust or in addition to a living revocable trust. Oh, I am not advocating the probate of anyone's entire estate. Use a rifle approach to probate. If you are using a living revocable trust, all of the trust's property will be free from probate. Property "left out of the trust" will be probated. In order to receive the advantages of probate, you don't need to probate all of your assets. Only probate a few of your assets. You could intentionally leave a piece of property out of your trust in order to have that property probated. For example, only the deed which is legally flawed, a car, or one small checking account needs to be probated, and you can use the probate system to your advantage. The rest of the estate, which you do not want to be subject to probate, can be handled by your living revocable trust. In this chapter you will learn about the advantages of probating some or all of your assets.

Using Probate to Close Out Creditors

Probate can be used to make the estate's creditors deal with you under a deadline, and that could be a valid reason to probate part of Dad's estate. Maybe Dad really did owe everybody in the county money. If you use probate, all of Dad's creditors have to step up and make a claim at the court within the prescribed time; otherwise, they are out of luck. They cannot show up two years later and try to collect from you. Without probate, the creditors could try to collect directly from the estate or the heirs for years after Dad dies.

The trustee of a living revocable trust is liable to have the trust pay all of Dad's debts—without the security of having a deadline after which nobody can show up and make a claim. If, however, a probate proceeding is held on a few of the estate assets, the estate can be protected against creditors, while most of the assets pass through the living revocable trust smoothly and quickly.

Using Probate to Avoid Lawsuits

Today, debts and creditors aren't the only concern. The architects, engineers, accountants, doctors, lawyers, and other professionals have a real fear of being hit by a legal principle known as "deferred liability." If an engineer designs a part for an airplane engine and the part fails after 10 years of use, there is going to be a big lawsuit. When the plane crashes, the engineer will be sued along with the airline manufacturer. The liability the engineer has for designing a defective part is "deferred" until the time when the part fails.

Even though the engineer has been dead five years when the part fails, he will be named in the lawsuit. Actually, his estate will be named in the lawsuit. However, if there has been a formal probate of his estate and the probate has been completed, there isn't any "estate" to sue. There isn't anybody to sue. The estate has been formally opened and closed. Actually, the notice and publication process in a simple, informal probate will be enough to prevent the lawsuit in many states.

Society has an interest in bringing Dad's affairs to a close, and probate is the way the law has chosen to write the last chapter. Once the gavel falls in the formal probate, Dad's business affairs on this earth are closed. It is over and can't be reopened. However, lawyers are always looking for a deep pocket to sue, and in some states the push is on to change the law so you can't ever close Dad's estate to certain liabilities.

ASSET PROTECTION TIP #4

To protect estate assets from lawsuits that might occur long after Dad dies, probate some part of the estate. Make sure the publication and notification process is carried out exactly, and have at least a formal opening to the probate process. This is critical if Dad was a professional that had to worry about deferred liability.

Clearing Up Property Titles Using Probate

Real property titles can be "clouded" for many reasons. Your family might have property where there is a missing link in the "chain of title," or there is a question about the boundaries of the property. If you are arguing with Mom's neighbor about which side of the fence the property line is on, you could sue Mom's neighbor and bring a quiet title action, or you could probate the title to the property when Mom dies. Anyone who has an argument over the property had better show up at Mom's probate, or they are out of luck. When the probate court transfers title, that title is free from all "clouds" or problems. Oh, there may still be a mortgage, but everything is cut, dried, and in order. Unless the neighbors understand the probate process, they could end up on the wrong side of the fence.

The Family Can Earn Money and Save Estate Taxes With Probate

Probate can actually save you money in some cases. The lawyer fees, personal representative fees, maintenance fees, cleaning fees, and everything else comes out of the estate before the estate tax is calculated.

Almost every American family has lost one or more of their children—they became lawyers. If cousin Vinnie really is a lawyer, have him handle the probate. The personal representative will almost always be a family member, and he or she can make a good fee. After Mom dies, hire the kids to clean her house and maintain the yard until it is sold.

You will be amazed how expensive yard-keeping kids can be these days. Basically, all of the money spent from the estate is moving directly back into the family. This money is "estate tax" deductible. It is cleaner to deduct administration expenses from the "estate" than it is to try to deduct trust fees. Trust fees are deductible, but the system of estate tax forms and deductions is set up for probate, so estate tax deductions work out "neater" for probates. Yes, the fees paid to the family members will be income to them, but the income tax may be cheaper than the estate tax. You will have to check with your accountant to see if your family will save money.

Estate taxes are covered in Chapter 19, but you need to know how important it is to whittle down the amount of estate exposed to estate taxes. The first dollar exposed to estate tax loses over 37 cents, and before long, every dollar is losing 55 cents to the tax. If the probate fees directly or indirectly go to the family and reduce the estate tax, there can be a big savings.

Probate Can Help Control Taxes

There are other very subtle advantages to probate. A probated estate can choose to have a fiscal tax year rather than a calendar tax year. This gives a probated estate the possibility of deferring income and saving income taxes. A living revocable trust has to use a calendar tax year for income tax reporting.

Additionally, a probated estate will have a $600 exemption on its income tax return. A simple trust only gets a $300 exemption when it files its tax return after Dad dies.

These are major arguments attorneys that hate living revocable trusts use against the trusts. The fact is, except in 2 or 3% of the cases, the arguments never come into play to any significant degree. For the 98% of the cases that aren't really affected, the possible savings are a couple of hundred dollars at the maximum.

Some of the other valid, but almost never applicable, advantages of wills over trusts include the deductibility of a loss generated when a probate estate sells property at a loss to an heir of the estate. The estate will get a tax deduction for the loss. Section 267 (b)(6) of the IRS Code says a trust won't get a deduction if the trustee sells property at a loss to a beneficiary. The trust could sell the property to someone other than a beneficiary and deduct the loss, thus avoiding the problem. Actually, I have never seen a will or a trust that says, "Sell my property to my kids when I die," so the situation seldom occurs.

If trusts accumulate income, they are subject to complex tax laws. They may have a lower tax rate than an individual, but the tax laws are very complicated. Probate estates can accumulate income and are not subject to the complex tax laws. The problem is easy to solve. Just write the trust and tell the trustee not to accumulate income. More or less, make the trust a "simple trust" (one that cannot accumulate income) instead of a "complex trust" (one that can accumulate income). Unless the estate is huge, the heirs or beneficiaries will probably want the income paid to them rather than accumulated.

You need to know what the advantages of a will are. If you can use a will and make the subtle advantages work for you, then go ahead and use a will as your basic estate planning document.

The tax advantages we have mentioned are so subtle that very few attorneys would ever even pick them up when they are working with an estate. The "advantages" a will and probate offer simply don't affect most estates, so a living revocable trust is a pretty safe bet.

To Probate or Not—The Decision Can Be Yours

You may have the impression that an estate is either probated or a living revocable trust is used, and the whole estate avoids probate. That impression is wrong. Only assets held by the trust avoid probate. In upcoming chapters, you will learn how to actually use the trust to avoid probate. However, having a living revocable trust doesn't guarantee you will avoid probate. In fact, most people who have a living revocable trust *do not* avoid probate. Don't worry, we will teach you how to control probate or to avoid probate, if you want to avoid probate. The decision should be yours. All you need to know is how to control the legal tools—a living revocable trust and probate.

If Dad has a small business that needs to qualify for the special estate tax advantages offered to small businesses that are being probated, fine; probate the business. When you get through with this book you should be able to orchestrate the living revocable trust and probate well enough to structure Dad's estate plan so that the business is probated and everything else Dad owned avoids probate. You can decide whether or not to take a specific asset to probate. Not bad, huh?

When you are weighing your decision (isn't it nice to have the decision?) about whether or not to deal with probate, you will certainly consider the financial and tax aspects of probate, but don't forget the emotional aspects. Is the time and pain worth the money you might gain in probate? For most estates there is no reason to even consider probate. So, avoid it!

Chapter

10

The Power of Trusts

Introducing a Secret to Wealth

Trusts are some of the oldest and best defined relationships known in the law. The Babylonians used trusts, and every society since then has used some sort of trust relationship. The basic concept of a trust is very easy to understand. One person (the "grantor") gives up property or "grants" property to another person (the trustee), who is "trusted" by the grantor. The trustee is trusted to take care of the property and use the property, not for himself, but for the "benefit" of a third person (the beneficiary). The terms "trustee" and "beneficiary" are standard in every trust. However, the term "grantor" is often replaced by "settlor," "creator," or "trustor." It becomes very confusing if the same document uses two or three terms to refer to the grantor. I always use the term "grantor."

A "trust" is simply an agreement—a relationship—the grantor has with the trustee. In this book, the word "trust" will refer to the written document that defines the relationship between the grantor and the trustee. There are many types of trusts. Each one is designed to achieve a specific purpose. A living revocable trust is a special type of trust used to avoid probate, reduce estate taxes, preserve your privacy, and manage your financial affairs. When you establish a living revocable trust for yourself, you will probably be the grantor, the trustee, and the beneficiary all at the same time.

The trustee actually owns the property or holds title to the property in his or her capacity as trustee, not in his or her capacity as an individual. So, when John Doe is acting as trustee for his own living revocable trust, he will open a checking account (he will hold title to the checking account) as follows: "John Doe, Trustee for the John Doe Living Revocable Trust dated July 4, 1976."

Although the trustee holds title to the property in his or her name as trustee, the law and everybody else recognizes that the property really doesn't belong to the trustee. The property belongs to the trust, and the trustee is just the caretaker. You don't have to worry that the trust property will be lost if the trustee gets sued or even goes bankrupt. Everybody knows the property isn't the trustee's. The trustee is just "holding title" to the property for the benefit of the beneficiary. The law honors the trustee/beneficiary relationship and protects the property from personal, legal, and financial problems the trustee may encounter.

The trust document tells the trustee what he or she is supposed to do with the property, and the trustee is bound by law to follow the exact instructions given by the trust. The trustee is bound by a "fiduciary duty" to handle the property exactly as the trust directs. Sometimes the trustee is referred to as a "fiduciary."

A fiduciary duty is a solemn responsibility imposed by law. The law doesn't lay out the day-to-day tasks trustees must perform to fulfill their responsibilities, but the law does set an exact standard (a very high standard) of conduct trustees must meet. A fiduciary relationship is one of the best defined relationships in our legal system. While people do serve as trustees all of the time and things work out OK, if they knew ahead of time what a solemn responsibility a trustee really has as a fiduciary, there is no way anyone would ever serve as a trustee. The fiduciary relationship is so well defined, and it protects the beneficiaries so well, that there is little or no reason to fear using a trust with a third party trustee.

In your living revocable trust, you will serve as your own trustee as long as you are alive and able to serve. You will also be the beneficiary, so there is absolutely no reason for you to be a afraid of using a living revocable trust. There is an exception to your ability to act alone as your own trustee. In the state of New York, attorneys have such a total control of probate that they have had a law passed so that you can't be your own trustee and avoid probate. Doesn't that make you love New York? The way around the problem is easy. Simply have your spouse, your brother, mother, uncle, or someone be a co-trustee with you.

Why Don't You Already Have a Living Revocable Trust?

If you aren't already using a living revocable trust, it's probably because you are not familiar enough with trusts to be comfortable using one. Living revocable trusts are becoming more and more popular, especially in the Western United States. I routinely teach classes about living revocable trusts and asset protection. Over the last decade, I have seen living revocable trusts become a viable estate planning tool in every state. Attorneys, banks, and people in general are becoming familiar with the living revocable trust concept and are embracing its use.

During the first years of my practice, I would have to visit the banks with my clients and show the bank people how to establish a trust account. The new accounts person at the bank wasn't used to having someone show up and open a checking account for a living revocable trust. I don't need to go to the banks with the clients anymore, because the banks have seen enough living revocable trusts that they understand what needs to be done. However, on the Eastern seaboard some banks still need a little coaching, because not as many people in the East use living revocable trusts. That's a shame, because the people in the East have the largest probate problems.

Many people I counsel in New York and other Eastern states say that their attorney said a living revocable trust wouldn't work in their state. Hogwash! You don't have to submit to the ritual of probate. A living revocable trust works in every state. With a few minor exceptions, the laws are very uniform throughout the United States. The living revocable trust works even in Canada, but it is used a little differently. Probate is such a deep tradition in the East that everyone has simply accepted it as the third sure thing in life, right behind death and taxes. As my lawyer friend in New York found out, probate isn't just a big business in New York, it is a huge business.

Living Revocable Trusts By a Different Name

In the Western United States, where the trusts are more popular, the terminology "living revocable trust" is becoming so popular with the masses that attorneys are calling the trust an "LRT." Lawyers used to call the trust an Inter Vivos Revocable Trust. "Inter vivos" is Latin for "between the living" and "revocable" simply means it can be changed or "revoked" by the grantor (you). The living revocable trust is also commonly called an "A-B Trust," a "C Trust," a "Family Trust," a "Shelter Trust," a "Common Trust," a "QTIP (Qualified Terminable Interest Property) Trust," and a dozen other names. Some books call it a "Loving Trust," because it is a trust you set up for the people you love. That is true. Establishing the trust is something you do for the people you love. Whatever name you call it by, the trust is the same. Don't be confused. To insure that you have to come to them to get the special named trust, many lawyers and authors have put their own special name on a living revocable trust.

Avoid The Set Up—A Testamentary Trust

Make sure you get a living revocable trust. I have had a number of clients proudly present me with a copy of their supposed living revocable trust, and the trust turns out to be a fraud. If you walk into a lawyer's office and say, "Here I am. Set me up." You just might get set up. You may not be given a living revocable trust. You might get a testamentary trust.

The testamentary trust can be a major set up, because not only do you pay the up front price of a trust, you have no chance of avoiding probate. A testamentary trust is basically a very complicated will. The trust isn't "established" until after your death and all of your property has been probated. After the probate, the property is given to the trust, which then holds the property for the beneficiaries or distributes it to them as directed by the trust. The trust and trustee are subject to the court's scrutiny just as if the property was being managed by a personal representative acting under a will. The testamentary trust can turn out to be a bigger nightmare and more expensive than a simple will and probate.

You can spot a testamentary trust, because the trust is created in the will. Clients often say that their will has a trust inside of it. That is true, but the trust isn't created until after their death and the probate. A living revocable trust is created as of a specific date, i.e. the date the trust is signed. Watch carefully to be sure you don't get a testamentary trust.

There is a very legitimate argument raging in the legal community. Some lawyers say living revocable trusts shouldn't be promoted, and the boiler room lawyers, who turn out living revocable trusts at the rate of 50 a day, should be shut down. They argue that boiler room lawyers are charging for a trust that avoids probate, when in reality the clients almost never avoid probate. The clients would have been better off getting a will or testamentary trust and admitting that their estate was going to go through probate. The bottom line is, their attorney never taught them how to use the trust, and/or they never understood what their responsibilities were. Unless you know how to use the trust and actually use it, you have wasted your money and you probably should have gotten a simple will. The simple will should be cheaper to set up than a living revocable trust.

If you are in a Uniform Probate Code state and have an attorney that will do the probate fast and cheap, then a testamentary trust may be just your ticket. In fact, the argument can be made that the testamentary trust will make life easier because you don't need to "use the trust" during your life. But, I find the arguments in favor of testamentary trusts to be hypocritical, because the same lawyers that argue against living revocable trusts charge as much for a will, which establishes a testamentary trust, as you would pay anywhere for a living revocable trust. With a testamentary trust, you can't avoid probate even if you want to avoid it. Your estate goes through probate—guaranteed. The fact is, a large percentage of lawyers will gouge the family during the probate process.

So You Want to Avoid Probate—You Have to Know How

One sure way to avoid probate is to enjoy life, prepay your funeral expenses, and budget your money so that you spend your last quarter calling the mortuary as you die in the phone booth. If you don't have anything when you die, there is nothing to "transfer." Thus, there is no probate. Of course, you don't want to die in a phone booth, and you want to take care of your family even after you die. Don't give up. Your living revocable trust really can avoid probate, help eliminate estate tax, and protect your property in the event you become incompetent. The trust will assure that the maximum amount of your estate ends up with your family and that you retain maximum control over your property—even after you die. The whole concept and operation of the trust is so simple that it will make you mad that you didn't start using a trust earlier.

Controlling Ownership

Before you start using a trust, you have to fully understand the abstract concept of ownership. Remember the discussion about ownership documents like deeds, signature cards for the bank accounts and safe deposit boxes, stocks, and bonds? If a dead person's name is on the ownership document, then the court has to give someone else the authority to sign for the dead person and transfer the property. The quest to obtain that authority and determine who should receive the property is the probate process.

The living revocable trust does an end run around this whole process. The trust makes it so that a dead person's name never shows up on an ownership document. The law and our society have said that the trust can own property.

The trust is treated just like a person by the law. It can own property, sue, get sued, be born or "created," and die just like a person. This is actually all an illusion, because a piece of paper (the trust) can't really own your house. Ownership, the right to sue, and everything else actually rests with the trustee, who is the warm body behind the piece of paper. But everybody knows that the property isn't really owned by the trustee; it's really owned by the trust. Can you see a circular argument here? Don't worry about it. I told you that the law doesn't have to be logical.

A Trust By Any Other Name Is Not Your Trust

Assume you and your spouse are named John and Mary Doe. After you have created your trust, you must make sure that the trust owns your property. Note that the trust is created by simply writing down the instructions you want to give the trustee concerning the property that will be "held" by the trust. Making the trust own property is easy.

If you want to own a bank account yourself, then you will go to the bank and open up a bank account in your name, i.e., "John Doe" or "Mary Doe." If you want to have the bank account owned by yourself and your spouse, you will open up the bank account in the name of "John Doe and/or Mary Doe." If you want your trust to own the bank account, you will open up the bank account in the name of your trust.

What do you name your trust? Name your trust as you would your child, i.e. anything you want. However, most people would not name their trust "Jim Doe." The normal name for the trust would be the "John and Mary Doe Living Revocable Trust, dated July 4, 1997." You could name the trust the "Upstitch Trust, dated July 4, 1997," or anything else. Note that your trust has two parts to its name. The first part is the part you make up, i.e.,

"The John and Mary Doe Living Revocable Trust." The second part is the date you created the trust, i.e., "dated July 4, 1997." Yes, you do have to have both parts of the name. People really mess up their trust when they don't have the date as part of the name. If you only had one name for yourself, you would always be messed up also.

I have a friend named "Susie." She went to court and had her birth name taken off her records, and she changed her name to "Susie." No, there aren't two names, only one. It is very awkward every time she introduces herself, because everyone waits for the second name. Only having one name has actually caused her a lot of problems. One day she had been to the beach and did not have her purse or driver's license because she had intentionally left them home so that they wouldn't get stolen. She was stopped by the police for a minor traffic violation. The conversation went something like this:

Police: *May I see your driver's license?*
Susie: *I am sorry sir, I left it home.*
Police: *What is your name?*
Susie: *Susie.*
Police: *What is your full name?*
Susie: *Susie.*
Police: *Don't be cute lady. What is your last name?*
Susie: *Susie. I don't have two names.*
Police: *Sure, lady. I'm calling for a backup.*

By the time all was said and done, Susie was hauled off in handcuffs, and she literally spent the night in jail. Even though she can't buy airline tickets, get credit cards, and do other simple things, she still only has one name.

Your trust is going to have two names. Right? It is named, "The <u>(something)</u> Trust, dated <u>(some date)</u>. You can create more than one trust, just like you can have more than one child. Each child will receive a different first name and the same last name, because that is just the way our society does the naming thing. Each trust you create will receive two names. The first name (The John and Mary Doe Living Revocable Trust) could be the same or different for each trust, but the second name, i.e., the date, will always be different.

So, when you want the bank account to be owned by the trust, you use the trust's name. Let's assume you will be the trustee (controller) for your own trust. The signature card at the bank will read something like this: "The John and Mary Doe Living Revocable Trust, dated July 4, 1997, John Doe, Trustee; Mary Doe, Trustee." You must always identify the trustee by name, because it is actually the trustee who holds title to the property. I will go into detail later about how to move each type of property into the trust.

I have been very specific as to how you should name your trust. Let me back peddle and say that there are numerous ways to name your trust. You shouldn't get nervous if the bank, brokerage house, or insurance company has a "required" way they want to see your trust named. In fact, the way you name your trust, or at least the way you write it down, varies from state to state. For example, Wyoming requires the beneficiaries to be named as part of the trust's name. Ask your local title insurance company or escrow company how they want to see your trust's name appear on a deed. Ask your stock broker how the brokerage company wants to see the name on their forms. After a while you will get a feel for the way your trust's name needs to be written down.

In most cases, the critical part is the date and the identification of the trustee. So, the trust's name on your stock account could read:

Doe Family Trust
John Doe and Mary Doe, Trustees
Under Agreement July 4, 1997
For the Benefit of the Doe Family

Lots of times the trust name is abbreviated so that it will fit into the space allocated on the deed or form. For example:

John Doe and Mary Doe, Trustees
U/A 7/4/97
FBO Doe Family

Abbreviations often used in reference to trusts:

U/A = Under Agreement
U/D = Under Date

U/D/T = Under Declaration of Trust
F/B/O = For the Benefit Of
Tr = Trust
Ttee = Trustee

The Trick—Why Trusts Avoid Probate

Here comes the probate trick. When your bank account is owned by your trust, i.e., it is in the name of your trust, and you die, did the owner of the account die? No, you, the trustee, the manager of the account died. The trust, that is the owner of the account, did not die. Will the account be probated? No! The owner isn't dead. Just the manager is dead. When the president, the manager, of IBM dies, does IBM have to probate all of its assets? No, the stockholders get together and elect a new president.

When you opened the account at the bank in the name of your trust, the bank, by letting you open the account, recognized your trust and agreed to recognize the trustees named in your trust. Of course the trust document has a section in it that appoints a new trustee, the "successor trustee," to act when you are dead. All you do is write down a statement in the trust that says that you want your wife or husband to be the sole trustee when you die and that you want Uncle Harry to be the successor trustee when both you and your spouse are dead.

OK, let's say you and your spouse both die in an automobile accident today. What happens at the bank? Uncle Harry walks into the bank tomorrow, and the conversation with the banker goes something like this:

Uncle Harry: *Hi, John and Mary were killed in an automobile accident last night.*

Banker: *Yeah, I read about it in the newspaper. Too bad!*

Uncle Harry: *I need to get into the bank account.*

Banker: *Drop dead, buddy. Go get me a probate order. I'll see you in a year and a half.*

Uncle Harry: *No, this is a trust account.*

Banker: *Oh, yeah.*

The banker goes into the back room to get the file. When you opened the account, the banker may have made a copy of all or part of the trust. Usually the banker doesn't actually want a copy of all the pages in your trust. It's best to supply the banker with a certification of the trust from your attorney or argue that the banker only needs a copy of the first and last pages, just to reference the trust. (When you have an attorney draft your trust, ask if a certification of the trust document is part of the deal.) If Uncle Harry has a copy of the death certificate and the trust, or the banker has his own copy of the trust, the banker will know Uncle Harry is the new trustee. The banker will ask for Uncle Harry's identification and simply say, "sign here."

Uncle Harry is into the bank account. No court order. No lawyer. No two year wait. No probate! When you died, there was an instantaneous transfer of power to the new trustee.

Oh, the money isn't Uncle Harry's now. It still belongs to the trust and Uncle Harry is now under the sacred fiduciary duty to follow your instructions and manage or distribute the property exactly according to the instructions you left behind in the trust.

You just eliminated probate. It was a slam dunk, but most people who get a living revocable trust never understand what you now have learned. You have to know why the trust works. The trust has to own the property. Most people forget to open the new checking account in the name of their trust, or they never change their existing checking account into the name of the trust. They are under the false impression that just because they have a piece of paper called a trust, they will not go through probate. You have to use the trust.

In 1976, Kristy's parents spent $2,600 for a living revocable trust, and they happened to get a good document. When I started to work with living revocable trusts in 1981, I looked at their trust. Although they had a good document, it would not have saved their family from probating everything when they died. The lawyer had not taught them how to use the trust. Just having a trust and understanding it isn't enough. You have to <u>USE</u> your trust. I had to go back and teach them how to put the bank accounts and real estate into the trust.

Actually, the lawyer who drafted their trust had made out a new deed transferring their house into the trust, and he had sent a letter to the bank notifying the bank that a trust had been created.

These were steps in the right direction, but Kristy's parents had bought more real estate and opened all new bank accounts. None of the new real estate or bank accounts were in the name of the trust. If they had died, everything would have gone through probate.

The goal of this book is to give you the information you need to draft your own living revocable trust, using two or three good form books. Or you can pick a good lawyer and get it done. Whatever you do to get it done is OK by me. But I have to stress, just giving you an understanding of the trust really isn't enough. I have to actually lead you through the steps you need to take in order to use the living revocable trust. It is a "living" dynamic document and concept. It isn't something that you just put in a safe deposit box and forget about. Whether you write it or a lawyer writes the trust, it doesn't matter. You have to know your trust inside and out and use it daily.

Chapter

11

Creating Your Trust

How to Choose Among Books, Computers, and Lawyers

Obviously you can have a living revocable trust and use it to good advantage. However, trusts have traditionally been something that wealthy people had. Middle income Americans couldn't afford to use a trust. That isn't true today. Two things, a new concept of trustees and the computer, have made the trust a very affordable and useful tool for everyone.

Trustees Need Not Cost a Dime

Almost everywhere in the United States, it has become acceptable for the grantor (you) to act as the trustee. You can act as your own trustee. Historically, your bank would usually act as the trustee of your trust. Some of you will remember that the banks all used to have a name something like "First Cheatem National Bank and Trust."

Fifty years ago almost all banks had the word "trust" in their name. The rich people did banking, and they had trusts. As the banks turned their marketing efforts to the middle class thirty years ago, they dropped the word "Trust" from their names. They probably reasoned that Ordinary Joe didn't have a trust, so in order to appeal to Ordinary Joe, they dropped any mention of trusts in their names. That was a big mistake, because today Ordinary Joe does have a trust, a living revocable trust, and trusts are a big draw for lawyers and financial planners.

In the good old days, the banks made money managing trusts for the rich. The bank was actually the trustee of most trusts. Each year the banks would charge between 0.5% and maybe 1% of the gross value of the trust in order to be the trustee of most trusts. All larger banks today still have "trust departments," and they manage lots of trusts. They still charge about the same rates to act as trustee. So, when the bank acts as trustee, there is an ongoing expense associated with a trust, and the service may be well worth the expense. However, when you act as your own trustee, there isn't any ongoing expense for you or your trust. With almost no maintenance fees associated with a living revocable trust, it is now affordable for everyone to have a living revocable trust.

The Easy Way to Write Your Own Trust

The expense of setting up a trust with a lawyer in days past was prohibitive. Trusts are usually long legal documents. Before the computer and word processing, it was very time consuming for the lawyer and very labor intensive for the law office to physically prepare the trust document. That made the trust very expensive. This is somewhat of an oversimplification, but today, lawyers simply use a computer to fill your name in the blanks and print the trust. Anyone can prepare a trust.

In 1988 I received a $160,000 grant from the federal government to develop a computer program that would let a non-lawyer draft a patent license agreement. The government wanted to speed the technology transfer process in order to improve our economic competitiveness with other countries. I pointed out that one of the major bottlenecks in technology transfer was the lawyer. Have you ever noticed that lawyers are like beavers? They both get into the mainstream of things and dam them up.

Since 1988, the computer program has had another $300,000 in improvements and is used by many Fortune 500 companies, universities, and major law firms when they draft a license for a patent. The computer program has been adapted so that you can prepare your own wills and living revocable trusts. The computer program makes it very easy for you to tailor a unique document to fit your circumstances.

Being able to act as your own trustee and set up the trust with a minimal expense means everyone can now use a trust and get all of its benefits.

Things to Consider When Deciding to Use an Attorney

Should you use an attorney to set up your trust? It's your decision. If you have enough knowledge to be comfortable setting up your own trust, then set up your own trust. If you have any reservations about your own work, use an attorney. Be careful! Don't be used by an attorney. It is always good to get a second opinion. So, whether you do your own work or use an attorney, try to get a second opinion from an attorney, your accountant, or someone. Actually, this book will help you do your own original work if you couple the knowledge you find here with a form book or computer program. Or you can use the information in this book to formulate your own "second opinion" on work done by an attorney.

I have a lot of reservations about using just any old attorney to draft your living revocable trust. Most attorneys were never exposed to a living revocable trust in law school, and they don't know any more about trusts than to go to a form book and fill in the blanks. Whether *Fortune Magazine* is correct or not when they state that only 1% of American lawyers know how to properly draft a living revocable trust, the fact is, not a lot of lawyers know what they are doing with a living revocable trust.

I have often become infuriated when I have read the trusts people have brought to me. They have paid $1000, $2000, $5000, $10,000, or more for a living revocable trust, and it is a piece of trash. The trust has language in it that the lawyer has inserted from a corporation or partnership document, and it is a mess.

If you do use this book and the computer program, you should be able to do a good job on your own trust. *However, if you draft your own trust, you take the risk of doing your own legal work.* If the only goal is to avoid probate, a home grown trust, used properly, will almost always work.

If you have a taxable estate, then more is at stake. You not only have to worry about avoiding probate, you also have to worry about eliminating estate taxes. Setting up the trust becomes more complicated, and a knowledgeable attorney or accountant should be used, at least for a second opinion on work you have done. In the case of a taxable estate, it would probably be worth your money to get professional help. Don't be penny wise and pound foolish. But, you can't just blindly trust your attorney or accountant, so study very carefully and make sure the professionals are doing a good job *for* you, not *on* you.

The great news is, when you finish this book, you will certainly know enough to easily determine whether your attorney or accountant knows much about living revocable trusts. You will be amazed when you figure out that you know more about living revocable trusts than many attorneys and accountants. Armed with your knowledge, you can effectively shop for an attorney to do your trust, if you want an attorney to do the trust. When you are shopping, if you know more than the attorney, it is time to get another attorney.

The best thing you can do is learn about trusts and how to use them, then get a good local attorney to help you through the rough spots. Yes, good attorneys are out there, and they are worth their weight in gold. Lest you forget their value, they will remind you in their billing statement. If you have the attorney actually set up the trust, don't forget to check the trust with your own knowledge.

Beware of Attorney Sweat Shops and Runners

Beware of the attorney who cranks out living revocable trusts at the rate of ten per day. The attorney is big into seminars or advertising. Insurance agents or financial planners mass market living revocable trusts for the attorney. The insurance agent, financial planner, credit union employee, or other person will "collect" the information the attorney needs, and then the attorney will give you a telephone call, if you are lucky. You may only see the attorney when you sign the trust, or you may never even see the attorney. You will sign the trust with the person who helped "collect" the information.

The "information collector" or "runner" is getting a kickback on the trust. The kickback could be as subtle as a sales pitch given to you by the attorney telling you to buy insurance or invest with the "runner." Often the "runner" makes more than the lawyer. Technically, it is illegal to have a runner bring the attorney business. It may be illegal, but a lot of attorneys do it anyway.

The sad part is, you aren't getting any more than a standard form. The long form that the information collector has you fill out isn't used for any purpose other than to get your personal information, name, address, etc., and to see if you have a taxable estate. If you have a taxable estate, the trust is exactly the same, but the price doubles.

How to Identify a Quick and Dirty Trust

Computers can easily be used to prepare the standard form, but even computers aren't fast enough for some lawyers. They type an "introductory page" that has your name, the kids' names, and other personal information, and then the rest of the trust pages are simply pulled out of bins and stapled onto the front page. Oh yeah, there is a signature page with your name on it stapled at the back. That is what you pay thousands of dollars for.

In the "staple-together trusts," there is a dead giveaway that tells you what happened. Each "section" or part of the trust is typed separately. This is obvious, because each section starts at the top of a new page and there is a lot of room left on the page that ends each section. This means that if one section does have to be changed, it can be changed without affecting the page numbering for the rest of the trust.

Ask to "see" a trust when you go to the attorney's office. You can spot the staple-together trusts. Ask to see two trusts, so that you can see how two people set up their trusts. You will get one trust, but you won't get two trusts, because the lawyer doesn't want to show you that all trusts are basically identical. Even with the most conscientious lawyers, there are only two or three parts of the trust that are ever changed. The rest of the trust is standard "boiler plate." In fact, the law requires the trust to have the same exact language in many of the sections, so those sections are never changed. Once you know what the boiler plate means and the two or three sections that can be changed, you have got the trust down. Then learn to use it, and you are home free.

Getting the Most Out of Your Lawyer

If you aren't the do-it-yourself type, and you want to have a lawyer draft your trust, that is OK. In fact, as a lawyer, I like that! When you work with a lawyer, here is what to expect, and here are some tips that can save you money.

Living revocable trusts do cost more than wills. The $2,600 Kristy's father paid for his living revocable trust was probably too much for what he got. I have seen cases where the clients were charged as little as $300 for their living revocable trust and other cases where the clients were charged over $10,000. In both cases, the clients got ripped off. The $300 cases almost always produce a worthless piece of paper for the clients, and the $10,000 cases cost thousands of dollars too much.

On a national average, living revocable trust packages drafted by good attorneys should cost somewhere between $1,000 and $2,000. The complexity of your estate, the number of assets in the estate, the value of the assets, the location of each asset, and how the assets are "owned" should be the primary considerations in determining how much the lawyer will charge for your trust. The price you are charged often doesn't correlate with the quality of the trust. The price usually correlates with your location, the good or bad conscience of the lawyer, and how much the attorney wants the work. Most attorneys quote a package price for the trust. If you are quoted a package price, make sure the package at least includes the living revocable trust, pour-over wills (Chapter 13), and initial funding of the trust (Chapter 12). The package may also include a trust certificate, a durable power of attorney (Chapter 14), a durable power of attorney for health care (Chapter 14), and a living will (Chapter 6).

Lawyers quote package prices when they want to charge a lot and know that the job won't take much time. If the going rate for the package is $1,500, and it only takes three hours, it is hard for the lawyer to justify a $500 an hour billing rate, so the lawyer simply charges a package price. Actually, if the package price deal is fair for your locality, don't begrudge your attorney his money. The $1,500 can be justified for many reasons. Believe me, it took more than three hours per trust for the first trusts the attorney set in place. I am honestly amazed at what my overhead runs, and mine is less than that of most attorneys. I admit, I have a hard time judging what legal work is worth. If the work is done right and it saves you $300,000 when Dad dies, it is worth every dime of $1,500, even if it only took the attorney three hours.

A quote on a package price gives you an open door. Bargain with the lawyer. Present yourself with all of the information in Appendices 2 and 3. Demonstrate that you know about trusts, that you already have written down exactly whom you want as your successor trustees, and that you know how you want the property to be distributed. Additionally, assure the lawyer that you can get the bank accounts changed, make out all of the schedules, shuttle the deeds around to be recorded, and basically use the trust. Obviously, you know what you are doing, and the lawyer won't have to spend as much time helping you. You will often get a discounted package price if you ask for the discount. You have to ask, or you will never get a discount. Remember, don't waste the lawyer's time with small talk.

Lawyers should be able to prepare your trust in about a week. You then need to review the trust and allow another week or so to have any revisions done. The whole process of setting up the trust and wills should take two or three weeks. When things were simple and the client was on his death bed, I have done the process in as little as two hours. Do your trust early, because if your lawyer is like me, he hates dealing with people who are actually dying. They might actually get in the last word.

Finding a Good Trust Attorney

Lawyers do specialize. In law school we are taught that as lawyers we can do anything. Actually, each area of law has its specialists. Patent law is the only area in law where the lawyer actually has to take a special Bar exam in addition to the standard Bar exam.

If you want to use an attorney, how do you find an attorney that will do a good job on your living revocable trust? Start by looking in the phone book. The yellow pages often categorize attorneys by specialty. Look for names of lawyers under "Estate Planning," "Tax and Estates," "Wills and Estates," "Probate," or similar categories. Then check to see if the same lawyers are listed under "Divorces" or "Ambulance Chasing."

Some lawyers do very well ambulance chasing. In fact, I once met a lawyer who had done so well ambulance chasing that he bought his own ambulance. OK, it's a joke, but it's no joke when an ambulance chaser tries to do your living revocable trust. If the lawyer advertises to do your living revocable trust and your divorce, go to a different lawyer for your living revocable trust and your divorce. When you have found the names of attorneys that only advertise under estate planning, then you need to check them out.

You can get some information about an attorney by contacting the State Bar Association. Each state has a Bar Association, which is simply the lawyers' union. Each lawyer has to belong to the Bar. Because you either belong to the Bar or you don't work, law is a union shop. The Bar has specialty subsections, such as tax and estate planning, bankruptcy, divorce, etc. A true trust attorney will belong to the tax and estate planning section of the state Bar.

After you have found some names from the phone book, you can call your state's Bar Association and ask if a specific attorney, John Doe, is a member of the tax and estate planning section of the Bar. The people in the Bar office should be able to tell you if John Doe is a member. If he is a member of the tax and estate planning section, then you have another indication that the lawyer might write good trusts. Generally, you can't just call up the Bar and ask for the lawyers who are in a specific section of the Bar. The people working at the Bar normally won't just read you the list of lawyers that belong to the estate planning section of the Bar. They should, however, look up the information for a specific name you give them.

Don't just call the Bar and ask them to recommend an attorney who does living revocable trusts. Starving lawyers pay the Bar to be on referral lists for people who are looking for attorneys. The referral list of lawyers is probably not the same as the list of lawyers that belong to the tax and estate planning section of the Bar. Good living revocable trust attorneys probably won't be on the list, because they aren't desperate for clients. So, use the Bar to check out specific lawyers. Don't call the Bar and simply ask for recommendations.

One more tip may be helpful if you are trying to locate the best trust attorney in town. Call up the offices of the big life insurance companies like New York Life, Northwest Mutual, Metropolitan Life, etc. (If you don't want to see an agent, you don't have to give them your name, but they really are very professional, in most cases.) Ask to speak to the office manager or general agent. You don't want to speak to some wet-behind-the-ears agent. You want the top dog. When you get to the top, just ask for his or her recommendation for the three or four most highly respected trust attorneys. Somebody who is a true professional and has been around in life insurance will know the good trust attorneys.

How to Make The Trust Legal—Filing Trusts

No, you don't need a lawyer's participation or signature on your trust to make it legal. No, your living revocable trust doesn't have to be filed anywhere. It isn't even filed anywhere after you die. The beauty of the trust is its privacy. Because it doesn't have to be "filed," nobody has to know what your trust says, how the property is distributed, or even what property is in the estate.

When Dad dies and you want to sell the house, acting as successor trustee, you will have to file some paperwork with the county recorder or similar office to show that you are the successor trustee and have the power to sign your name as successor trustee. Check with the recorder to see what they need. Sometimes they will file a copy of the first page, the page that appoints you as successor trustee, and the signature page of the trust. In other situations you will file an affidavit claiming you are the successor trustee. Scroll 11.1 is an example of a successor trustee's affidavit. All title insurance companies or escrow companies in your area will know exactly what to do, and if you use them when you sell the house, they will prepare all of the papers. But, whatever is actually filed doesn't destroy the trust's privacy, and the trust avoids probate. So, don't complain.

Trusts normally are not witnessed. That means they do not require witnesses to the signatures, as a will does. Technically, a trust doesn't even have to be written down. A verbal agreement can form the relationship necessary to establish a trust between the grantor and the trustee. But don't even think of establishing a trust without having the agreement in writing. Simply having the grantor and trustee sign the trust that is dated is sufficient to formalize a written trust. However, almost every living revocable trust you see will have the signatures notarized. Notarizing the signatures is a good idea. Go ahead and have your trust notarized, because that is what society is coming to expect.

The simple act of signing the trust makes it "legal," and society will recognize the trust as an independent legal entity, almost as if it were an independent person. I've had people argue with me, saying that something more had to be done to create such a powerful thing as a trust. Nope. If you write it down, sign it, and notarize it, you have formalized your trust to the max.

Affidavit of Successor Trustee

I, John H. Doe, of legal age being first duly sworn depose and say that Daddy D. Doe, the decedent, mentioned in the attached certificate of death is the same person as the Daddy D. Doe named as one of the trustees in that certain Living Revocable Trust titled: The Daddy D. and Mommy M. Doe Living Revocable Trust U/A October 10, 1986.

I, John H. Doe, further depose and say that I am the successor trustee of the Daddy D. and Mommy M. Doe Living Revocable Trust U/A October 10, 1986.

____
John H. Doe

State of Nevada)
: ss
County of Washoe)

BEFORE ME, the undersigned, a Notary Public in and for said County and State, personally appeared John H. Doe, personally known to me or proved to me on the basis of satisfactory evidence to be the person whose name is subscribed to the within instrument and acknowledged to me that he executed the same in his authorized capacity, and that, by his signature on the instrument, the person executed the instrument.

SUBSCRIBED AND SWORN TO before me the 10th day of October, 1997.

WITNESS my hand and official seal.

____
Notary Public in and for said County and State

Scroll 11.1—Affidavit of Successor Trustee. Use the form your bank or title insurance company wants you to use.

Of course, you also want the written text of your trust to follow the laws which will make it "legal," avoid probate, give your trustee the most power, and provide you with all of the possible estate tax advantages. Many trusts will avoid probate, but they don't meet all the IRS requirements necessary to get all the neat tax advantages available to your trust. Unless the trust is written just the way the IRS says it has to be written, it really won't help when it comes time to pay the tax man.

Trusts Are Easy to Change

One of the nicest aspects of a living revocable trust is the ease with which the trust can be changed. You are always in control. You can have a little part of the trust changed. You can rewrite the whole trust, or you can just revoke it entirely.

Maybe you already have a trust, and you want to change something after reading this book. If you get a living revocable trust today and change your mind tomorrow, no problem. Trusts are easy to amend. You don't have to use a lawyer, but it is a good idea, because an innocent little amendment can easily mess up what the whole trust was intended to achieve. Yes, the amendment should be notarized if your original trust was notarized. The notary isn't necessary, but it is a good idea.

There will be language in your living revocable trust which states that you can amend or revoke the trust. Any amendment should refer to the part of the trust which gives you the power to amend the trust.

Amendments are usually used to just change a small part of the trust. Maybe you have changed your mind about how old the kids have to be when they receive their share of the trust. Maybe you want to choose different trustees. There are dozens of reasons the trust might have to be amended.

Expect to amend the trust. Your expectations in life, your plans, and your desires change rapidly. Even though living revocable trusts are flexible and generally cover many points, it is unrealistic to think that the trust will exactly meet your desires ten years after it is written. Fine, write a new one. Isn't it a blessing to have another ten years of life? Living long enough to "have to" be bothered by the task of writing another living revocable trust really isn't a disaster.

Sometimes, so many things in your trust need to be changed that it is easier to amend the trust by "restating" the trust. When a trust is "restated," the whole document is trashed, and a new trust is written to replace the old one. It is often better to "restate" the trust than to revoke the trust and start over by writing a new trust. From a legal standpoint, totally restating the trust by amendment is very different than revoking the trust and writing a new trust. No, there isn't any less paperwork, but the property owned by the original trust can be automatically "picked" up by the restated trust. Because the owner didn't change, new deeds and bank signature cards are not necessary with the restated trust. Only the rules by which the property is managed changed. However, you should let the banker know about the restatement so that there aren't any surprises when you die.

The name of the trust can reflect the fact that the trust has been amended or restated. So the name of your trust may read, "The John T. and Mary S. Doe Living Revocable Trust under Agreement December 4, 1990, as amended October 24, 1992." However, the same name and date you have always used is sufficient, even after the trust has been amended.

Chapter

12

Funding Your Trust

Successful Trust Management

When lawyers explain trusts, they say that the trust should be "funded." What they mean is, the trust has to own the property. That means it has to own all of the property that would normally require your signature to sell or transfer while you are alive or after you have died. Just having Gramps write on a piece of paper, "I hereby fund my trust with $10 and other good and valuable consideration" isn't going to help at all. If the trust is funded with a piece of real estate, that means the trust owns the piece of real estate. How does the trust "own" the home, car, and bank account?

In the last several years more people have started to actually use living revocable trusts. The public is becoming more familiar with the trust, and they know the trust has to be funded. Ten years ago, a majority of the trusts that people showed me were "unfunded." Most of the people who had trusts didn't have any idea that the trust had to be funded, and the rest of them didn't know how to fund the trust, even though they knew it was supposed to be funded. Their trusts were, of course, useless, and they had wasted their hard-earned money. A large part of this chapter will be dedicated to showing you how to fund your trust.

In order to totally avoid probate, your trust has to be fully funded. It has to own all of your property.

Why Your Trust Must Own Your Property

The terminology "all of your property" must be clarified. The trust has to own only the property that has an ownership document, i.e., property that requires your signature in order to be sold, such as your house, car, stocks, bonds, etc. The toaster, microwave, riding lawn mower, diamond ring, and clothes don't need to be "owned" by the trust. Ownership of these kinds of "property" is evidenced by possession, not a piece of paper.

I always tell my clients that they don't have to worry about making the trust own anything that their neighbor could physically sell at a garage sale when they were out of town. Your neighbor couldn't sell your car at a garage sale unless he or she had the title with your signature on the transfer line.

The Ownership Hang-Ups of Americans

Ownership is a major issue with Americans. It is a psychological hang-up we have. We have to "own" things. If you are going to use a living revocable trust, you will have to get over that hang-up. You can control the property, but you can't technically own it. You will use the property just as you always did. You can buy, sell, rent, burn, build, and do anything else you could when you "owned" the property, but technically it isn't yours.

Some people, especially older people, cannot live with the thought of losing ownership, even though it is explained that they will still have control, and life will go on just as it always has. If the emotional price is higher than the monetary savings using a living revocable trust might yield, then don't establish a trust. I have talked several families out of establishing a trust for Mom and Dad, because Mom and Dad couldn't be comfortable giving up "ownership" of the property they had worked their whole lives for. They felt as though they were losing all of their security, and establishing the trust wasn't worth stripping them of their psychological security blanket.

Your Trust is Like a Company, But It is Not a Company

A trust is not a company and should never be confused with a company. However, the concept of a company can help you understand the relationship between ownership and control. Lots of people have a small company, and they buy their car or computer in the name of the small company. The company then owns the car and the computer, but the person who has the small company drives the car and uses the computer as his "personal" car or computer. If they want to buy a new car, they "have the company sell the old car," and "they have the company buy a new car." They don't own the car, but they control the car, as if it were their own. The concept of ownership and control functions about the same way for a trust.

Using Schedules in Trusts

Many lawyers will "fund" your trust by using what is called a "schedule." You should not rely on a schedule to fund your trust.

If your trust is using a schedule to "fund" itself, the text of your trust will say that the trust owns everything "listed on the 'Schedule A' which is attached to the trust." The schedule is just a list of property that goes along with your trust. The schedule is usually known as "Schedule A" because it is the first schedule talked about in the trust. Of course, the schedule could be known as Schedule A, Schedule B, Schedule Green Shoes, or by any other name. Not all trusts call the property list a "Schedule." The property list is sometimes referred to by a term such as "Exhibit," "Appendix," "Addendum," or some other term. It doesn't matter what your trust calls the property list.

In some cases, the schedule is securely and irremovably attached at the back of your trust using staples or some other binding technique. However, often the schedule is just placed in the ringed binder or folder with the trust papers and wills. Unless it is securely, physically attached to the trust papers, the schedule should clearly state that it is part of your trust. It should refer to your trust by the trust's name, including the date. Scroll 12.1 is a short example of a schedule that would accompany John and Mary Doe's trust. The schedule should simply be a listing of property, including your car, boat, bank account, certificate of deposit, stock certificate, and almost everything else you own. Note that the house and the real estate are transferred by deeds, not by the schedule. There is usually a place for your signature at the end of the property list. Sometimes there is also a notary public attestation following your signature. Not all unattached schedules are signed and notarized, but it is a good idea to have them as "official" and clear as possible.

In theory, the trust actually does "own" everything listed on the property schedule. You signed the trust, which states that you are transferring ownership of all of the property listed on the schedule. By signing the trust, ownership of the property listed on the schedule is being transferred from you as a joint tenant, tenant in common, or sole owner to the trust. If you want to get technical, the trust owns the property, but the property is actually transferred to the trustee, as custodian (fiduciary) acting on behalf of the trust. The trust document itself may act as the transfer document. Either the trust will have language of conveyance in it or the schedule will have language of conveyance. In order to officially make the schedule work, the trust will have to be recorded along with the schedule. Privacy is one of the main advantages of a trust, and so nobody wants to have their trust recorded, because that totally blows their privacy.

The Problems with Schedules

In many cases, the lawyer carefully makes out the list, has you sign, pats you on the head, and says, "Run along. You don't have anything to worry about because all of your property is listed on the schedule, and that means it is protected by the trust." This is exactly what happened to my father-in-law.

Schedule "A"

The below listed property is hereby transferred, conveyed, assigned and delivered to John H. Doe and Mary A. Doe as Trustees, and their successor Trustees, subject to the terms and conditions of the John H. and Mary A. Doe Living Revocable Trust dated the 1st of September, 1997, and signed by the Undersigned:

1. The following accounts in the following institutions together with all future additions, interest or accumulations therein and also including all new accounts and the accumulations and the future additions of interest or the accumulation in any and all other financial institutions in which new accounts are opened in the future:

   Invest Your Money Here Bank of Nevada
   1001 Main Street
   Carson City, NV 89701
   Safe Deposit Box #222
   Checking Account #99-754-333-1
   Savings Accounts #22-4456-7-88

2. The following owned vehicles

   1959 Chevrolet Corvette
   VIN #EL024246VI81S12

3. The following securities, stocks, and other investments.

   IBM Stock Certificate #694231026
   Ford Stock Certificate #12431C

DATED the 1st day of September, 1997.

____
John H. Doe

____
Mary A. Doe

State of Nevada)
: ss
County of Washoe)

BEFORE ME, the undersigned, a Notary Public in and for said County and State, personally appeared John H. Doe and Mary A. Doe, personally known to me or proved to me on the basis of satisfactory evidence to be the persons whose names are subscribed to the within instrument and acknowledged to me that they executed the same in their authorized capacities, and that, by their signature on the instrument, the persons executed the instrument.

SUBSCRIBED AND SWORN TO before me the 1st day of September, 1997.

WITNESS my hand and official seal.

____
Notary Public in and for
said County and State

Scroll 12.1—Property Schedule Accompanying John H. and Mary A. Doe Trust

So, does the schedule work? Do you really avoid probate? In theory, yes. In reality, no. It is a setup and a trap. The trap closes in a scenario something like the following:

Dad's bank account is carefully listed on his trust's property schedule, and if he is like most people, he will never tell the bank about the trust. What happens when Dad dies? After his death, the successor trustee, you, his oldest daughter, go into the bank and say, "Hi, Dad died last night, and I need to get into the checking account." The banker looks up the signature card. The signature card shows that the account is in the name of Mom and Dad as joint tenants with rights of survivorship. The banker is an old friend of Dad's, and he knows Mom died last year and Dad died yesterday. He tells you that he is sorry, but he will have to have a probate order, a letters testamentary, before he can let you get into the bank account or safe deposit box.

When the banker says "probate order," you retort that Dad had a living revocable trust, and there shouldn't be any probate. This is news to the banker. To prove your point, you whip out a copy of the trust for the banker, and say, "Look, the bank account is listed right there on Schedule A." After a quick consultation with the branch manager and a rush call to the bank's half-baked attorney in the home office, the banker says how sorry he is, but that the attorney said that you still need a probate order.

The banker was Dad's friend. He really does want to believe you, but maybe the trust isn't real. Maybe someone forged Dad's signature. Maybe Dad revoked his trust and decided trusts were garbage. Maybe Dad left a will that he established only three weeks ago. The bank's attorney is very good at playing the "maybe game."

The maybe game is going to wear out your patience very quickly. In frustration, you finally scream, "OK. I am calling my lawyer." The trap closes!

Your call to the lawyer that drafted Dad's trust confirms your suspicions that the bank's lawyer is a turkey. Your lawyer points to the checking account listed on the property schedules and assures you that everything will be worked out when he calls the bank's lawyer. After running his clock for 2 hours at $165/hour, your lawyer calls you up and reconfirms your suspicion that the bank's lawyer is a turkey. In fact, your lawyer is so livid that he informs you he has already started to file the papers needed to sue the bank. But, there is no need to be concerned, because there is absolutely no question—the checking account is listed on the property schedule, and you will win the suit against the bank.

Needless to say, you are now livid. You are breathing lawsuit with every breath. Can you sue the attorney who drafted the trust? No, probably not. The attorney prepared a schedule for Dad and pushed him out the door assuring him everything was fine. However, on Dad's way out the door, the attorney handed Dad a copy of all of his paperwork. The lawyer never told Dad he needed to do a lot of homework. Dad was supposed to read the papers and follow the instructions. The first four pages of the paperwork were a cover letter from the attorney that clearly stated it was Dad's responsibility to contact the bank, file the deed (which is now nowhere to be found), and do all of the other things required, in addition to simply listing the property on Schedule A, to effectively transfer property to the trust and avoid probate. So, as far as the attorney is concerned, this mess with the bank is all Dad's fault.

Before the banker will help you, you are going to have to prove to the bank that this was Dad's real trust, that it hadn't been revoked, and so on. When your lawyer said you will win the lawsuit with the bank, he was right. After all the legal hairs are split, the court will determine that the trust is for real and will tell the bank that Dad's trust really does own the checking account. Isn't that nice? To get into Dad's bank account, you didn't need a probate order, all you had to do was sue the bank. When your lawyer says he is suing the bank, if you are smart, you will immediately back out of the lawsuit and hire a different attorney to probate Dad's estate.

It will probably be faster, easier and cheaper to go through probate instead of suing the bank. Besides, why go to the trouble of suing the bank, when you will have to go through probate anyway, because you can't find the deed transferring Dad's house into the trust. Dad never recorded the deed. You either have to find the deed or probate the property. Because you don't have the deed and there is no record of the deed, you will have to get a probate order to sell the house. All of the existing records show the house is jointly owned by Mom and Dad. Because Mom's name is still on the deed, you will be lucky if you don't have to probate Mom's estate too, or bring a quiet title action to get Mom's name off the deed.

What went wrong? The problem has nothing to do with the trust itself. Dad just didn't do his homework. He was never told that only listing the property on the schedule could cause problems. Dad never really understood what had to be done, because the lawyer ushered him out of the office before he could even ask a question. Dad should have recorded the deed or put it in a safe place where you could find it. Obviously, just listing the bank account on Schedule A wasn't enough. Dad needed to do something else at the bank. Dad had to go into the bank after he got his trust and change the signature card from his name to the trust's name.

When Dad changes the signature card, the banker will often want a copy of part of the trust, or he will want a summary of the trust. In rare cases, the banker will want to keep a full copy of the trust. Let the banker have whatever he wants. It will be kept relatively private in your bank file.

When the banker changes the name on the signature card and the safe deposit box, he is agreeing to honor the terms of the trust. He will copy part of the trust so that he can identify the trust when you show up with it after Dad has died. Trusts are private, not secret. The banker has a copy he got from Dad, so he knows that the trust was what Dad wanted.

When the bank knows about the trust, things will go smoothly after Dad dies. You will show up at the bank with the trust document and Dad's death certificate. The banker will examine the trust to make sure it is the one Dad had when he came in to change the account to a trust account. Sure enough, everything matches up, so the bank is secure in transferring power to you as the named successor trustee. The banker simply says, "Sign here," and you are home free.

Just listing the property on a "schedule" attached to the trust may be technically sufficient to fund the trust. But in order to make the trust work smoothly and provide the benefits it promises, the property all has to be owned by the trust and actually titled in the name of the trust. I don't know how many times I have already written this in this book, but it can't be overstated.

The situation may arise where you have to deal with a trust that has only been funded by a schedule. The schedule may even list the real property. All may not be lost. To complete the transfer of the property into the trust, the schedule and the trust will probably have to be recorded. Exactly where you "record" them depends upon state laws. Recording the trust "blows" its privacy aspects, but the trust can still save you from a messy probate proceeding in many cases.

Making Your Trust Avoid Probate

Here are a few hints on procedures required to place property in the name of your trust.

One of the major objections lawyers have with living revocable trusts is the "complexity," time, and expense of moving property into the trust's ownership. Even if you have a trust, there will be recording fees (on the order of $20) that will be charged to record a deed showing that property is being transferred into the trust. This is the same recording fee that will be required when a deed is recorded following a probate proceeding. Yes, when the trust is used the filing fee has to be paid now rather than 25 years down the road—there is a time value to money. But that fee is nothing compared to the attorney's fees in probate.

I have never had a client come back to me and say the complexity of dealing with the trust was too much to handle. Once you learn how to buy and sell property, open bank accounts and brokerage accounts, and generally how to act as a trustee, dealing with that property is almost exactly like dealing with your own property.

Checking Accounts

The bank should not change your account number, make you print new checks, or charge you anything to change the signature card. Some banks are stubborn, and they require you to open a new account with a new number and new checks, but there isn't any law requiring them to do that. Your checks do not need to have the name of the trust on them. Anything can be printed on the check. It's the signature card that controls what happens.

Safe Deposit Box

Make sure the signature card for the safe deposit box is changed to the name of the trust. The safe deposit box should be easy to change.

Savings Accounts

Don't forget to change each savings account, even the one your grandpa opened for you when you were five years old.

Certificates of Deposit

In order to change the name on a Certificate of Deposit (CD), a new CD must be issued. If you cash in the CD early, you will have a penalty and lose money. I counsel clients to wait to change their CDs that are short term or that are coming due within a few months after the trust is established. Wait until the CD comes up for renewal, then have the next CD issued in the name of the trust. Unless there is some reason to think you will not live to see the CD mature, it is probably worth the bet to wait for the CD to mature before changing it to show that your trust owns it. But remember, it is a bet. If you die before the name on the CD is changed, the CD will have to be probated. Watch to make sure the bank doesn't automatically roll your old CD into a new one before you get a chance to change the name on the new CD.

Stocks

Your stock broker will have to change the name on any stock certificates you hold. When a name is changed, there is often a transfer fee charged by the company which manages the stock for the corporation that issues the stock. The transfer fees often cannot be avoided if a new certificate is issued in your trust's name. That is unfortunate, but changing the certificate now is much cheaper than the probate fees will be if the certificate has to be probated. You might note that the same charge will be exacted from your estate to issue a new certificate after you die, but that is on top of the probate fees.

One "trick" which may save some costs is to open a brokerage account in your trust's name and then deposit the certificate into the account. The broker holds the account. Stock certificates are usually not issued to the brokerage account. Therefore, transfer fees are reduced or are totally eliminated.

If you already have a brokerage account at a brokerage house, the account will have to be changed to reflect the trust's ownership. Your broker will help you change the name on the account. As I have said before, the SEC (Securities and Exchange Commission) requires the broker to keep a copy of your trust or a detailed summary of the trust, i.e., a "trust certificate."

S corporation stock is a special type of stock used by small corporations. If you bought your stock through a stock broker, it won't be S corporation stock. However, if you own stock in an S corporation, a big red caution flag needs to go up right here. Transfer of S corporation stock into the living trust may jeopardize the corporation's "S" election with the IRS after the trust becomes irrevocable at your death. The living revocable trust can hold the S corporation stock for a maximum of two years after your death. Almost every estate will distribute the stock within the two year period. But, if you have your wealth in a company that is an S corporation, you need to consider the S corporation problem of distributing stock from a living revocable trust.

Treasury Bonds/Notes

One year, an elderly lady and her daughter came to me on April 1st with a $32,000 problem. The local banker and attorney had helped her put a simple living revocable trust into place. It was a simple trust, and the banker and lawyer had been smart enough to know that the trust had to be funded.

All the lady owned was about $100,000 in treasury bonds. She and her husband had spent their lives saving these bonds. The banker and lawyer figured that the only way you could get the trust to own the bonds was to have her sell the bonds and then reinvest all of the money in new bonds that would be purchased in the name of the trust.

The banker and lawyer had set her up for a disaster. When she sold the bonds, it triggered the income tax on all fifty years worth of earnings from the bonds. There isn't any tax until you sell; then the tax hits. She paid $32,000 in income tax that year, and there wasn't a thing I could do about it.

All the banker and lawyer had to do to change the name on the bonds was use Form PD F 1851, "Request for Reissue of United States Savings Bonds/Notes in the Name of Trustee or Personal Trust Estate." Form PD 4633 is used for treasury bills. The Federal Reserve bank uses the forms to change the name on the bonds or the bills without triggering any income tax problems. Your banker can help you get the Federal Reserve change papers.

Whenever you are changing the title on an asset, you must be concerned about the tax consequences. The good news is, almost all assets can be transferred to the living revocable trust without any adverse tax effects.

Cars

Cars, trucks, and other motor vehicles have a title that will require your signature if they are sold or otherwise transferred. They should be transferred to your trust's ownership. The rub comes with the Department of Motor Vehicles. Some states require a sales tax or transfer tax every time the title on a car or truck is changed. If your state doesn't understand what a living revocable trust is and let you move the title to your car without charging a tax, then don't transfer the car to your trust. Check with your state Department of Motor Vehicles and ask how they recommend moving title of your car into the name of your trust.

For small estates, the laws in most states leave a loophole or two open so that a car can be transferred without a probate proceeding. In such transfers, filing a simple affidavit will allow the car title to be moved after the owner dies.

Your next car will obviously be purchased in your trust's name. The trust's name will actually be the named owner on the car's title.

The last time I bought a car, the dealer asked if I wanted title in my name alone or as a joint tenant with my wife. I said neither. He responded, "You want your wife to own the car?" "Nope," I said. "I want it in the name of my trust, which is a division of our joint trust." When I rattled off a name that had 29 words in it, the dealer said I must be joking. I assured him that I was serious. He promptly told me to drop dead, and explained that the box on the title form was only large enough to have 4 or 5 words. I said that I understood, but explained that I wasn't going to buy a car unless it could be purchased in the name of the trust. Funny thing, the dealer and the salesman figured out how to put all 29 words on the title. They did abbreviate some words. For example, Tr = trust, and U/A = under agreement. The title read something like this: "The John H. Doe Trust, a separate division of the John T. and Mary S. Doe Trust under agreement July 4, 1990, as amended September 6, 1992."

Houses

Real estate is transferred using a deed. Usually a quitclaim deed or transfer deed is used to transfer title from you to your trust. The quitclaim deed is sufficient, because it transfers all rights that you have in the property. Warranty deeds are often used to transfer title when you are buying a house. The seller is giving you a warranty or guarantee that the title to the house can be transferred. When you use a quitclaim deed, you aren't guaranteeing that the title will be good, but if you can't trust yourself not to cheat yourself, well, whom can you trust?

You can get a sample of a quitclaim deed at the local office supply store. An example is shown in Scroll 12.2. (next page.)

"Warranty deeds" or "grant deeds" are considered "cleaner" by many lawyers, escrow companies, and title insurance companies. The warranty deeds make warranties that the quitclaim deeds don't make, and it may be a good idea to keep the warranties "running" along the chain of title to the property. Call your local title insurance company and ask if a quitclaim deed is sufficient or if they would rather see a warranty deed. While you have got them on the phone, ask the title company employees how they want to see the name of your trust put on a deed in your state.

Do you record the deed? The answer depends upon where you live. Most states recognize that the living revocable trust is an extension of you and that the transfer from you to your trust isn't the type of transfer which triggers a property tax reassessment. Some states view the change as a transfer which has tax consequences.

Mail to:
John H. Doe
598 Doezer Street
Sparks, NV 89431

Quitclaim Deed

For the sum of Ten ($10.00) Dollars and other good and valuable consideration, John H. Doe and Mary A. Doe, Grantors of Sparks, County of Washoe, State of Nevada, hereby Quitclaim to John H. Doe and Mary A. Doe as Trustees of the John H. and Mary A. Doe Living Revocable Trust, under agreement dated the 1st day of September, 1997, and the survivor thereof and successors thereto, with full power and authority to assign, sell, transfer, convey, encumber and mortgage the following described tract of land located in Washoe County, State of Nevada.

Commencing at the Southeast Corner of Lot 2, Block 7, Plat "A," Sparks City Survey; and running thence North 8 rods; thence West 3 rods; thence South 8 rods; thence East 3 rods to beginning.

DATED the 1st day of September, 1997.

____
John H. Doe

____
Mary A. Doe

State of Nevada)
: ss
County of Washoe)

BEFORE ME, the undersigned, a Notary Public in and for said County and State, personally appeared John H. Doe and Mary A. Doe, personally known to me or proved to me on the basis of satisfactory evidence to be the persons whose names are subscribed to the within instrument and acknowledged to me that they executed the same in their authorized capacities, and that, by their signature on the instrument, the persons executed the instrument.

SUBSCRIBED AND SWORN TO before me the 1st day of September, 1997.

WITNESS my hand and official seal.

____
Notary Public in and for
said County and State

Scroll 12.2—Quitclaim Example

A local attorney, the people who work in title companies, or the people who record deeds (the county recorder's office) can probably help you find out what happens in your state. In fact, the county recorder's office can be a big help in making out new deeds. Call and ask the recorder how they want the trust's name on the deed and what tax consequences filing a new deed will have. If you don't get the new employee in the office, you can get a lot of tips from the recorder's office. Hopefully, you will get the same information from the recorder's office and the title company. If there is going to be a tax problem when the deed is recorded, you simply make out the deed, deliver it, and don't record it.

In most states a deed is valid even though it is never recorded. You could check with a local title company to find out whether or not your state requires deeds to be recorded in order to be valid. Unless state law dictates otherwise, recording doesn't make the transfer any more valid or legal. However, if the deed isn't recorded and it is later lost, then you are back to a probate proceeding. Recording a deed puts the transfer on public record and protects you if the deed is later lost.

Some states, such as California, have very specific procedures that must be followed in order to transfer real estate into a living revocable trust and avoid a property tax reevaluation. First, the deed must be prepared. You can use either a quitclaim deed or a "warranty deed" ("grant deed"). There is no such thing as a "change deed" or "transfer deed." Second, a form called a "preliminary change in ownership form" must be filed with the county where the property is located. You can get a copy of the form from the County Recorder's Office.

If you are transferring the property to your living revocable trust, all you need is the deed and preliminary change in ownership form. Transferring property to a family member requires a third step to be exempt from the property tax reevaluation. An additional page must be filed with the preliminary change in ownership form, which specifically claims an exemption. The extra sheet must claim a spouse to spouse, parent to child, or child to parent transfer.

You need to check with your state or county property tax officers and find out the exact procedure you will need to follow in order to avoid the property tax reevaluation trap, if it even applies in your state.

The transfer of a piece of real estate to a living revocable trust does not affect the mortgage on the property. Many loan agreements have "due-on-sale" clauses, which adversely affect the mortgage if the property is sold. Most lenders recognize that a transfer to a living revocable trust doesn't affect their security in the loan, and they pretty much ignore your transfer of the real estate to your living revocable trust. If some lender gets real nasty with you about the transfer of your home to your living revocable trust, then whip out federal law 12 CFR 591.5 and point out that federal law bars the lender from accelerating the mortgage on your personal residence because you transferred it to your living revocable trust. If the property is something other than your personal residence, then you had better walk softly, and don't make waves. Only the transfer of your personal residence is protected by federal laws so that the lender cannot accelerate the mortgage. However, most lenders will grant permission to transfer any piece of real estate to a living revocable trust without affecting the mortgage. If there is a problem, make out a deed to the trust without telling the lender, and don't record the deed. Make sure you deliver the deed to the trustee (yourself), and tell your successor trustees about the deed.

HUD (Housing and Urban Development) loans are not available on property purchased in the name of a living revocable trust. If you want a HUD, FANNIE MAE, or FREDDY MAC loan, purchase the real estate in your name and/or your spouse's name, just as you normally would. Then later, have a quitclaim deed made out to move the property into your trust. You will not record the quitclaim deed. Put it in a safe place, and let your successor trustees know where it is so that they can retrieve the deed after your death, and avoid probating the property.

How to Handle Real Estate

The same considerations that apply to your home apply to your investment real estate. If you are willing to hold the property in your own name, there usually isn't any reason that the property shouldn't be moved to the ownership of your living revocable trust.

Real estate investors often have to leverage their investments. One investment will be "pledged" or put up as collateral in order to induce the bank to make an additional loan on another piece of property. You often also pledge assets. For example, you may have to use your home as security to get a loan for a new car. If your trust "owns" your house, how do you use the house as security for another loan?

Some lenders will not lend against property owned by a living revocable trust. That is just their policy, and in my opinion, it is a bad policy. Unfortunately, banks don't pay a lot of attention to me, so my opinion isn't worth much.

In the "powers of trustees" section in your living revocable trust, the trust should give the trustee, you, authority to pledge the trust property. The trust can "put up" the trust property as security for your loan, just as your father could "put up" his house as security for your loan. Many lenders know what a living revocable trust is and will accept the trust's property as security in exactly the same way they would accept property owned directly by you. Other lenders aren't as congenial, and for no legal or justifiable reason they will make you transfer the property out of the trust before they will accept it as security.

ASSET PROTECTION TIP #5

When you apply for a loan for any reason, never pledge more property than is absolutely necessary to secure the loan. The property listed as security can readily be taken by the lender if you default on the loan. Of course, you never think that you will default on the loan, but it does happen.

When you apply for a loan, find out what the banker will require as the minimum amount of security necessary for you to be approved for the loan.

To persuade the banker to tell you the minimum amount of security you need to pledge, you may need to make the banker think you will have a hard time coming up with enough property. However you do it, you need to determine the minimum amount of property necessary to secure the loan. When you find out what the minimum is, don't list any assets other than those necessary to meet the minimum security amounts. Don't brag to the banker about your wealth. If you say you have $6 million in property, the banker isn't dumb. He will want all $6 million as security. Flashing around big asset sheets is stupid. Keep your wealth private. It could save you a lot of grief someday.

Using Homesteads to Protect Your Home

When your personal residence is placed into a trust, it usually loses its "homestead" protection. Many states have laws called "homestead laws" which will "protect" your house and some minimal amount of personal property such as clothing. The laws are designed to prevent people from taking your last dime through a lawsuit or bankruptcy procedure. Florida and Texas have the most effective homestead laws.

When your house is transferred to ownership of the trust, technically it is not yours anymore. The trust owns it. Because homestead laws only protect "your" house, in most states they will not protect a house owned by the trust. The law isn't consistent. Because you don't "own" the house, the law won't let you use the homestead laws to protect the house. Yet, the law says that you can lose the house in a lawsuit or bankruptcy, even if it is owned by the trust, because technically you still "own" the house under the lawsuit and bankruptcy laws. It doesn't matter if the trust owns the house; the trust can't protect it from your personal legal problems under most laws. Aren't you learning to love the law?

Don't concern yourself too much with the homestead laws. In fact, in most states you can pretty much ignore the homestead laws because they don't protect enough to worry about. Most states protect only minimal amounts—amounts in the range of $6,000, $10,000 or $15,000. The rarely used homestead laws simply do not offer enough protection to influence most people's estate planning and the decision to put a house into a living revocable trust.

However, Florida and Texas have traditionally protected 100% of the personal residence, and if you are living in one of those states and are planning on lawsuits and bankruptcy, the homestead rights should be preserved. Check with your local attorney to see what, if any, homestead rights your state laws afford you and what effect putting your house in a living revocable trust has on those rights.

Also, check the rules that must be followed in order to claim protection under the homestead laws. The homestead protection may not be available to you when you need it if you don't take the necessary steps to qualify you for the protection.

The bottom line is, you probably shouldn't give up the probate protection and privacy of a living revocable trust to save the homestead rights. Your chance of cashing in on the probate savings is 100%, while your chance of ever using the homestead protection is very small. I don't know anyone who has claimed the homestead protection, but I know lots of people who have died and used a living revocable trust to avoid an expensive probate mess.

Retirement Plans, IRAs and Life Insurance

For tax reasons, your spouse, if you are married, should usually be listed as the primary beneficiary on your retirement plans, IRAs and life insurance. This is particularly important on retirement plans and IRAs. The trust will substantially impact the way the IRS taxes the benefits, if the trust is the primary beneficiary. Naming the trust as the secondary beneficiary is commonly done, and the consequences are just not as dire as naming the trust the primary beneficiary. If your retirement plan and the IRA are only moderate sized, your living trust would probably be a good choice as the secondary beneficiary. If you have a lot of money in the retirement plan or IRA, you need the advice of someone who knows a lot about the tax laws as they will be applied to your particular situation.

It is almost always a good idea to list your trust as the secondary beneficiary of your life insurance policies. Make sure that you actually make the changes with the insurance company and the entity that holds your retirement plan and the IRA funds, if you are making your trust the secondary beneficiary. Also, check with your fire and casualty insurance company to see how you can use your trust to avoid probate if your insurance policy has to make payments on any claims after your death. You may have to fill out a change of beneficiary form for each company or have your trust put on your casualty policy as an additional insured, but this is another case where it is worth the effort to "cross the t's and dot the i's."

Your life insurance face values are included in your assets as part of your total estate. If you have a taxable estate, you should be using an irrevocable insurance trust to hold your life insurance. This is a special type of trust used to avoid all estate taxes on life insurance. Life insurance trusts are very different from living revocable trusts, but they work great. You can totally avoid estate taxes on any amount of life insurance. That's not a good deal, that's a great deal!

Moving Keepsakes To the Kids Without a Fight

By now you have a totally negative impression of trust "schedules." Wrong! It's my fault. I'm sorry. I have only tried to impress upon you that the property requiring your signature to transfer or sell must be placed in your trust's name while you are alive. Otherwise, there may be a problem after your death.

I recommend that every client have a schedule, attached to the trust, which disposes of the little personal items. Do you remember the personal letter associated with the will? It prevented the family fights over the dollies and doilies. Many states do not allow your will to incorporate a personal letter into your estate plan. Actually, all states will allow you to write a will which refers to a document, such as a letter, which is in existence at the time the will is written. But, your personal letter is something you want to be able to write and rewrite after your will goes into effect.

You need to know whether or not your state's law allows you to write a personal letter after your will is written. Call the probate clerk at the court, or call your local lawyer.

The use of a second will, a holographic will, in addition to your formal will, has already been discussed in detail. This second will can be used to list the little personal things. It does not have to be in existence when the formal will is executed, and you can rip it up and write out a new one any time you want. However, your state may not recognize holographic wills, and the "second will" concept is even foreign to most lawyers because everyone thinks you can have only one will—"your last will and testament." The lawyer that says you can have only one will doesn't know any better or is lying.

By the way, you do know how to tell if a lawyer is lying? (His lips are moving.) Everybody knows the answer to that riddle. It is easy. This next riddle is harder. Do you know what a good dead lawyer does? (He lies still.)

Sorry, where were we? Oh yes, we were discussing the personal letter. If your state won't let you have one with your will, don't panic. If your state won't let you have a holographic will, don't worry. In fact, you don't even have to bother checking to see if your state will allow a personal letter with your will or a holographic will, because every state will permit your trust to have a schedule that disposes of your personal property. I always call the personal property schedule, "Schedule B." You could call it "Schedule Dollies and Doilies." It can be called by any name.

The text of your trust must refer to the schedule. For example the trust will read as shown in Scroll 12.3 (next page). The schedule should refer specifically to the trust. It should state that it is a list disposing of your personal property. An example of a "Schedule B" is shown in Scroll 12.4 (page 189).

The schedule of personal property is easy to make. However, it does require a little more formality than the personal letter. Whereas the will's personal letter only has to be signed and dated, the "Schedule B" will have to be signed, dated, and notarized each time it is changed.

Schedule B Language in a Living Revocable Trust

John and Mary may dispose of personal property by making a Schedule "B" and identifying it as part of this Trust Agreement. All personal properties listed on the Schedule "B" are to be distributed to the person or persons designated, and the items shall be conveyed to the persons in addition to their distributive share, if any, as described in the provisions of this Trust.

Scroll 12.3—Sample Language Referencing Schedule B

Schedule "B"

The personal property listed below is hereby transferred, conveyed, assigned and delivered to John H. Doe and Mary A. Doe as Trustees and their successor Trustees subject to the terms and conditions of the John H. and Mary A. Doe Living Revocable Trust dated the 1st of August, 1997, and signed by John H. Doe and Mary A. Doe, as Grantors. This personal property shall be distributed, according to the Trust Agreement, to the individuals indicated on this schedule.

PROPERTY DESCRIPTION	NAME
1. Antique sewing machine in walnut cabinet	Jane Doe Roberts
2. Shot gun, serial #468942	Johnny Doe
3. Oak dining room table with cabriole legs	Joan Doe
4. Six oak dining chairs with pink needlepoint	Joan Doe
5.	
6.	

DATED the 1st day of August, 19 97 .

____
John H. Doe

____
Mary A. Doe

State of Nevada)
: ss
County of Washoe)

BEFORE ME, the undersigned, a Notary Public in and for said County and State, personally appeared John H. Doe and Mary A. Doe, personally known to me or proved to me on the basis of satisfactory evidence to be the persons whose names are subscribed to the within instrument and acknowledged to me that they executed the same in their authorized capacities, and that, by their signature on the instrument, the persons executed the instrument.

SUBSCRIBED AND SWORN TO before me the 1st day of August, 1997.

WITNESS my hand and official seal.

____
Notary Public in and for said County and State

Scroll 12.4—Sample Schedule B distributing personal property under a living revocable trust

The property schedule, or any other schedule used with a trust, has a minor legal problem that is almost always overlooked by lawyers. In many states, the laws will not let you refer to a second document in your trust, contract, or any other paper, unless the second document is in existence at the time the document referring to it is created. There is a whole field of law surrounding the ideas about documents referring to other documents. This field of law is called the "Doctrine of Independent Significance." You don't really care about the doctrine, but you do want to have the power to rip up your Schedule B and write out a new one next week.

Don't be concerned; the problem can be overcome by making a mini amendment to your trust each time you want to make out a new schedule. The form you want to use to make the amendment is shown in Scroll 12.5, and an example of the Amended Schedule B is shown in Scroll 12.6 (page 192). By using the forms, you can change your schedule as often as you want, and there won't be any problem with the "Doctrine of Independent Significance." Your lawyer may not have thought this one all the way through, but it works. It lets you do what you want to do—get rid of the dollies and doilies and change your mind every week without going back to see your lawyer.

I recommend that you stop worrying about putting a personal letter in your will and go directly to the use of a schedule in your living revocable trust. Your living revocable trust may actually be permitting you to dispose of the dollies and doilies in a way that is impossible with a will.

You may feel that you can't decide what personal property should go to what person. As hard as it is, you need to make the decisions. Just do your best, and write them down. If you have written a complete list of personal property, then when you die, the kids can't be mad at each other. One child didn't "steal" the vase from another child. You personally gave the vase to a specific person. If you were wrong, and Jim really wants the vase after you gave it to Jane, Jim and Jane can straighten things out if they agree. But if there isn't an agreement, you, not Jane, are the culprit that cheated Jim out of the vase. Jim can be as mad at you as he wants to be. What is he going to do? All he can do is go out and jump up and down on your grave. He can't be mad at Jane, because she didn't cheat him at all. A personal property list will assure your interest in preserving your family relationships after you are gone.

Third Amendment to John H. and Mary A. Doe Living Revocable Trust

This, the third amendment to the John H. and Mary A. Doe Living Revocable Trust, dated the 1st day of August, 1997, is made on this, the 10th day of October, 1997, and executed in duplicate between John H. Doe and Mary A. Doe, acting in their capacities as Grantors, and John H. Doe and Mary A. Doe, acting in their capacities as Trustees.

WHEREAS, the Grantors and Trustees entered into a trust agreement dated the 1st day of August, 1997, hereinafter referred to as the "Trust Agreement," and whereas Article 2(C) of the Trust Agreement provided that the Grantors reserved the right to amend the Trust Agreement in any manner or revoke in whole or in part the Trust Agreement, and whereas the Grantors are desirous of modifying and amending the Trust Agreement and the Trustees are agreeable to the modification and amendments contained herein.

NOW THEREFORE, IT IS AGREED:

FIRST

Schedule B, attached to the Trust Agreement as part of the Second Amendment, dated the 15th day of September, 1997, is hereby revoked in its entirety and a new Schedule B, which is attached to this amendment and made a part hereof, is substituted in lieu thereof.

SECOND

The Trust Agreement and any prior amendments, if any not revoked or amended hereby, shall in all other respects remain in full force and effect.

In witness whereof, the Grantors and the Trustees have executed this Third Amendment to the Trust Agreement.

Dated the _10th_ day of _October_, 1997.

______________________	______________________
John H. Doe, Grantor	John H. Doe, Trustee
______________________	______________________
Mary A. Doe, Grantor	Mary A. Doe, Trustee

State of Nevada)
: ss
County of Washoe)

BEFORE ME, the undersigned, a Notary Public in and for said County and State, personally appeared John H. Doe and Mary A. Doe, personally known to me or proved to me on the basis of satisfactory evidence to be the persons whose names are subscribed to the within instrument and acknowledged to me that they executed the same in their authorized capacities, and that, by their signature on the instrument, the persons executed the instrument.

SUBSCRIBED AND SWORN TO before me the 10th day of October, 1997.

WITNESS my hand and official seal.

____
Notary Public in and for said County and State

Scroll 12.5—Trust Amendment authorizing a new Schedule B

You, or you and your spouse, should sit down every year or two and redo the personal property distribution on Schedule B or your personal letter. Most of the distributions won't change, but they still need to be reviewed. Remember, the family fight is over the family heirlooms or the property which has memories attached. The Polyanna game that belonged to Great Grandma is more significant than the color TV.

Third Amendment

Schedule "B"

The personal property listed below is hereby transferred, conveyed, assigned and delivered to John H. Doe and Mary A. Doe as Trustees and their successor Trustees subject to the terms and conditions of the John H. and Mary A. Doe Living Revocable Trust dated, as amended, this, the 10th day of October, 1997, and signed by John H. Doe and Mary A. Doe, as Grantors. This personal property shall be distributed, according to the Trust Agreement, to the individuals indicated on this schedule.

PROPERTY DESCRIPTION	NAME
1. Antique sewing machine in walnut cabinet	Jane Doe Roberts
2. Shot gun, serial #468942	Johnny Doe
3. Oak dining room table with cabriole legs	Martha Doe
4. Six oak dining chairs with pink needlepoint	Martha Doe
5.	

DATED the _10th_ day of _October_, 19_97_.

____

John H. Doe

____

Mary A. Doe

State of Nevada)
: ss
County of Washoe)

BEFORE ME, the undersigned, a Notary Public in and for said County and State, personally appeared John H. Doe and Mary A. Doe, personally known to me or proved to me on the basis of satisfactory evidence to be the persons whose names are subscribed to the within instrument and acknowledged to me that they executed the same in their authorized capacities, and that, by their signature on the instrument, the persons executed the instrument.

SUBSCRIBED AND SWORN TO before me the 10th day of October, 1997.

WITNESS my hand and official seal.

____

Notary Public in and for said County and State

Scroll 12.6—Amended Schedule B sample

How to Buy Property with a Trust

Once your trust is in place, you will purchase property in the name of the trust, not in your own name. When you open a new bank account or purchase stock or other assets, transact all of the business in the name of your trust. When assets are purchased directly in the name of the trust, you do not have to go back and write down the description of the new assets on a schedule.

The schedules are simply being used to try to move property, which isn't purchased in the name of the trust, into the trust. If an asset is purchased in the name of the trust, there isn't any legal advantage achieved by placing the item on a schedule. More or less, the schedule is not necessary to invoke the power of the trust over the item and to avoid probate. However, it is a good idea to maintain complete records which will lead the successor trustee to all of the trust assets. Therefore, it is a good management technique to maintain the schedule or some sort of an inventory, even if the assets are originally purchased in the name of the trust and the schedule or inventory doesn't have any influence over the asset or its ownership by the trust.

Trusts Give You Prestige

Buying property in the name of your trust is fun. Who uses trusts? Rich people do. Trusts are the tools of the wealthy. A strange thing happens when you start to use a trust. People will start to treat you differently.

Kristy and I have the name of our trust printed on our checks. No, the trust's name doesn't have to be on the checks, but it does have to be on the signature card as the owner of the account. But, just for fun we had the trust name put on the check.

When you go to the store and use a check, the clerk always asks you for two forms of ID. When Kristy goes to the store and uses a check, the clerk hardly ever asks her for ID. In fact, I can stand there and question the clerk. "Hey, don't you need two forms of ID from her?" The clerk will pick up the check and read, "The Lee R. and Kristy S. Phillips Living Revocable Trust,

U/A July 4, 1994," and then look at Kristy and say "Lady, you must be rich." That always helps her ego, but it hurts the bank account because the clerk takes the check.

Your Biggest Mistake is to Think Your Estate is Too Small For a Trust

The biggest mistake you can make is to conclude that you don't have enough property to have a living revocable trust. That is wrong. You might not have enough property to justify paying big bucks for the trust, but even if you have a small estate, you need the protection of the trust. Probate is often more devastating to small estates than it is to big estates. Of course, people with larger estates critically need the protection of the trust. It doesn't matter if you are old or young, married or single, or whether or not you have children or grandchildren; you should at least investigate using the trust for yourself. Whether you admit it or not, you do have a moral obligation to your family, your loved ones, to take care of your business affairs, and the living revocable trust forms an excellent basic plan for most people.

I have seen people actually gain wealth by using the trust. No, I am not talking about the probate and tax savings. What I am talking about is very subtle. If you believe something and you start to act the part, does your belief often come to pass? If you use the tools of the wealthy, people who watch you will conclude you must be wealthy, and they will start to discuss ideas and opportunities with you. Your world will change, and you will be in a position to accumulate greater wealth.

Chapter

13

Making Your Will & Trust Work Together

The Value of Pour-Over Wills

Even though you have a living revocable trust, your estate plan will also include a will. The will is a companion to your living revocable trust. It has to refer to the trust and give preference and support to the power of the trust. If you have a will before you get a living revocable trust, a new will must be prepared at the time your trust is prepared.

The companion will is called a "pour-over will." The will acts as a safety net underneath the living revocable trust. Hopefully, the will will not really enter into the picture when you die, but it is there to protect you and your family if something goes wrong with your trust. It automatically "kicks into action" if your trust wasn't prepared properly, or you didn't use your living revocable trust the way you should have used it.

The pour-over will works just like any other will. All property that is subject to the will's control, i.e., all property that is not owned by your living revocable trust, will be subject to probate. The probate process is exactly the same as it would be if there was just a regular old run-of-the-mill will in place. The will is called a "pour-over will," because it directs the personal representative to give all of the property, after it is probated, to the trustee of the living revocable trust. The property can then be distributed to the heirs or beneficiaries according to the terms of the trust. Thus, after the probate, the property is "poured over" into the living revocable trust.

Yes, You Still Have to Use Your Trust

I talk to a lot of clients who feel that they have a living revocable trust, and because they have a pour-over will which protects them, they don't need to use the trust or worry about it. The attorney that drafted Kristy's parents' trust actually told her parents not to worry about using the trust because their pour-over wills would take care of everything when they died.

I am not sure I would go so far as to say that the attorney intentionally led them astray, but look at what would have happened. The lawyer would have received his $2,600 for drafting the trust and pour-over wills. Then, if I hadn't looked at the trust later, the trust wouldn't have avoided probate, because when they died, nothing would have been owned by the trust. Thus, everything would have had to be probated. Of course, when there is a probate, the family usually goes back to the attorney that originally did the trust and wills. In this case, the attorney would have made out like a bandit because he got the fee for the trust (much higher than the fee for a simple will) and he would have had a fat probate to handle. A setup? You be the judge.

Even careful people who are trained to use their trust forget to place some small piece of property, such as a stock certificate or a certificate of deposit, in their trust. That asset may have to be probated. But the financial and emotional costs of probating one certificate of deposit aren't anything like probating a full estate.

Can you see how important it is to use your living revocable trust during your lifetime and not rely on the pour-over will? If you do need the will to help manage property, it is a nice tool to have. But the object of the game is to use the trust so that the will never comes into play.

Pour-Over Wills Don't Create Testamentary Trusts

The pour-over will does not create a testamentary trust. The pour-over will does not create the trust at all. It is only a companion to your living revocable trust. Remember, a testamentary trust is a trust which is actually created by the will and is "funded," only after the probate, with the probated property.

Guardians and Conservators—Make It Easy For the Kids

When minor children are involved, the pour-over wills are usually used to appoint guardians for the children. The provision appointing a guardian in the pour-over will is exactly the same as it is in any other type of will. Even if you have a trust, a court proceeding will be required to officially empower the guardians you have selected in your will. But, if the living revocable trust is used properly and there isn't any property to probate, the process of going to court and having a guardian appointed isn't too bad. When the court doesn't have to worry about property and money, the probate proceeding appointing guardians is an open and shut case unless someone challenges the will.

In some cases, living revocable trusts can actually eliminate the need for guardianships and conservatorships. One common problem that can be eliminated occurs when someone leaves property in a will to a minor or an incompetent person. Because the property is left under a will, the court will have control of the property, and the court will see to it that a conservator is appointed to protect the property. The conservatorship appointment is required even if the minor or incompetent has good parents or a court appointed guardian. For example, if Grandpa leaves money in his will to the grandchildren, the parents will have to be appointed, as part of Grandpa's probate proceeding, as conservators over the money. Until the money is finally distributed to the grandchildren when they are old enough, the parents will have to report periodically to the court and account for the money.

Leaving money to the grandchildren in a living revocable trust and directing the trustee to pay the money to the grandchildren's parents would avoid the necessity of such conservatorship appointments. Trusts should give the trustee numerous avenues to get the money to the grandchildren. For example, trust funds can be moved to help the beneficiary in any one of the following ways:

1. The trustee can move funds directly to the beneficiary.
2. The trustee can give funds to the beneficiary's legally appointed guardian.
3. The trustee can give funds to a relative or friend of the beneficiary for the care, support, and education of the beneficiary.
4. The trustee can use funds directly for the beneficiary's care, support, and education.
5. The trustee can also give funds to the beneficiary's custodian under a "Uniform Gift to Minor's Act."

A minor child presents one problem that has to be worked out. The adult incompetent presents another. What happens when Mom or Dad becomes incompetent? The solutions to the problems caused by minors and the problems caused by adult incompetents are a little different. A legal tool called a "power of attorney" can be used to help avoid conservatorship appointments when one of your adult family members becomes incompetent. It will be used in addition to your will and living revocable trust.

Chapter

14

Obtaining Power Beyond Your Trust

Implementing a Power of Attorney

A "power of attorney" is a powerful legal tool. In fact, when clients hear about a power of attorney, they often question the need for a living revocable trust and a will. They get the impression everything can be covered by a power of attorney. A power of attorney is simply a written statement which transfers control of property to another person. If you are going to leave town and need to sell your car, you could give a power of attorney to someone authorizing them to sell the car in your absence. If you wanted to, you could give someone power of attorney over all of your property. This would be considered a "general" power of attorney.

Power of attorney arrangements are great, but they cannot be used in place of a will or living revocable trust for three main reasons.

First, all powers of attorney fail when the "principal," i.e., the person who creates the power of attorney, dies. The law says that if the principal is dead, the power of attorney is no longer valid. The law says so, and that is that. No power of attorney can be used to control or distribute property after the principal dies. There are no ifs, ands, or buts about it.

Second, the power of attorney used in most situations becomes void when the "principal" becomes incompetent. When the principal becomes incompetent, the person designated to act under the power of attorney, the "agent," automatically loses all power to act. The law simply says that the power of attorney is void as soon as the principal becomes incompetent.

Third, when you give an agent power of attorney over your property, the agent is not controlled by the strong "fiduciary relationship" which controls a trustee. The agent has full power to do whatever he or she wants to do with the property, irrespective of whether or not his or her actions are in your best interests. However, a fiduciary (trustee) must perform those acts which are in your (the beneficiary's) best interest. So, the best protection for you and your family is provided by the trust's fiduciary restraints on the trustee, not by the sheer, unchecked power given an agent by a power of attorney.

Give Yourself Light in Your Family's Darkest Moments

A special type of power of attorney called a "durable power of attorney" has been created by new laws that have now been passed in every state. The durable power of attorney "endures" the incompetency of the principal, and the agent has power to act even though the principal is incompetent. You should definitely have a durable power of attorney as part of your legal arsenal.

You need a durable power of attorney to support your living revocable trust, but it should be made clear that the durable power of attorney is not a substitute for your will or your living revocable trust.

Property which is owned by your living revocable trust will be under the control of your successor trustee when you become incompetent or die. Property held in your trust will not be controlled by the agent appointed in your durable power of attorney.

Only property you "own," i.e., property not in your trust, will be controlled by your agent when you become incompetent. Your trust should describe the criteria under which you will be considered incompetent. Therefore, when you become incompetent, there shouldn't be any need to go to court and have you declared incompetent. Your trust will automatically transfer power to your successor trustee when the criteria of your incompetency are met. How you define those criteria is described at the end of Chapter 16 in detail.

The same type of criteria will be used in your durable power of attorney to describe when you are incompetent. When the criteria are met, the agent you have appointed in the power of attorney will have the power to act. His authority will "spring" into existence. Thus, the lawyers call this transition of power a "springing power."

In your durable power of attorney, the agent should be given broad authority or power over all of your property which is not held in your trust. In fact, your durable power of attorney could authorize the agent to transfer ownership of your property to your living revocable trust. This will allow the agent to move the property, prior to your death, so that it won't have to be probated if you die. Just because your agent can move property to your living revocable trust, that is no excuse for not moving the property prior to your incompetency. And who knows, you may just die and skip the whole incompetency thing.

In addition to managing property, your agent must be given power to act on your behalf with the gas company, electric company, your credit card companies, and other companies and agencies you do business with. Have you ever tried to deal with the utility company on behalf of someone else? It is impossible without a power of attorney.

Some of my clients dismiss the need for a durable power of attorney. The facts are that at age 25 you are almost ten times more likely to be incompetent next month than you are to be dead next month. Even at age 65, you are almost five times more likely to be incompetent tomorrow than you are to be dead tomorrow. Over 80% of all people are incompetent and need a durable power of attorney for at least 90 days during their life. You should have a durable power of attorney as a part of your estate planning package, and your trust should be used to the maximum.

You can easily determine whether or not a power of attorney is the common type of power of attorney or a durable power of attorney. If it is a durable power of attorney, it will have a "durability provision" some place in the document. The provision will have language in it which reads something like that shown in Scroll 14.1.

Durable Power of Attorney for Health Care—Use One

Durable powers of attorney can be used to authorize your agent to manage your property. In almost all states, they can now also be used to manage your health care. A living will (discussed in Chapter 6) is the directive that lets you die with dignity and tells the doctors to unplug the machines, but it doesn't direct your medical treatment unless death is certain. How is your medical care directed during a major illness?

Kristy and I have come to the conclusion that someone, other than the doctors and hospital staff, has to direct your medical treatment if you are seriously ill. Someone, a family member or friend, should be with you almost continuously while you are hospitalized.

We have observed that the level of medical care is substantially better when a third party is there watching and actively representing your interests. Sick people cannot physically or mentally direct their own medical treatment. They need help. Having someone else there watching could be the difference between life and death. We know from experience how important it is to have a fully active, thinking person present at the hospital.

Durability Provision

This Durable Power of Attorney shall not be affected by the subsequent disability or incapability of the principal. Notwithstanding any provision herein to the contrary, my agent shall take no action under this instrument unless (1) I am deemed to be incapacitated as defined herein, or (2) I have executed a certificate that authorizes my agent to act under this Durable Power of Attorney.

Scroll 14.1—Language used in a power of attorney to make it a "durable" power of attorney

When our son was three years old, he went to the hospital to have his tonsils out. The nurses said he would get his pre-operation series of shots at about 4:00 a.m. (Of course, we had to pump them to get that information.) Kristy said she wanted to be with him when he received the shots. The nurses said she was crazy to get up that early. She left the hospital about 11:00 p.m. the night before and was back by 4:00 a.m. At about 5:00 a.m., she watched the nurse give our son all of his shots to "dry him out" and prepare him for surgery.

At 7:30 a.m., another nurse came in and started to prepare a bunch of needles to give our son a lot of shots. Kristy asked what the shots were for. The nurse said they were the shots necessary to prepare him for surgery. Kristy told the nurse he had already had the shots. The nurse looked at our son's chart and told her to stand aside because he hadn't had the shots. The chart indicated that he still needed the shots.

Kristy and the nurse got into a verbal war. The situation got nasty. Supervisors and doctors came because Kristy got loud and physical. She started using the "L" word and the "S" word (lawyer and sue). The hospital finally called the night nurse who had gone home at 6:00 a.m. Sure enough, she had forgotten to write down that she gave our son all of his shots.

My doctor friends tell me that if our son had received two full sets of pre-operation shots, there was a high probability that he would have died when the anesthetic was administered. We would have never known why he died. There was no written record. We would have been told that our son had had one of those rare, horrible reactions to the anesthetic that couldn't be helped—one of those horrible reactions to the anesthetic like the reaction that recently killed the three year old girl that lived through the block, when she had her tonsils out. Maybe she did have a rare reaction to the anesthetic—maybe she didn't.

My cancer treatment was long, but Kristy was always there. Her presence got me medical attention I would not have received otherwise and probably saved my life on at least two occasions. I have witnessed many situations where a sick person in a hospital has been actively defended by a family member, and the sick person's life has definitely or most likely been saved.

I have strong feelings about how the hospital scene should be handled. The hospitals and doctors can be rude, arrogant, and very cold. Of course, if you are helping someone in the hospital, it is best to "get along" by using the old charm techniques, and charm usually works. However, if push comes to shove, it is wise to have a durable power of attorney for health care backing up your position.

The durable power of attorney for health care legally appoints someone (your agent) as the person who the doctors and hospitals are obligated to deal with. Your agent has the legal right to see all of your medical records, hire and fire doctors, move you to a different hospital, and do all of the other things that it would be impossible to do without the legal backing of the durable power of attorney for health care.

The durable power of attorney for health care can be a separate legal document, or it can be part of the durable power of attorney which allows your appointed agent to manage your property.

The same factors that should be considered when naming your trustee should be considered when naming your agent under a durable power of attorney and a durable power of attorney for health care. The same factors that go into deciding how you would be declared incompetent under your trust should be used to prepare the language determining your incompetency under your durable power of attorney.

Actually, the agent named in your durable power of attorney and the agent named in your durable power of attorney for health care will probably be the same person you named as trustee under your living revocable trust. Can you see how the durable power of attorney documents and living revocable trust dovetail together to form your complete legal plan? The living will, durable power of attorney, and durable power of attorney for health care are part of your plan for life. The living revocable trust helps both during your life and after your death.

Chapter

15

Living Trust Advantages

Getting the Most From Your Trust

Of course, avoiding probate and being able to control your wealth, both during your life and after you die, are the big advantages of living revocable trusts. There are also many other significant advantages you can obtain by using your trust.

The Trust Protects Your Privacy

Everyone believes the right to privacy is a freedom guaranteed by the United States Constitution. Protecting your privacy is becoming increasingly more difficult. Since computers have been used to track us, Big Brother is always watching. Trusts have traditionally been used to protect the privacy of the super wealthy. A living revocable trust very effectively protects your privacy.

Because assets owned by the trust are not exposed to probate, they don't have to be inventoried for the courts. If the trust is meticulously used, there won't be any probate at all, and there won't be any notices in the newspapers. Papers won't be filed at the court, and strangers won't be able to find out what Dad really owned. The scam investors will never know you got Uncle Big Bucks's million bucks.

When you use your trust, the people you deal with will require you to show them the trust, and they may even want a copy of the trust. That is to be expected. For years the SEC (Securities and Exchange Commission) required your stock broker to obtain a copy of your trust when you opened a brokerage account. Now the SEC has decided that they have too much paper, so they require the broker to obtain a "summary" of the trust. Banks will often copy part of the trust for your file. They have to be able to identify the trust when a successor trustee shows up and wants to get into your (your trust's) bank account.

Of course, the broker, the bank, and others will keep your trust private, just as they keep your account records private. Having a broker or a bank take a copy of the trust is not asking for the trouble you get when you file a will at the courthouse.

You should retain an originally signed copy of your trust. The lawyer will keep a photocopy or a second originally signed copy of your trust. Because some people you deal with as trustee will want to see an original signature, it is important that you have an originally signed copy. Additionally, if you have the original, it leaves you free to amend the trust, revoke the trust, or even work with another attorney without ever having to contact the attorney that drafted the trust. The trust is yours, not the attorney's.

Trusting the Ex Out

You have already learned how to write the guardianship section of a simple will. The same guardianship provision will be put in your pour-over will, and the court will get involved in the appointment of the guardian. The courts will generally honor your choice of guardians. However, a problem may occur when you are divorced and are the custodial parent of the children. When you die, you may not want the kids to go live with your ex.

You may not have a choice. If you have been divorced and your children have not been officially adopted into your new family when you remarry, or if you don't remarry, the "ex" can usually obtain custody or guardianship of the kids when you die. Even though your will appoints someone else as a guardian, the court controls the guardianship appointment, and the ex can often step in.

You, not the court, control the appointment of your substitute or "successor" trustee. Without a request from the successor trustee or the beneficiary(ies), the court isn't arbitrarily going to change the appointment of the trustee who takes over your trust when you die. Please take careful notice! The trustee of the trust and the guardian for the kids do not have to be the same person. Of course, the same person generally acts as both trustee and guardian, but in cases where there has been a divorce and there are custody concerns, the money and the kids can effectively be separated by the living revocable trust.

My former secretary lived in great fear that she would die and her ex-husband would obtain custody of the children. We established a living revocable trust for her which turned all of her property over to a trustee she chose. She trusted her trustee to help her children and not just turn money over to her ex if he got custody of the children.

Obviously, the trust itself directed the trustee to hold the money for the children's benefit and not give it directly to the children or the ex. You can use your trust to control the flow of money and property very effectively after your death. Your trust can very carefully lay out all of the ways the trustee can use the trust funds for the children.

Control the money and you can usually control the situation. In my secretary's case, it's a pretty safe bet that her ex will not fight to become guardian for the children if there isn't even the smell of money associated with the kids.

The living revocable trust allows you to retain the maximum amount of control over your financial affairs, even after you are dead. The trustee can respond quickly to the needs of the family, placing funds exactly where you have directed them to go.

Incompetency—Trusts Save Money and Heartache

The living revocable trust is a lifesaver when Dad or Mom becomes incompetent. It can also be a lifesaver when you become incompetent. When you become incompetent, that doesn't mean you will be hauled off to the loony bin; it just means that you can't handle your own business affairs.

The law allows you to use your trust and designate the conditions under which control will be passed to your designated "successor" trustee. Your successor trustee will control all of your trust's property. Yes, your durable power of attorney will allow your appointed agent to control all of your "other" property. Because your durable power of attorney will not avoid probate when you die, hopefully there won't be any "other" property to be controlled by your agent. Only the trust will allow your family to avoid the nightmare of probate.

There are numerous variables to consider when you define the conditions of incompetency in your trust and durable power of attorney. The variables will be discussed in detail at the end of Chapter 16. When the conditions (however you define them) are met, control of your trust automatically transfers, and your successor trustee will have full control over all of the trust property. Likewise, your agent is automatically authorized to act.

If you are managing all of your financial affairs through your trust and also use a durable power of attorney, there won't be any need for your family to go to court to have you declared incompetent and have someone appointed as your conservator. Should a guardian or a conservator have to be appointed, his duties will be easy because he will not have to continually report all of your financial affairs to the court. This protects your privacy. Your competitors, the grabby relatives, and all of the nosey neighbors don't even need to know you are not acting on your own behalf.

We didn't have a living revocable trust or durable power of attorney when I had cancer. My incompetency during that period was real, and it caused big problems. I tried to conduct business when I wasn't really "with it." When a catastrophic illness like cancer strikes, your life is totally out of control. You want to be normal more than anything else, and even if life is far from normal, you will try to act normal.

When I was sick, I had people "pass" documents to me for my signature. Because I was in isolation, I couldn't have visitors. (I didn't have any white blood cells to fight infection, and even a cold would have been deadly.) All papers were presented by the nurses or Kristy, who had to be washed, gowned, and masked before entering the room. Two conflicting papers were signed. When the second paper was signed, I had no idea that I had signed the first document.

The legal battle over the two papers stopped just short of the Supreme Court of Utah. The stress and concern we went through fighting the legal battle undoubtedly slowed my physical recovery and prevented our lives from returning to normal for months after I returned home to recover. The legal system was destroying our lives over a seemingly minor problem, and I was a lawyer.

Everything had happened so innocently. We learned the value of good attorneys. The mess was finally resolved when it was proved that on the day I signed one of the documents, I had been given 14 types of drugs, including 120 milligrams of morphine. When your body organs are shutting down in preparation for death, the pain can be extreme, and massive amounts of morphine are appropriate. I learned about pain.

The judge presiding over our legal battle finally agreed I was incompetent when I signed my name. In retrospect, Kristy should have gone to court and had me declared incompetent. But, who would have been appointed as my guardian and conservator? Kristy? Kristy was under such intense emotional trauma that there were periods of time, long periods of time, when she shouldn't have even driven a car. At best, if she had been appointed, she would have simply gone through the motions of "conducting business."

So, who should have been appointed? How long would it have taken, and how much would it have cost? How could Kristy justify the expense when the monthly hospital bills were each as much as a mortgage on a home? My body was obviously being destroyed. How could my family admit that my mind was also gone? That would simply add disgrace and embarrassment to physical tragedy.

My clients will often refuse to have Mom declared incompetent. The emotional stress and embarrassment isn't worth it. To declare someone incompetent, there basically has to be a trial. Witnesses have to be subpoenaed. Often, Mom has to be subpoenaed. Just the trauma of being subpoenaed is too much for Mom.

No matter how many times you have been subpoenaed, it doesn't feel good to open the door and have the sheriff poke a paper in your face and say "sign here." Even if you haven't done anything wrong, it can be embarrassing, unnerving, and destructive to your privacy.

Believe me, when a sheriff's car shows up in your driveway, there goes all your privacy. I have been served with subpoenas dozens of times. While I was in law school, my little chemistry laboratory had the contract to do the forensic chemistry work for law enforcement agencies in the southern half of Utah. I knew all of the officers because they brought me the evidence that needed to be analyzed, and they delivered the subpoenas when I was required to appear in court to testify concerning an analysis.

Whenever a drug bust went down, there was a fatal accident, or something happened that required the chemical analysis of evidence, the police either took me to the scene or immediately brought the evidence to me. The chain of evidence couldn't be broken. I had to have physical control of the evidence as soon as possible.

Two days after we moved up on Pill Hill, the police happened to converge on our home. There were two police cars, a highway patrol cruiser, and a sheriff's van all parked out in front at once. That blew our privacy in the neighborhood. The gossip went wild. We were amazed at the excuses neighbors used to come over and see what we were doing.

The whole legal process of subpoenas, testimony, judicial decisions, lawyers, and hassles required to declare someone incompetent makes the living revocable trust look mighty good when someone in the family goes down.

Often people who are incompetent are only incompetent for a period of time. I am fine now. (OK, it is debatable, but I can fool most of the people most of the time.) Believe it or not, the legal process of having someone declared sane, after he has been declared incompetent, is as bad as the incompetency hearing. The living revocable trust should look even better than mighty good because the successor trustee can simply step aside when control should be handed back to you, the original trustee.

Trusts Can Avoid the Will Contest Problems

Because your living revocable trust is a very flexible legal tool, it can be changed any time you want. It is also a very stable legal tool. Maybe it is just because there are far fewer trusts than there are wills, but I don't see the challenges to trusts that I see brought against wills.

The common challenges to wills include: (1) This will isn't real, (2) Dad was incompetent when he made out the will, (3) Dad forgot me in the will—it was a mistake, and (4) The will doesn't square with letters, statements, and other evidence showing Dad's intentions. Here are some arguments that trustees can use to overcome these challenges if their trust is ever challenged.

This isn't the real thing. No! It must be the real trust because the bank has a copy of part of it, and the broker has a whole copy. Additionally, Dad filed pages 1, 3, and 40 with the title insurance company when he sold the house, because he had to verify that he had the trust and he was the acting trustee.

Dad was crazy. No! Dad may have been sick and worried about dying when he made out the trust five years back. His competency might have even been questioned, but every time he used the trust during the last five years when he was well, that use ratified his trust. The broker will testify that Dad was just fine when he opened his brokerage account in the name of the trust and talked to him about the trust.

If Dad really is only half there and is going to die hours after the trust or will is made out, maybe you had better go with the will. Dad is making a "contract" when he signs the trust, and the law says he has to be a lot more competent to make a contract than he does to make a simple will. The bottom line is: Don't wait and end up doing deathbed planning.

No mistake. Dad certainly didn't make a mistake when he left you out of the distribution terms of the trust. The summary of the trust or "certification of the trust" that he filled out at the broker's office, three years after he had the trust written, lists the beneficiaries, and you weren't on that list. That was no mistake at the broker's office, and he wasn't on his death bed.

Can you see how the common attacks used against a will are easily set aside when a trust is involved? Yes, Dad's trust is private, and yet, many people have had dealings with the trust. Remember, it may be private, but it isn't secret. It isn't some mystery document that is brought out of the crypt when Dad dies. It is a living document. Dad referred to it often.

Trusts Can Be Sued

If you get in trouble while you are alive, your living revocable trust can be sued. The bad news is, your living revocable trust is actually a poor asset protection tool when it gets sued. Limited asset protection can be achieved by using your living revocable trust in certain ways. Asset protection techniques using your living revocable trust will be discussed in Chapters 19, 20, and 21.

Avoid Probate In All States

America is mobile. You will probably live in two or three states. As a result, you can easily end up owning property in more than one state. My friend Ray owns property in more than one state. He lives in California, but he has a wonderful cabin in the mountains by a lake in Utah. It is a place where the family holds a "reunion" every summer. Actually, after the 15 grand kids have all tried to sleep together in a one room loft for a week, everyone feels that they have been a little too reunioned, but the moments at the cabin are precious to everyone. Ray put together a living revocable trust and very carefully placed his California property and the Utah cabin into the trust. By doing this, he has saved the family a probate headache in California as well as one in Utah. Without the living revocable trust, there would be a probate in both states.

Probate courts only have jurisdiction over the property in the state where they are located. Therefore, a different probate proceeding must be conducted in every state where the deceased owned property. As discussed earlier, the probate in the state where the deceased was a resident is called the primary probate, and the probates in other states are called ancillary probates. All of the probates are avoided when the property is brought together under the ownership umbrella of the living revocable trust. Only one trust is required. It simply owns property in more than one state in the same way that you can own property in more than one state.

Income Taxes—No Problem, Trusts Help

You do not have to file trust income tax returns in the name of your living revocable trust, as long as the trust is revocable and you and/or your spouse are the trustee(s). That's the good news. The bad news is, you still have to pay your income taxes. You will file your own 1040 form just as you always have. The government doesn't even want to know that you have a living revocable trust. They reason that since your trust is revocable, you can get the property back at any time. It was your property before you put it into the trust, and you can get it back or use it however you want. Therefore, it must be "yours." So the IRS will tax all of the income just as they did before you got your living revocable trust. Whenever anyone asks for a tax I.D. number for your living revocable trust, just give them your social security number.

Your trust receives its income from the same places you do. It receives income from investments, from paychecks which are deposited into the trust's account, and from various other sources. The text of your trust will direct the trustee to "pay" the beneficiaries (you) all of the "income" from the trust quarterly or at least annually. This does not mean that the trust writes you a check for the amount of the trust's income. It simply means that you have to claim the income on your 1040 tax return every quarter, or at least annually, just as you would if the income had come to you directly. Because your living revocable trust has to "pay" you all of the income, it cannot "accumulate" income. Trusts that cannot accumulate income are called "simple trusts."

When you die, your trust becomes irrevocable. If you or your spouse dies and the "Decedent's Trust" is created, the Decedent's Trust becomes irrevocable. The Decedent's Trust is explained in Chapter 19 on estate taxes. An irrevocable trust is required to have its own tax I.D. number. Form SS-4 from the IRS allows you to file for the trust's tax I.D. number and the trust (irrevocable trust) will file its income taxes using form 1041.

An irrevocable trust with its very own tax I.D. number can accumulate income, if its trust document allows for accumulation. When a trust accumulates income and pays it to the beneficiaries later, the tax laws applied to the trust and the beneficiaries are incredibly complex. Lawyers call trusts that can accumulate income "complex trusts." No, it's not a joke. Such trusts are referred to as complex trusts or "accumulation trusts."

In my distant past, I taught tax preparers in a big national firm about living revocable trusts, because they were encountering them in their tax work. Almost any file drawer I opened in the tax preparation offices had several tax files for living revocable trusts that had tax I.D. numbers and had been filing tax returns. In most of the cases I saw, the trust should not have had a tax I.D. number or been filing tax returns because the grantor hadn't died and was still acting as trustee. The trust was still revocable. (When you and your spouse both die, your entire trust will automatically become irrevocable.) The lawyers had set up their clients by preparing the living revocable trusts and then filing for tax I.D. numbers. The lawyers could then make an extra $1,000 or so a year by preparing the tax return for the trusts. After a couple of years, when the clients couldn't afford a thousand dollars to prepare the tax returns, they would take the trust to tax preparers and have them file the returns.

This is all wrong! In fact, if you are acting as trustee of your own living *revocable* trust, it is now illegal for you to have the living revocable trust file a tax return. Don't do it! *Irrevocable* trusts must file a 1041 tax return each year. This will be discussed later in detail. Living revocable trusts that were established before 1980 were required to file a 1041 form. If you do happen to have an old timer living revocable trust created prior to 1980 or which filed a 1041 form prior to November 24, 1981, you can keep filing a 1041 for your trust, or you can file a final 1041 form and start just filing your personal 1040 forms.

The Subtle Advantages of Trusts

A living revocable trust has numerous advantages that everyone can take advantage of, and it also has some subtle advantages that can really help in certain circumstances.

Obviously, it will save a lot of money—possibly thousands of dollars—in probate costs, and it moves that money directly to your loved ones. Lawyers charge more to prepare living revocable trusts than they do simple wills, but the real cost of the will also includes the cost of probating the assets which are subject to the will. When you look at the big picture, a living revocable trust is relatively inexpensive, especially if you don't need help funding the trust and will do all of the legwork yourself.

A living revocable trust is easy to establish, and it facilitates the smooth, quick transfer of power and property at your death or incompetency. Your instructions are carried out, giving you control over your property even though you aren't there to act. The courts, the lawyers, and the public are excluded from your affairs. Because everything is controlled, private, and in order, the emotional trauma you and your family experience is alleviated in times of crisis.

Yes, you actually maintain full power and control over all of your affairs until you voluntarily give up control or can no longer act for yourself. You don't need to be afraid of losing control, because in the trust itself you have defined the conditions under which you can no longer act. Only your defined conditions are used. Other conditions, such as the court's conditions, have not been imposed upon you.

Once you set your living revocable trust in place, life goes on just as it always has for you. Funny thing, when the checking account is owned by your living revocable trust, the checks bounce just as high as they always did. The mortgage is still on the house, even though the house is owned by the trust. The kids still need money for college. Nothing changes except the fear and worry.

Whether you will admit it or not, subconsciously you worry about placing your affairs in order. Once the living revocable trust is in place, and it has been properly funded, a satisfaction, security, and peace that are hard to describe settle over you, and life actually gets better.

Chapter

16

Trust Provisions Unique to You

Selecting Your Trustee

Most parts or "provisions" of a trust are the same in every trust. The language used in those provisions is language which complies with the law or IRS regulations, and the language should be the same in every trust. If a lawyer usually puts out a 30 page trust for a client, about 26 pages are going to be exactly the same for every client. In this chapter, you will learn about the parts of the trust you can change, and I will show you some of the ways my clients often want to change their trust provisions. This will give you ideas, so that you can think about the way you want your trust to read.

Trustees and Successor Trustees—Go Ahead, Change Your Mind

You will probably be the trustee for your trust as long as you are alive and can function effectively. When you act as your trust's trustee, you will continue to conduct your financial affairs just as you have always done.

If you have a joint trust (a trust designed for a married couple where there is only one trust document addressing the desires of both husband and wife), the trustee position can be shared between you and your spouse. You can both be the trustee, and you can each have full control, just as you do now if you own property jointly. Couples that have a separate trust for him and a separate trust for her will have him act as trustee for his trust and her act as trustee for her trust.

You could have anyone or even a company, such as a bank, act as your trustee. Actually, you probably don't want someone else acting as trustee while you are able to act for yourself. There are, however, circumstances when it becomes very nice to have someone other than yourself acting as trustee. For example, if you are out of town for an extended period of time, your trustee can manage all of your affairs.

The Bank—It's Not Necessary

A close friend of mine is halfway around the world serving a three-year mission for his church. He created a trust that gave the trustee authority to handle all of his financial affairs for three years. When the three years are up, all of the power to handle the affairs automatically reverts back to him and his wife. His bank was to act as trustee, and the bank would have done a good job as trustee. However, everything blew up hours before he flew out.

The bank understands what a fiduciary duty means, and they got cold feet. My friend was a senior, high-powered attorney the bank used whenever it had a $100 million lawsuit on its hands. For some reason, the bank decided there might be a conflict of interest or some problem if the bank acted as trustee. So, the bank said "no" at the last possible moment. It wasn't necessary to have the bank act as trustee.

At 2:00 a.m. we found a notary public, and I became the trustee of my friend's trust. Now I am landlord, accountant, tax preparer, financial advisor, and regular old grunt man, or "trustee." Everything has actually worked well. The good news is that the three years are over. The bad news is that he extended for a fourth year.

You, Yourself, and the Family—All the Trustees You Need?

Most of my clients set up their trust so that they are the trustee, and then when a new trustee is needed, because of death or incompetency, a family member is designated as the successor trustee. If the client has older children, one of the children is usually designated as the successor trustee.

When Kristy and I first set up our living revocable trust, our children were young. So we named our fathers as successor trustees. Of course, we are the original trustees, and I will assume, throughout our discussion of trustees, that you will be the original trustee of your living revocable trust. Our fathers are designated to act jointly as successor trustees. Both of them will have to agree on the actions that will be taken after Kristy and I are gone.

Some people want two or three people to share the trustee's position. There isn't anything wrong with that. However, I always counsel them about the problems that arise whenever a committee is given a task to do. Business goes much faster, and it often avoids hurt feelings if only one person is designated to act at any one time as trustee.

Yes, two or more successor trustees acting together can cause problems, but many of the problems can be solved by simply having the written trust document address the problems up front. The trust should have a provision which lays down the rules to resolve a deadlock between the co-trustees. It should also clearly state how many signatures are required to conduct trust business. Only one signature is necessary, but the trust could be written to require all checking accounts owned by the trust to have two signatures on the checks.

Your trust will actually list a number of successor trustees. You should have a first choice, a second choice, etc. If a number of possibilities are listed and for some reason the first choice can't serve as trustee, then there are one or two backup choices.

How to Pick the Best Trustee

Factors you should consider, when choosing individuals to put on your list of successor trustees, include:

1. Where is the person? If all of your property is in Vermont and your oldest child lives in Florida, that child might not be your first choice for trustee. The trustee is required to manage the property. Long distance management can be done, but it isn't easy, and it is more expensive than local management.

2. Does the person have money sense? The trustee handles financial matters. If the person you are considering naming as trustee is a spendthrift, you probably don't want him acting as trustee. Spendthrifts (people who can't handle money) don't make good trustees. Be sure to consider not only the money habits of the person you are designating as trustee, but also the money habits of the designated trustee's spouse. The spouse technically has nothing to do with the trust or the trustee's actions, but I have seen many cases where the trustee was influenced by his or her spouse.

3. Is the person fair and honest? When you appoint an individual as trustee, you surely want him to treat the beneficiaries fairly. Yes, the trustee is under the fiduciary duty to treat the beneficiaries fairly, but things will go a whole lot smoother if the basic nature of the trustee is to be fair and honest. You don't have to worry about corporate trustees being honest. They had better be honest, or you will sue them. So, the questions to ask are: "How deep are the corporate pockets? How much do you get when you sue?"

4. What is the general health of the person? Obviously, your choice as trustee should be someone who can physically and mentally handle the job. Don't forget to evaluate the mental factors. What is the person's stress load? Does he have the time to be trustee?

5. Does the person have a reasonable legal understanding? Your trustee should at least be able to understand legal actions. No, he doesn't have to be an attorney, but some people just don't

have the patience or ability to put up with the legal system, and they don't make good trustees. Chances are, the trustee won't ever have to deal directly with lawyers and courts, but you want someone who can go to bat for the trust if he has to fight a legal battle.

These five factors, and others that may be important to you, should all be weighed when you choose an individual as trustee or successor trustee. Weighing the factors will help you to determine the order of names on your list of successor trustees.

Anyone can serve as trustee, as long as he can legally act. If you are naming one of your children as successor trustee, be sensitive, as you were when you named them as personal representatives. I suggest you put all of your children on the list. Sure, only the first one or two on the list are really in the running to become successor trustee, but won't it make each child feel good to see his or her name on the list, even if the name is way down the list? Why hurt someone's feelings by leaving his name off the list just because there isn't really much of a chance he will ever serve?

Your first choice as successor trustee should be the best person for the job. That isn't automatically your oldest child. All factors must be considered and weighed.

Don't forget that your successor trustee probably isn't going to have to start acting as trustee tomorrow. It might be 10 years before your successor trustee steps in and takes over. If your children are great kids, but they are only young teenagers, they obviously can't legally act today as trustees. However, consider putting them first on your list of trustees, because when you need a successor trustee ten years from now, your then 27 year old son or daughter might be just the person you want. Naming your teenage children as possible successor trustees won't hurt anything. If for any reason your first choice for the designated successor trustee can't act, or refuses to act when needed, the designation drops to the next choice down the list until someone is found who can act. Make sure that somewhere down the list, you name somebody who really could act if you needed a successor trustee tomorrow.

Some situations make it advisable to get an independent person or even a corporation (bank) to act as successor trustee. When the kids hate each other or have a high probability of having problems with each other, it's probably best to go outside of the family to recruit a successor trustee. Stand back and realistically evaluate your family. Can the kids pull together? Will having a child act as trustee break up the family? The problems and expenses of a corporate trustee are small costs compared to the emotional costs when family relationships are destroyed. Using family members as successor trustees usually works well, but it can be a total disaster. Will it work well or be a disaster for your family?

It is possible to choose a family member as a co-successor trustee to act with the bank or other independent trustee. This not only provides some family input into the trustee's position, but also provides for an independent trustee who can wield a heavy hand if necessary.

The choice of trustees is yours and yours alone. Sometimes an attorney will push you to appoint him or a bank as the successor trustee. A bank is actually frequently recommended, because the bank refers clients to the attorney. In exchange, the attorney lines the bank up as trustee. The attorney's job is only to counsel you, not push you.

Remember, your choices can be changed, and they should be reviewed every year. Look at whom your designated successor trustee marries. A spouse can influence even the best choice for trustee. If your son or daughter goes bad or has problems, get his or her name off the list as successor trustee, or at least put his or her name at the bottom of the list.

As the original trustee of your trust, you can transfer control of the trust to the designated trustee any time you wish. All it takes to transfer control is a written notarized statement which says what you want to do. Trusts are amazingly flexible. You are in total control and can do whatever you want. When a husband and wife are acting as joint or co-trustees, the trust can be written so that all power automatically transfers to the survivor when one spouse dies.

No matter whom you designate as your successor trustee, it is a good idea to talk to him about your intentions to have him act as your trustee. He may not want to be the trustee, so let him tell you up front so that you can appoint someone else.

Your successor trustee will do all of the legwork to clean up your estate after you die. He will perform the same function as the personal representative does, except that the successor trustee will not have to answer to the probate court. The successor trustee will have instant access to all of your property, and he can handle all of your affairs. The transfer of power from you, as the original trustee, is instantaneous, private, and without cost.

Give your designated successor trustees a copy of the trust, if you want. Make sure they have a copy of this book and have an understanding of how to use a trust. If you choose a bank as your successor trustee, talk to the bank and make sure you know that they want your trust. If you have a small trust estate, many banks simply refuse to act as your trustee. Find out now what the bank will or won't do for you.

Advantages of Using Corporate Trustees

Corporate trustees (banks) often don't want to handle the little Mom and Pop living revocable trust. If the trust estate (all of the property the trust owns) is small, there simply isn't enough money in the fees to make it worth their while, because the fees are usually set as a percentage of the trust estate. Go down and talk to the bank to see if they will act as your trustee. Check out the professionals. What is their reputation? How big is their trust portfolio? With whom will you and your family deal? Are you comfortable? If you are not comfortable, don't do it.

There are some cost disadvantages associated with having a professional trustee, but there are also some real advantages. Some advantages include:

Stability

I almost always have my clients list one of the big banks in town as the last name on their list of successor trustees. If for some reason nobody up the list can act as trustee, the bank, or at least its successor entity, will probably be there 20 years from now. Banks are open every day (well, most days), and they don't get sick or die.

Professional Stature

Good or bad, the banks and trust corporations manage lots of trusts, and they know what to do. They have full legal, accounting, and investment support. All of the reports, taxes, distributions, and other housekeeping details associated with management of the trust are easily performed by professional trustees.

Objectivity

The banks aren't afraid to make the hard decisions. They simply carry out the instructions you give them in the trust document you wrote. The bank may be cold and strict, but sometimes that is exactly what will save your family relationships. Your kids can be mad at the bank, but they can't be mad at each other because only the bank is involved in pulling off the "dirty deed."

Investment/Management Skills

The primary function of a professional trustee is to protect the trust estate. Making money for the trust is not a goal of the professional. As a result, your money will be invested very, very conservatively. This can be very frustrating to beneficiaries that like the higher income generating investments. Remember, income potential is directly related to risk potential. If the bank loses money from the trust, it could be held liable to replace the money, so they just don't take any chances.

Using a Bank While You Are Alive

Having the bank act as successor trustee after you die has some advantages, and in a limited number of cases, the bank should be considered as the original trustee. One advantage of the professional trustee is the freedom you can achieve by not having to control every aspect of your financial affairs. If you name a bank or professional trustee as your original trustee, you certainly want to maintain enough control to direct the trustee or fire the trustee and get a new one. In a living revocable trust, you can easily maintain such control. In the trust, you just write down the rights you want to reserve to yourself, including the right to fire the trustee. The trust document controls everything, so what it says becomes very important. When trustees agree to take the management reins, they are agreeing that they will follow exactly the instructions written in the trust document.

Two of my clients, an older couple, have a lot of real estate in town. They have the bank act as trustee. Of course, the bank hires a management company to manage all of the properties. Sure, it costs money to hire the management company, and the bank gets its trustee's fee, but my clients never have a worry or a concern. Money just shows up in their bank account from the rents. They love having the bank act as trustee.

Keeping Maintenance Charges Low or Zero

Banks act as the trustee for many trusts, but today, very few living revocable trusts are managed by a bank. Unless you have a special situation, you will manage your own living revocable trust as long as possible, and when you need a successor trustee to step in, your choice will most likely be a family member or friend. You could pay your successor trustee if you wanted, but family members and friends usually don't charge to act as trustee. Of course, you don't charge your own trust to act as trustee. Therefore, once the trust is established, there really aren't any maintenance charges required to keep your living revocable trust in place.

Once the attorney finishes his work and you have established your living revocable trust, the attorney doesn't need to be involved anymore, unless (1) the laws change and the trust has to be changed to comply with the new laws, or (2) you change your mind. Historically, it seems that Congress likes to address new estate planning laws in a big way about every 10 years. Maybe clients are like Congressmen; I find they like to change their minds about every 10 years. Go ahead, change your trust. It might cost a little money, but it is easy to do, and it will set your mind at ease.

Does Your Trustee Need to Be Bonded?

Bonding the trustee is basically just the act of purchasing an insurance policy to assure that the trustee will do a good job and not run off with the trust funds. Bonding isn't a huge cost, but it is a cost most of my clients don't want to spend. Therefore, I put a provision in the trust document which says that the grantor will not require the trustee to be bonded. If you are acting as trustee, obviously you wouldn't bond yourself. Most professional trustees are already bonded because they have to be bonded in order to meet all of the federal and state regulations imposed on banks and trust companies.

Avoid Courts When Someone Becomes Incompetent

In the trust document itself and in your durable power of attorney, you have the opportunity to set the standard by which you will be considered incompetent. Once the standard is met, the successor or backup trustee named in your trust can step in and manage all of the trust's property for your benefit and the benefit of the other beneficiaries described in the trust. Similarly, once the standard is met, your agent in your durable power of attorney will have control over your property and affairs that are not governed by your successor trustee.

The trust and durable power of attorney could say that you will be considered incompetent the first time you forget your wedding anniversary or your driver's license number, but those criteria aren't too realistic. Most trusts and durable powers of attorney tie the competency test to the opinion of your family members and your attending physicians. Usually the documents simply require an affidavit saying that you are incompetent and the signatures of your spouse and one or two of the doctors who are treating you. The affidavit is a simple, short one or two paragraph statement which states that you are incompetent. It is signed by the designated attestors and notarized.

You can put as many criteria in the standard as you want. Maybe you will want the approval of your personal physician, an independent psychologist, your spouse, and each of your children. Some people use a religious leader who knows them as someone who has to agree to their incompetency.

Obviously, you could put so many criteria in the standard that it would end up being easier to go to court and have the judge decide when you are incompetent. You don't want to overburden your family, successor trustee, and agent with ridiculous criteria, but you need to feel assured that your right to act for yourself as an individual and as trustee is protected as long as you can competently act. You have to find the balance point where you are comfortable and still don't overburden the family. The criteria you define will depend upon how much you trust the people involved and their ability to make the best choices for you.

Assuming that your trust and durable power of attorney are in order when incompetency occurs, the transfer of power to your successor trustee and agent will be immediate and private without any extra costs for courts, lawyers, or anyone else. Note that your spouse or child is probably going to be your successor trustee and your agent. Armed with the trust, the durable power of attorney, the affidavit, and the proper personal identification, the successor trustee/agent shouldn't have any problems actually taking control of your trust assets and other property.

Control can just as easily be transferred back to you when you are once again able to act for yourself. The same standard used to declare you incompetent can be used to dictate when control should be transferred back to you.

Remember that the trustee can handle only matters relating to property already owned by your trust before you become incompetent. The durable power of attorney will have to be used to empower your agent to handle all of your property which is not owned by your living revocable trust. The trust and durable power of attorney obviously work together to help your family during your incompetency. They substantially lower your family's stress level at a time when it is critical. The living revocable trust, durable power of attorney, and durable power of attorney for health care become your best investment when a family member goes down in a catastrophic disaster such as an accident or illness.

Chapter

17

Transferring Property Using Your Trust

How to Protect Your Heirs

A beneficiary is the person who receives the benefit of the trust's property, and the beneficiary is a necessary player in all trusts. Of course, you will be the beneficiary of your living revocable trust. If you are married, your spouse will also be a beneficiary. During your lifetime, you and your spouse have the benefit of your trust, and your children have an indirect benefit through you. The trust is yours, and it is for your benefit. If for some weird reason the trust isn't meeting your needs, get rid of the trust.

Your primary responsibility is to provide for your welfare and your spouse's welfare during your lives. Don't get so caught up in "planning" for the disposal of property upon your death that you forget that your living revocable trust is a part of your life. Focus on what you and your spouse will need during your lifetime. Your living revocable trust should actually make life easier for you. View your trust and your planning in a bigger picture than just the events following your death.

Nevertheless, planning to dispose of property at your death is the classic use of a living revocable trust. Deciding which people or institutions will receive the benefit of your fortune, whether it is large or small, is an important decision that must be made in order to establish your living revocable trust. If you are like most people, your natural desire is to take care of your family. In my opinion, that is great!

However, when clients say they don't want to leave anything to their children or grandchildren, it is not my place, as a lawyer, to talk them out of their decision. A lawyer's job is to act as scribe for you, the client. Oh sure, the lawyer should counsel you by giving you the pros and cons of doing something a specific way. The lawyer can guide you by giving you different options, but it is up to you to decide what you want to do, whom you want as your successor trustees and beneficiaries, and how you want your trust property managed. Consciously or subconsciously attorneys "guide" clients to make decisions that fit the language they already have in their word processors.

I feel strongly that clients shouldn't be made to fit the forms. The forms should be made to fit the client. The computer program I have created provides you and the attorney with the language necessary to fulfill many of the options possible in drafting living revocable trusts. This is important because it eliminates the biases encountered when a "fill-in-the-blank" system is used. Using the computer program, it is easy to make the forms fit a person's specific needs.

You can leave your property to anyone you want. You can leave it all to your kids, to your dog, to your church, to the IRS, or to me. It doesn't matter. Do exactly what you want to do. A trust can be used to do anything except something that is illegal. The trust is invalid by law if it is established to accomplish an illegal purpose.

Most people want to have everything used to support their spouse. Then when the surviving spouse dies, they want everything to be divided equally among the children. Your living revocable trust can accomplish that easily, but there are several options to consider when the dispositive provisions of your trust (the provisions that "give away" your property after your death) are prepared. The dispositive portion of your trust should be unique to you. It is the most difficult part of the trust to write. There are many traps.

How to Protect the Surviving Spouse

In planning to move your property after your death, I suggest you first focus your attention on your spouse, if you are married. You must have a lot of wealth before I would recommend giving property away when you or your spouse dies and one of you is still alive. Sufficient property should be held after one spouse dies to assure that the surviving spouse has adequate wealth to see him or her through until he or she dies. The problem is that nobody can say how long it will be until the surviving spouse dies. The safe bet is to hold everything for the surviving spouse.

A lot of the estate planning techniques require a best guess as to which spouse will die first. I have learned that you should not try to guess who is going to die first. More than once I have had a couple ask me to do their estate planning. As the couple sits in my office, it seems obvious to everyone that one spouse has one foot in the grave, and the other spouse is fit as a fiddle. Then three months later, the fit spouse is dead, and the sickly spouse lives on, and on, and on.

If you are married, your trust will usually openly state that all of the property is to be held for the surviving spouse and the children. The trustee can usually use the trust property to support the surviving spouse and children in any way the trustee deems best. Tax laws place a very minor restriction on how the trustee can use the property and still have it be protected from estate taxes. The estate tax aspects of living revocable trusts will be explained in Chapter 19.

Note that the surviving spouse will probably take over as sole trustee after his or her spouse dies. This leaves the surviving spouse in full control over all of the trust property, and as long as he or she follows the IRS rules, he or she can basically do anything and still protect the maximum amount of property from estate taxes.

If you are single, obviously you don't have to worry about protecting the lifestyle of a surviving spouse, and you can focus all of your attention on the distribution of property after your death.

Leaving It All to the Kids

Who are "the kids"? Your trust must define who your children are. Yes, that sounds stupid, but I am afraid Bill Clinton's family has a real inheritance problem. Other than Bill, who really are Clinton kids? You might remember that during Bill Clinton's first year in office he discovered that his father had a son by one woman and a daughter by another woman that Bill knew nothing about. Undoubtedly, you don't have that kind of a problem in your family. But, what about the Indian child who lived with you during her high school years and who is still considered "part of the family?" If there is a second marriage, will his kids, her kids, or our kids be "the kids"?

Tragedy occurs when the attorney has used the standard boiler plate language and defined children as "natural issue or adopted children." After the second marriage, for example, Dad never legally adopted Mom's daughter from her first marriage, but certainly the child is part of the family. After all, Dad, Mom's second husband, raised her ever since she was 2 years old. Assume Mom dies leaving everything to Dad. Dad dies leaving it all to his children, using the standard boiler plate language. The oldest daughter is left out. She wasn't Dad's "natural issue or adopted child."

Most of my clients want to leave as much of their property as possible to their children. It is, or at least it has been, the American way to scrimp, save, and fight, to give the next generation a better lifestyle. Nearly all of my older clients (75 to 90 years old) have sacrificed to leave even more to their children than they received from their parents, so that the children will have a better lifestyle than they had. Many of my retirement age clients (55 to 75 years old) have helped their children go to college and buy their houses, and now they don't care if there is anything left for the kids. My middle-aged clients (35 to 55 years old) don't know whether they want to help their kids or not, and my younger clients (25 to 35 years old) don't even know who their kids are. Obviously, these are generalizations which many will argue are inaccurate, and they are probably right, but I hope America isn't leaving the spirit of sacrifice behind, buried in some entitlement trash heap.

Ways to Divide the Property—Shares

Assuming you want to leave it all to your children, there are only two ways you can do it. First, you can leave your wealth, your trust property, to the children and simply have each child's share given to the child upon your death (assuming your spouse is already dead). Second, you can keep the child's share in your trust and give all or part of the share to the child when certain conditions are met.

The word "share" is a term of art used in trusts. It simply means the part of the trust which a beneficiary is entitled to receive. Remember that the trust property will consist of everything you own. If the trust doesn't already own the property before you die, your "pour-over will" will dump or "pour over" all of your property into the trust. Remember also that the property which comes into the trust through the will has to be probated, so you want the trust to own all of the property before you die.

First of all, your trust needs to define each child's share. Your trust may simply state that "...all of the trust property shall be divided into equal shares so as to provide one share for each living child and one share for each deceased child who died leaving 'issue,' i.e., descendants." This statement leaves property to your grandchildren if their father or mother (your son or daughter) is dead. Most clients want to pass on a share to the grandchildren if their parent is dead, but you don't need to leave anything to the grandchildren if you don't want. Be aware that there is a horrible tax assessed if you leave a large amount (over $1 million) to your grandchildren or great-grandchildren while your child is still alive. If it is left to the grandchildren while your children (their parent) is still alive, you will be "skipping a generation," and the IRS will impose heavy taxes. If you have a chance of leaving this much money to the grandchildren, you need to get to a big time tax and estate planning lawyer immediately.

Lawyers have developed a couple of elaborate systems to describe how property is left to your grandchildren when their parent (your son or daughter) has died prior to your death. One is called "per stirpes" or "by representation" and the other is called "per capita."

One Way To Leave Property—By Right of Representation—Per Stirpes

The most common technique for determining who gets what part of an estate is "by right of representation." The term "per stirpes" is often used by lawyers. Per stirpes is simply the Latin term for "to take by the roots" or "by right of representation." This technique says that if the parent is dead, a descendant stands in the shoes of his or her parent.

Refer to Diagram 17.1. Assume that Dad's first son dies before Dad dies. If Dad's trust or will says that the shares will be divided "by right of representation" or "per stirpes," then upon Dad's death, Son 2 and Daughter 1 will each receive a third of Dad's estate. Son 1's two children will each receive a sixth of Dad's estate, which combined is the third share Son 1 would have received if he had been alive. More or less, the grandchildren will receive the share their parent would have received if the parent hadn't died prior to your death.

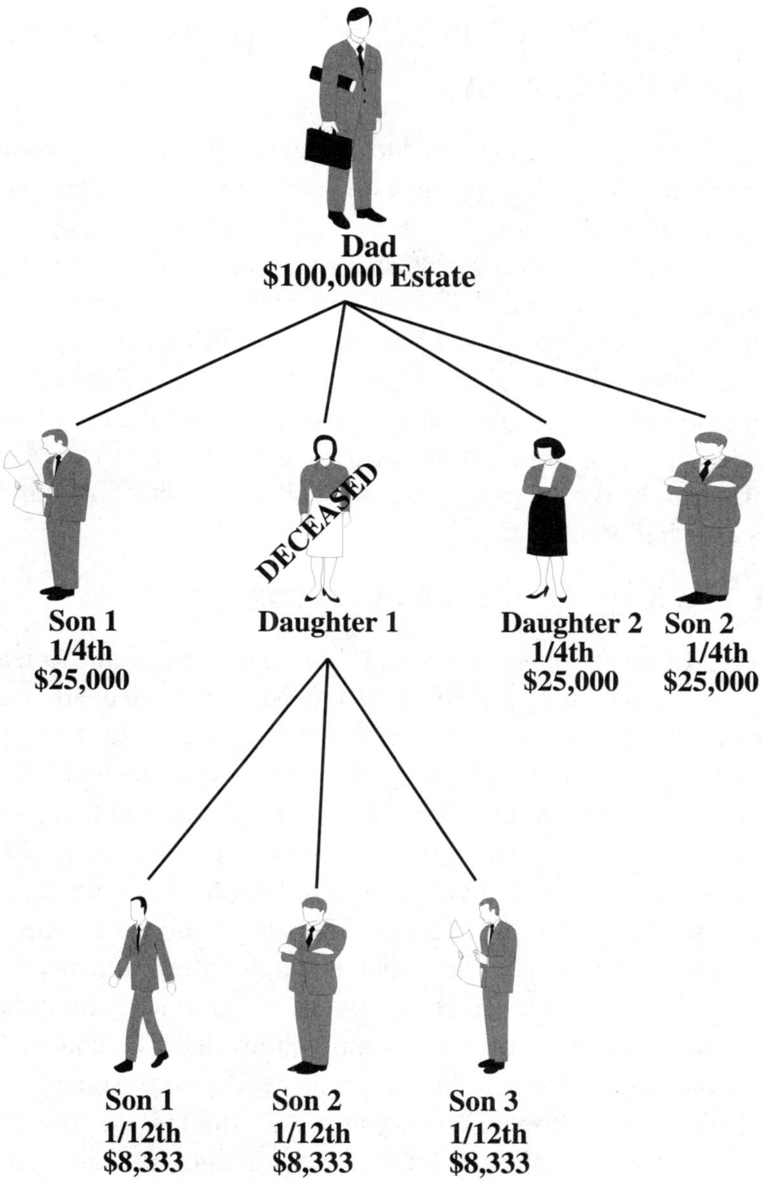

Diagram 17.1—A "Per Stirpes" or "By Representation" distribution pattern assuming a $100,000 estate. Children of a deceased family member stand in the place of the deceased parent and share what their parent would have received.

A Second Way To Leave Property—By Pro Rata—Per Capita

Dividing property up by the per capita technique isn't nearly as common as division per stirpes. Distributing property per capita is also known as a distribution by share or pro rata among all of the descendants. The words share and share alike are usually used in a per capita distribution description when a pro rata or per capital technique is used. Diagram 17.2 shows that each qualifying descendant receives the same share. Each child of your deceased son (your grandchildren) will receive a share of your estate not equal to that share which their parent (your deceased son) would have received, but equal to the share that your surviving children will receive.

A Trick in Writing Your Trust

At first thought, you may think you do not want to leave equal shares to the children. You may want to leave the house to one child, the summer cabin to another, and the boat to a third child. That can certainly be done, because you can instruct the trustee to do absolutely anything you want with the trust property after you die. But before you divide up the trust property one piece at a time, I advise you to rethink because planning to leave property like this is a trap. The disposition is so specific that the plan may backfire. For example, after you make the trust, you might sell the house and move into a condominium. At the time of your death, the summer home hasn't changed, but the boat has a hole in it, and it's a piece of junk. Actually, the boat isn't the 28-foot ski boat you had in mind when you wrote your trust. You sold that boat because at age 70, water skiing didn't sound like a good idea, and you bought a 10 foot aluminum fishing boat with a 5 horsepower Evinrude motor. The money that was left over from the sale of the boat was spent on two trips to Hawaii. So, when you die, who gets what?

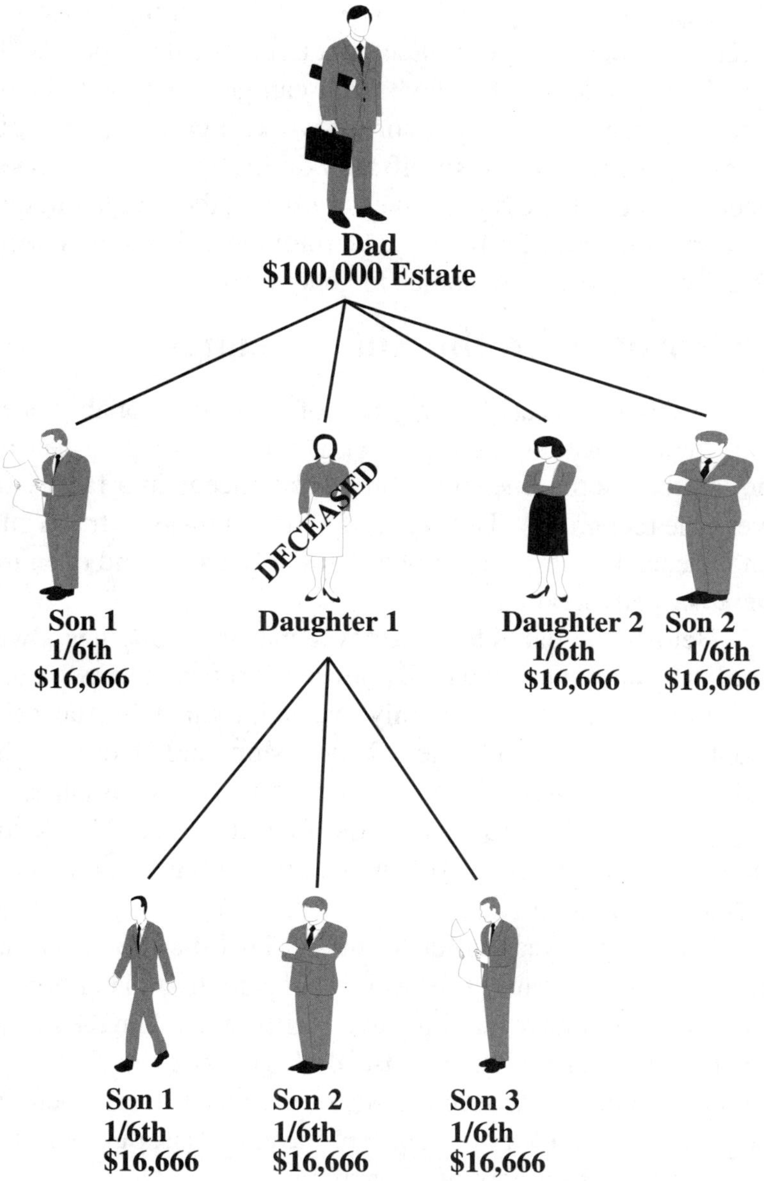

Diagram 17.2—A "Pro Rata" or "Per Capita" distribution pattern assuming a $100,000 estate. Children of a deceased family member receive an equal share with all other family members entitled to receive a share of Dad's estate.

Can you see my point? The trick in writing a trust is to specifically describe your intent, but not make it so specific that your intent is defeated. Maybe you can get away with leaving specific pieces of real estate or art work to certain people, but generally it isn't wise to specifically divide up the trust property piece by piece. Unless you have very strong feelings about moving certain pieces of property to certain individuals, it is best to describe the creation of shares in general terms.

Be Sensitive To the Kid's Feelings

"Who gets what?" is only part of the trap. Probably one of your major goals in passing on your estate is keeping peace in the family. Sometimes there are special needs in a family that everyone recognizes. But generally, the only way to try to guarantee peace is to treat everyone absolutely equal, and even then there isn't any guarantee.

Beth is the daughter that never married. She has always lived in an apartment and really never had much. Her two brothers and her sister are all happily married, financially successful people with their own homes. When Mom and Dad died, they had their estate divided into not four, but five equal parts, and they gave one share to each of the four children. The "extra" share they gave to Beth so that she could finally have a down payment for a home.

Today, two years after Mom and Dad died, Beth is more alone than ever because she has lost her parents, and her brothers and sister won't have anything to do with her. When they do see her, they are very bitter because Beth got an extra share. For example, to cover the minor costs of the recent family reunion, they billed her not for one fourth of the expenses, but two fifths, which is now "her share of everything."

Mom and Dad's plan wasn't totally equal, but in their minds, it was fair. The problem is the greed of Beth's brothers and sister, not Mom and Dad's plan. Their plan might have worked well if they had "sold" the plan to the family before they died. But, when you make out your plan, you shouldn't have to "sell" the plan to your kids. It really isn't any of the kids' business. Family matters are always sensitive, and there is no right or wrong way to handle family problems. Use your best judgment, be patient, and try your best.

How to Give Unequal Shares

When the trust is divided into shares, the shares don't all have to be equal. Some clients want to leave $100,000 to Joe, $20,000 to each of the 5 grandchildren, and $50,000 to a charity. I almost insist that you don't break up your wealth like this. You can't guarantee that you will have enough money to fulfill all of your directions. One long hospital stay can wipe out most people's fortune. If there isn't enough money, how does the trustee divide up what is left? When you die with $100,000 in your total estate, does the trustee give the $100,000 to Joe and nothing to anyone else?

It is better simply to direct the trustee to give Joe 40% of the trust property, each grandchild 8%, and the charity 20%. With these directions, the trustee can carry out your intentions, no matter how much property is left when you die.

But even when you give shares of 40% to Joe, 8% to each of the grandchildren, and 20% to the charity, there is still a trap. It would actually be best to say that the grandchildren will receive "40% of the trust property divided into equal shares so as to provide one share for each living grandchild or deceased grandchild who shall leave issue then living." Using this wording, you will probably achieve what you wanted and avoid the additional trap.

Here's the trap. What happens if another grandchild shows up after you write the trust? If you said each grandchild should receive an 8% share. That assumes 5 grandchildren (8 x 5 = 40). You are in big trouble if you end up having more than 5 grandchildren. It is possible that your son or daughter may add a caboose onto their family, and suddenly you have 6 grandchildren. Giving an 8% share to each grandchild means that you are giving away 108% (40 + 48 + 20 = 108) of your trust. That won't work, but simply by saying that 40% goes equally to the grandchildren, you avoid the trap. You will avoid the trap not only when another grandchild is added, but also when a grandchild dies prior to your death.

Additional restrictions could be placed in your trust in order to get even closer to your actual intentions. For example, the distribution to Joe could be limited to 40% of the trust or $100,000 whichever is less. By doing this, you have limited Joe's distribution to a maximum of $100,000.

When you are writing the trust, try to keep your distributions as simple as possible. It is very easy to leave a loose end or create a trap without even knowing it. A good lawyer or writer should be able to write your trust so that it will be general, thus avoiding most of the traps, and will still make the trust achieve whatever you want.

Unfortunately, even lawyers get into trouble if they are blindly using the standard form books. The form books simply give you a standard form, and they never tell you where the traps are when the form has to be altered. Of course, because each person's situation is unique, the form always has to be altered. You are unique. You could write your own trust. You certainly have the right to write your own living revocable trust, and if someone points out the traps to you, the task of writing your own trust is really quite simple.

Protecting the Youngest Children

Often it isn't appropriate to divide up shares and give everyone his part immediately after you die. Three factors should be considered. The factors are: (1) the age of the beneficiaries, (2) the money smarts of the beneficiaries, and (3) the special needs of each beneficiary.

If all of your children are already middle aged when you write the trust, it is appropriate to write the trust so that it simply divides up the shares and gives each child his or her share.

If your children are young, you should consider keeping all of the trust property in your living revocable trust after you die. The trustee can then "dish it out" to help the children as they grow older. Many trusts say that the trust property should be divided into shares in order to provide one share for each of the children. Then the shares are to be held in the trust or put into a separate trust for each child. I recommend you consider keeping the property all in one "pot" within your living revocable trust until the youngest child reaches a specific age, such as 25 years. Don't have the trust divided up into shares as soon as you die. If the trust property is divided into equal shares at the time of your death, you may be cheating your younger children.

This is how the younger children get cheated. Assume you have 4 children, ages 16 (the caboose), 22, 25, and 27. Also, assume your total estate equals $100,000. If you were to die and have the estate divided into equal shares and each child's share distributed to the child when he or she reached age 25, watch what would happen.

The 27-year-old is a medical doctor, is still single, and has a new house complete with a new Porsche. The 25-year-old daughter is a college graduate, married to a guy who owns a business his dad set up. Her biggest problem is deciding what clothes to wear on their upcoming cruise. The 22-year-old daughter is a college senior in business management, single, and on track for a great position with P&G. The 16-year-old is a high school junior, driving your old Sunbird. He is hoping to go to Stanford to study electrical engineering.

You have always helped your children. In fact, you have paid their college tuition and their living expenses when they were at school. Until they marry, you maintain them on your insurance, buy most of their clothes, provide them with computers, send them to Europe for a special class, and see to virtually all of their needs. Your children are good kids, and you actually receive a great deal of satisfaction from helping them.

When you die, if each child gets an equal share of the trust, the older children get a real windfall, when compared to your 16 year old. Each child will get $25,000 which he can use however he wants. What does $25,000 mean to each one of your children when you die? The 27-year-old will throw in $25,000 of his own money and buy a BMW to drive when his Porsche is in the shop. The 25-year-old will blow her $25,000 on an extra cruise and a trip to Europe. The 22-year-old will use her $25,000 as a huge down payment for a new house. Your 16-year-old gets his $25,000, which he will have to use to finish high school, go to college at Stanford, and get married. Whom are we kidding? Your 16-year-old's inheritance won't even get him through high school and the first year at Stanford. And yet you paid all of the other children's college expenses that they couldn't cover with a scholarship.

Taking a crass look at the situation, your death was a little financial bonus for the older children, and it destroyed all the hopes and dreams of your youngest child. Wouldn't it be appropriate to expend a fair share of your estate placing the 16-year-old in the position you have placed your older children? The older children have enjoyed your companionship through hard times and have been cloaked by your earning capacity and wealth as they have grown up. When you provide for the needs of your younger children, even though everything isn't divided "equally," it may be divided fairly. In most cases I have observed, the older children understand, and as long as they are remembered with a distribution of the personal items and an equal share of whatever is left after the youngest child reaches a specific point, they are usually satisfied. Of course, there is always a family like Beth's. You need to do whatever you feel is right.

Even though the estate isn't divided into shares until the youngest child reaches age 25, the older children can still get a benefit from the trust. While the trust is holding everything, the trustee can use the property to help any one of the children. When your 22-year-old needs a house down payment, the trustee can distribute enough to enable her to make the down payment. The amount the 22-year-old gets for the down payment can be considered an advance against her share, a loan from the trust, or just a reduction in the trust value and not considered when shares are finally divided up. Decide what you want to happen, and write that into the trust. Actually, if I were to write down the wording for 25 distribution scenarios, the chances are over 95% that you could use one of the wordings and achieve exactly what you want because there really are only so many scenarios.

All of the little considerations I am bringing up may seem tedious, but your lawyer will often fail to tell you what can be done. When I tell my clients about the little considerations, they usually say, "Oh yeah, that is a good idea."

Protecting the Kids From Themselves

Even if the children are all older and on their own, it may be wise to retain at least part of their share in trust. Are your children mature enough to handle a distribution of their share? Most people who get a life insurance payout or a large distribution from an estate "blow the wad" within a short period.

If the children need to be taught about saving money, your trust can help. At your death, have the trustee dish out only part of the share set aside for each child. When the child (your 25-year-old son or daughter) gets the first third of his share, there will be a race to the toy store. He will buy a jet ski, a big screen television, and the tickets for a trip. The distribution will be gone, and he will have the same financial problems he had before he got the first distribution from your trust. By the time he gets the second or third distribution, several years down the road, maybe he will have figured out that he should spend his distribution in a financially prudent manner.

When the possibilities of retaining wealth within the trust are explained and the process is understood, many of my clients want their trust to be divided into a share for each child, and they want the shares to be held in their living revocable trust. The trust might say that each child will receive a third of his or her share at age 25, with other distributions at ages 30 and 35. Of course, any age could be used, and any percentage of the share could be distributed at any point.

The trustee will retain all of the money or property in the trust until the trust directs the trustee to make a distribution. While the trustee is holding part of a child's share in the trust, the trustee can use the money to help the child in specific circumstances. The trustee is able to pay college tuition, wedding costs, a down payment on a home, or whatever else the trustee feels is a "wise" use of the child's share being held in trust.

By having the trustee control part of the child's share and make distributions over a longer period of time, you have prevented the child from blowing all of his inheritance within a year after you are gone. A simple will cannot protect the child from his own poor judgment, but the trust can. Under a simple will, once property has cleared the probate court, the judge hands the money over to your older child or the guardian for your younger child. It doesn't matter whether your child is a spendthrift, is on drugs, is a gambler, or is problem prone. The court doesn't care whether or not the money lasts a week.

One of my clients has a couple of spendthrift children. Actually, his "children" are all over 40 years old. When I wrote his trust with him, he was adamant that the children were never to receive an outright distribution from his trust. That could certainly be done; however, after a lengthy discussion, he decided to have the trustee start distributing each child's share when he or she reached the age of 55. I pointed out that a person should learn something about handling money before he dies, and age 55 is late enough in life to start loosening the apron strings. The client has died now, and the trust is still "sitting on the shares." The beneficiaries do receive benefits from their shares, but they don't have their hands on the money.

Contingency Plans If The Kids Are Gone

Your living revocable trust should have a contingency distribution provision. This provision gives the trustee instructions to follow in the event all of your children, all of your grandchildren, and all of your heirs have died before the trust property is all distributed. If your children are all married and living in different states, and you have married grandchildren, the chances of all of your heirs being dead when the trust is supposed to be distributed aren't very big. Nevertheless, your trust must provide for a disaster. It does happen.

I remember exactly where I was and what I was doing when I heard the tragic news. I was in the little office I opened after being sick, sitting at the computer struggling with a provision in a living revocable trust. The telephone rang, and it was Kristy. She blurted out that Leland (the cardiologist that saved my life), his wife Mary, the kids, all of them, were dead. Their New Year's ski trip ended when their Jeep wagon slid on the ice in front of a big truck.

The funeral was held in the biggest church in town. Leland was the chairman of the hospital. Mary did everything. She was very involved in the community. The high school students, junior high school students, and grade school students were there by the hundreds to pay their respects to their deceased friends. The caskets lined the front of the church. When the police escort finally pulled away, the line of hearses stretched for a full block. I remember. I have never seen anything like that before or since.

Yes, Leland had a living revocable trust and other irrevocable trusts. His estate was well structured to cover this disaster. Your living revocable trust can cover a disaster like Leland's in several ways. If all of your children and grandchildren are dead, all of the trust property can be moved to your parents and/or your spouse's parents. If none of the parents are living, it can be moved to your brothers and sisters and/or your spouse's brothers and sisters, or it can be moved to some or all of the nieces and nephews. You can give the trust property to a charity. You can direct the trustee to do anything, but your instructions have to be written in your trust.

Rather than outright "giving" the property to your parents, consider holding the property in your trust for as long as your parents live. The trustee can use the trust property to benefit your parents, but your parents will not own the property. The trust still owns the property. By carefully maintaining the trust outside of your parents' ownership and control, the trust property will not be included in their estate when they die, thus avoiding a probate and possibly saving a lot in estate taxes. Additionally, the trust property can be shielded from an attack when a parent goes into a rest home. The trust can be distributed, as you direct, after your parents have died.

If you want to solve the Medicaid problem, you have to start working on it now; the law requires the trust to be established at least five years before the government will help pay any of the bills. The laws in relation to the rest home change every few months. It's a nightmare. You need to know that the government is working very hard to see to it that you get squeezed for every dime before they have to put up any of the money you have paid into the system.

ASSET PROTECTION TIP #6

You should know that your living revocable trust will not protect your property from the government if you or your spouse go into a rest home. When a family member goes into a rest home or long term care facility, the government makes the family liquidate all of their assets and essentially spend all of their money before any government aid is used to help pay the bills. Even if you have paid into the system all of your life, the government will not help pay the rest home bills unless your family has spent all of its money. When a family member is sick and needs long term care, losing all of the family wealth is a major problem you may be facing. The standard living revocable trust does not meet the government rules which protect a person's property and satisfy the Medicaid requirements. A special type of trust, called a Medicaid Trust, can be used to preserve the family wealth when a family member goes in the rest home. When you use a Medicaid Trust, know that you have strict rules to follow and know that the government is going to change the rules.

Planning to Help Your Son or Daughter-In-Law

Sons-in-law and daughters-in-law are often not included in trust distribution patterns. Your son's or daughter's children, your grandchildren, are usually designated to receive the share their parent would have received if he or she predeceases you. However, your son's wife and your daughter's husband usually aren't given any inheritance. Why not let them inherit? Because, indirectly they will benefit if their children are provided with an inheritance. If your son-in-law or daughter-in-law is unable to make his or her own way in the world, even when the children are provided for, you may want to leave some part of the trust to him or her directly. It's your option.

Control Your Property After You Die

Whether you are protecting your children, providing help for your parents, or achieving some other goal, your living revocable trust doesn't just have to stop after your death. The trust can be used to help your family members long after your death. This is especially important if there is a possibility that minor children will be receiving the benefit of the trust property.

A probate proceeding would be required to appoint a conservator/guardian for a minor child who is designated to receive a share of your estate directly. When the share is held in trust until the child is old enough to receive the property directly, there is no need for such a probate proceeding. The trustee will see to your child's needs, using the trust property. Because the property isn't under the child's control, there isn't any need for a conservator to be appointed.

The trust document will undoubtedly give the trustee broad discretion to distribute trust property for the child's benefit. The trustee could give the property to the child's guardian, pay the child's expenses directly, or give the money to a friend or grandparent of the child to be used for the child. Any instruction you desire can be put in the trust.

Leaving Property to a Charity

There was a plaque on the door of my hospital room. It read, "This Room was Donated By..." and then there was a person's name. Without that person's donation to the university hospital, there may not have been space for me. Someone else's generosity has paved the way for you to go to school, read library books, get specialized medical treatment, worship as you wish, walk through beautiful forests and gardens, and maybe even live and breathe.

Your living revocable trust is perhaps the most flexible way to make a gift to charity. There are literally thousands of places you can make a gift to help others. You can even give away your body organs. Property which passes through your living revocable trust is not subject to probate, so the charity will receive a much larger gift from you if your living revocable trust is properly used.

There are other trusts, called charitable remainder trusts, which are used to make larger gifts to charities. The charitable remainder trust can have some big tax advantages for you while you are alive. Because you get extra income and benefits during your life and the charity gets what is left after you are gone, it is a win-win situation. The government wants to encourage charitable giving. Uncle Sam is willing to give you an incentive to entice you to give to your favorite worthy cause. As a result, Congress has made the charitable remainder trust a sweet deal.

Contact the university, hospital, society, or group to which you want to leave a gift, and their attorneys will help you set up a charitable remainder trust. Because the attorney may be donating his or her time, or because the charity will pay the legal bills to secure your gift, it often doesn't cost you anything to have the legal work done.

Things to Consider When You Disinherit a Child

You can certainly disinherit anyone you want. I did a trust 10 years ago for an older couple, the Smiths, who had a wayward son. This kid was more than wayward; he was off the deep end. His parents disinherited him, his wife, and his children.

I always quiz clients extensively when they want to disinherit a family member because it is a serious matter. Disinheriting someone has repercussions far beyond the financial considerations. You have slammed, humiliated, and disowned a child as your final act. You can never come back and say you were sorry.

Thank goodness the Smiths lived well into their 90's. We had a chance to change their trust. Their son somehow found his way back and has become a prized son in the family. The prodigal son did return. The trust was changed, and all is well. But, a huge tragedy would have occurred if the son had come back, and the Smiths had not changed their wills and trust.

To disinherit someone, the trust must clearly state that you want to disinherit the person. As long as it is clear and there is no possibility of a mistake, the designated person will be disinherited. Lots of clients want to leave one dollar to the person they want to disinherit. They have heard that you have to leave a dollar to the person in order to make everything legal. Go ahead and leave one dollar to the person you want to disinherit. Although it doesn't hurt, it isn't necessary.

The old "one dollar" language is used to overcome challenges to a will that tries to disinherit someone just by leaving them off the list of children. The person who is "left off" can come back and argue, "Dad never intended to disinherit me. Dad just made a mistake, or there was just a typographical error and the secretary forgot to type my name on the list." The courts often buy the argument. However, if the person's name is stated, and it is clearly stated that he is to be disinherited and receive no share of the will and trust, there isn't any need to leave one dime to the person.

A Special Type of Trust—A Children's Trust Has Big Advantages

When a share is held in your trust for a child, the trust is often considered a "children's trust." I prefer not to call the share being held for a child a children's trust. It is just a share of a living revocable trust being held for a child. A "children's trust" is a term of art in the law with a separate meaning. Using the term "children's trust" in reference to a child's share of a living revocable trust is confusing. A children's trust refers to an irrevocable trust established under Section 2503 of the IRS code. 2503 trusts are very different from living revocable trusts.

After You Die, Your Trust Becomes Irrevocable

At your death, your trust does change. Your trust becomes irrevocable. Nobody can go in and change the trust, and it cannot be revoked. When it becomes irrevocable, upon your death, the trust is no longer an "extension of you," as it was when you were alive. The trust becomes an entity unto itself. It has to get a tax identification number and start filing its own income tax returns. It becomes a "legal person" with almost all of the rights and obligations you had as a living person.

Make Sure Your Trust Ends Legally

Just like a person, your trust has to "die" sometime. The trust must ultimately distribute all of the property, and when all of the property is gone, the trust doesn't have any further function, so it "dies" or "terminates." The trust is in a trap if the trust writer has fixed the time of its termination on an uncertain event. For example, the trust's termination cannot be tied to the youngest child finishing college, the marriage of all of your children, or the birth of your first great grandchild. These events may never take place. Without a certain end to the trust, the trust is invalid, by law in most jurisdictions.

Very strict, very complicated laws have been concocted that set the life of a trust to a certain maximum. One of the laws used in a number of jurisdictions states that the trust can't go on "in perpetuity" (forever). The trust document must actually define a specific time when the final distribution will occur. Even though there are some jurisdictions that have laws which will allow special types of trusts to go on indefinitely, all living trusts should fix a time when they will terminate.

To make sure that the trust "dies" before the law requires, trusts often have a "perpetuities savings clause." This clause is just a fail-safe mechanism to make sure the trust complies with the laws and ends appropriately. The trust should never have to rely on the perpetuities savings clause because it should terminate timely according to its own terms.

You can control when the trust terminates by simply writing your desires in the trust document. If you have young children when you write your trust, your trust will probably be written so that it ends when your children are all a certain age or have all died. If your children are already older, or you do not have children, when you write your trust, you will probably simply have the trust terminate after your death when the assets are distributed within a reasonable time.

Chapter

18

Provisions Every Trust Should Have

Directing Trustees and Protecting Assets

Only a few sections of a living revocable trust document are routinely changed to reflect your individual desires. Most of the trust provisions read exactly the same way in each trust the lawyer "drafts." The perpetuities savings clause is going to be exactly the same in every trust.

If 98% of your trust reads exactly the same as your brother's trust, that doesn't mean the attorney did a bad job or doesn't care about you. It simply means that the language of trusts has been developed over the years, and everybody uses the same language. Cases (lawsuits) that have come up over the years have forced the courts to "interpret" the standard language used in trusts. Lawyers can trust language the courts have already blessed, so it is usually best to use the same language in every trust. The law is basically built on tradition, and tradition dictates that you do it the same way every time.

This chapter will detail some of the common "standard" provisions that will probably appear in your living revocable trust and cannot be changed. These provisions include the provisions granting "power" to the trustees, spendthrift provisions, governing law provisions, insurance provisions, and others.

What Powers Should You Give Trustees?

Whether you are acting or someone else is acting as trustee, your trust has to "empower" the trustee and authorize everything the trustee does. Your trust should have a big laundry list of acts the trustee can perform. The list will give the trustee power to open bank accounts, own stock, buy or sell real estate, sue someone, and collect insurance. The list will actually run on and on for pages.

One grand old client I had blew his stack when he saw this list. He insisted that the list was garbage and didn't need to be in the trust. He didn't want his trust to be all full of legal gobbledy gook. I had to put my foot down. We went head to head arguing over the list.

He argued that, at a minimum, if the powers couldn't be removed, the trust could simply reference the "powers" that were set out in the state's statute. Each state has passed laws that govern trusts and trustees acting within the state. Part of each law is a list of powers that permit a trustee to do business in the state. Some trusts don't list out all of the trustee powers. They simply say that the trustee shall have those powers listed in the state statute.

Each state law also says that your trust document can give the trustee more power or less power than the state statute authorizes. All you have to do is write down in your trust exactly what powers you want the trustee to have. Maybe it is just my ego coming through, but I argued that I could write a set of powers that would be better than the ones the state wrote, and the powers I would give the trustee would make life much easier for the trustee. In order to keep the bank, stockbroker, title insurance company, and everybody else satisfied, the trustee powers need to be all laid out in the trust. I won the argument, but he got the last laugh.

When this old gentleman came to me and asked me to write his trust, he laid down some rules for me. He was quite a famous author and composer who had taught at a major university, and I figured that it would be an honor to write his trust and have him teach me about writing. I agreed to his rules.

I was to write his trust without a sentence over 40 words long. He also set a limit on the maximum number of letters that could be used in a word and the maximum number of commas in a sentence, and he said that the trust had to be written in plain English—not legal language.

He read the first draft copy of the living revocable trust I prepared for him, and he applied every rule. He ruthlessly applied the rules to the second copy, and the third copy, and the fourth copy, and the tenth copy, and the fifteenth copy.

Oh yes, I should tell you that he had made me agree up front to a set price for the trust. My patience and my pocketbook were stretched, as the days turned to weeks, and the weeks to months as this process dragged on and on. He challenged every sentence, asking, "What does it mean?" "Why is it there?" "Is it necessary?"

He died a few years ago, and his living revocable trust worked flawlessly. My experience with him helped me learn to draft trusts written in plain English. I am honored to have known this great author and had him teach me. He got me though. He got me where it really hurts a lawyer. When I added up all of the hours I had spent on his trust and compared them with the price he held me to, he got me for about $4.50 an hour. But, I did win the argument over the powers of trustees, and his trust has a long list of powers—a carefully drafted long list of powers.

How to Use State Law to Your Advantage

As I just explained, each state has laws governing trusts and trustees. Your trust should have a section that identifies which state law will govern the trust. The state named is almost always the state where you are a resident, but any state could be selected. Laws of the selected state will be used by the court, wherever the court is located, to interpret the trust document.

In your trust you should probably name the state where you live and where your trust will be owning property. With a few exceptions, state laws are surprisingly uniform. It is usually best to pick the state where you are a resident, because by choosing to have the local laws applied to your trust, you may save some headaches. Local people, such as your real estate agents, bankers, and insurance agents, will be more comfortable dealing with your trust, because they will already know how local state law affects their dealings with your living revocable trust.

ASSET PROTECTION TIP #7

Your trust should have a good "spendthrift" provision in it. A spendthrift provision is usually only one or two paragraphs long. It simply states that a beneficiary's interest or "share" in the trust cannot be legally attacked, because of the beneficiary's acts, while the trustee has control over the share. The interest could, however, be attacked when the trustee transfers the property held in the share to the beneficiary's ownership. But, as long as the trust has the property, it is protected from all of the stupid things the beneficiary might do. The beneficiary's share cannot be attacked if the beneficiary declares bankruptcy, gets sued, gets divorced, tries to take out a loan and pledge the share as collateral, dies, or does something else stupid.

Many trusts don't include a spendthrift provision. This is a big mistake, because without the provision, the beneficiary's share is in jeopardy. If the trust has a spendthrift provision, the judge deciding a lawsuit can protect the trust and preserve the beneficiary's share. If the trust doesn't have a spendthrift provision in it, the judge will have to attack the beneficiary's share to satisfy a judgment against the beneficiary.

Words in your trust are critical. Just leaving out a few words in the trust will force the judge to attack the trust in order to satisfy the divorce, bankruptcy, creditors or others who might have a claim against the beneficiary. Yet, if the words are there, the judge can protect the trust property. Isn't the law fun?

Scroll 18.1 shows a spendthrift provision. Your trust had better have one, and it had better read something like the one shown here.

Spendthrift Provision

Except as otherwise provided in this Trust Agreement, all payments of principal and income which are payable, or will become payable, to the beneficiary of any Trust created by this Agreement shall not be subject to anticipation, assignment, pledge, sale, or transfer in any manner. Nor shall any beneficiary have the power to anticipate or encumber any such interest. Nor shall such interest, while in the possession of the Trustees, be liable for, or subject to, the debts, contracts, obligations, liabilities or torts of any beneficiary. Such interests shall also be free from any claim, control, or interference of the spouse of a married beneficiary, or the parent of a beneficiary.

Scroll 18.1—Sample Spendthrift Provision

Directions to Pay Taxes

Two things are certain in life—death and taxes. Your living revocable trust will undoubtedly have instructions that direct the trustee to pay the taxes due. The trustee will be instructed to use certain property to pay the taxes with, and he or she will be told the order in which debts and taxes should be paid. These instructions are the same in nearly every living revocable trust, because they are designed to give the trustee the maximum flexibility allowed by the law.

Just because your trust carefully addresses what the trustee will do when it is time to pay the tax man, that doesn't mean your estate will have to actually pay any estate taxes. In fact, if you use the living revocable trust properly, hopefully there won't be any taxes to pay.

Chapter 19 deals with taxes and shows you how your living revocable trust can help save you big taxes.

Allowing Your Trust to Deal With Life Insurance

Living revocable trusts will often have a special provision that tells the trustee how to deal with insurance companies and your insurance policies. The trust should authorize the trustee to pay insurance premiums, buy new insurance policies, collect insurance benefits, and do whatever needs to be done to manage the insurance.

The trustee may be handling more than just life insurance. The trustee may be handling your auto insurance and trying to collect after your fatal accident. He may have to wrap up your malpractice insurance. He may have to ... He may have to ... The list goes on and on.

Make sure your trust lays out all of the instructions and tells the trustee exactly what to do with insurance. Insurance is one of the most important parts of your financial planning. At some time, it may well become the central focus of your entire financial life.

I remember years ago listening to a radio call-in show. A lady caller had recounted a tragic story of a father's death. He had left a wife and little children. The lady caller pressed the talk show host demanding that society, the government, provide a way to take care of a family left to provide for themselves. The host finally ended the lady's tirade when he simply said, "Lady, our society does have a way to take care of a family that has lost their breadwinner. It's called life insurance."

There is one problem with life insurance. Life insurance is taxed. Your agent may have told you that there won't be any tax on the life insurance proceeds when your family receives the money. The agent is right, but wrong. When your family gets the life insurance, after you die, there won't be any income tax due on the money. It isn't income to your family; it is replacement of a loss—you. But, but, but, the life insurance money is exposed to the estate tax. It is not uncommon for the tax to be 55%. That is a huge loss!

However, if you use the law, the loss can be totally prevented! Use an insurance trust. It is an irrevocable trust which is specifically designed to hold life insurance and pass it to your heirs without ever being exposed to estate taxes. Although living revocable trusts can help with estate taxes, as you will learn in the next chapter, they are not irrevocable life insurance trusts. Life insurance trusts are very powerful. If you have a taxable estate (including life insurance), you had better make a beeline to your favorite estate planning attorney and get a life insurance trust in place. If you are in the position where your estate is a taxable estate and you are married, the living revocable trust can solve your federal estate tax problems if you don't have over twice the exemption equivalent value (see Appendix 1). A standard will setup isn't going to solve any of your problems.

Chapter

19

Avoiding Estate Taxes

How to Keep Every Dime

Husbands and wives with the standard will setup always have about the same estate plan. He has a will that says he loves his wife, and when he dies, she is to receive everything. Her will mirrors his. It states that the husband will receive everything when she dies. Both wills say that whatever is left, after the husband and wife are both dead, will be distributed to the children or one of the other relatives. If you have husband and wife wills, this is surely what your wills say. Oh, it may take 10 pages to say it, but the husband and wife wills always read the same. Lawyers call this type of will setup a "John loves Mary estate." It is a disaster. It is an estate tax disaster!

Estate taxes have nothing to do with probate. The fight in probate is over ownership. The fight in estate taxes is over value. You now know how your living revocable trust will help your family avoid probate. Your living revocable trust can also help avoid estate taxes.

So far in this book, almost nothing has been said about estate taxes. The value of the property in the estate will determine how much tax will be assessed by the IRS. The same estate tax will be imposed on assets held in a living revocable trust and assets held by individuals, whether or not they have a will. Estate taxes aren't cheap. They kick in at a rate of 37%, and the rate moves to 55% very quickly.

All property owned by Dad will be taxed when he dies. Yes, for purposes of the estate tax calculations, Dad owns everything in his living revocable trust, just like he would own it if the property wasn't in the trust. Have I made a mistake? If the trust property is owned by the trust, how can the IRS say Dad owns it and include the property in Dad's estate? No, there isn't a mistake. The IRS can do whatever it wants. Our great country was born out of a war fought to put down a taxing agency that could do whatever it wanted. Actually, in spite of what some individual IRS agents think, the IRS does have to follow the laws. Of course, you also have to follow the laws. OK then, if the trust property is taxed just as if it wasn't in the trust, then how can the trust help your family avoid estate taxes? What is the catch?

The Tax Disaster

Assume you have the John Loves Mary will setup, or you don't have wills for you and your spouse, or your trust doesn't have the magic IRS words in it that follow the law. You lose, and your family loses big. Here's how it works.

Wham! You die in the automobile accident. Your will says you love your spouse and everything you have goes to the beloved spouse. This sets up the John Loves Mary trap.

When you die everything transfers to your spouse. No problem! No tax! The law says that property (almost all property) passing between spouses, when one spouse dies, is simply a deduction for the deceased spouse's estate. The deceased spouse's estate gets to deduct from the value of the estate all the property which is given to the surviving spouse. The deduction wipes out the tax problem at the time the property is transferred to the surviving spouse. This is called the unlimited marital deduction. You can pass a trillion dollars to your spouse when you die, and there isn't any estate tax on the trillion dollars. The deduction is unlimited. So, when one spouse dies, all of the property that is passed to the surviving spouse passes estate tax free. Not a bad deal, right?

You died at the scene of the accident. Now, assume your spouse dies on the way to the hospital in the ambulance or your spouse dies 30 days later, two years later, or 10 years later. It doesn't matter how much time passes between your death and your spouse's death. When the surviving spouse dies, wham! The trap locks shut. His or her will says that all of the property goes to the kids. The IRS has your family right where they want them—stuck in the trap. It's going to cost your family big bucks to get out of the trap. How does this tax trap your family?

Let's say you have an estate worth $900,000. I'm not crazy; you may well have an estate worth $900,000. That doesn't mean you are rich. In fact, you may consider yourself quite poor and still have a $900,000 estate. You are probably worth more dead than you are alive, and that doesn't mean your mug is on a wanted poster down at the post office.

A nice house, some savings, a good retirement plan, a little business, and a life insurance policy almost certainly guarantees a $900,000 estate. Use Appendix 3 and get a feel for what you are worth dead.

OK then, when you died in the accident everything went to your spouse, the surviving spouse. No tax. That means your spouse has it all—all $900,000. When your spouse dies in the ambulance, everything—all $900,000—goes to the kids.

Remember that the magic number (exemption equivalent) for federal estate tax changes every year. The exemption equivalent is the value of property you can transfer, either by gift or at death, or a combination of the two, and not have to actually pay any federal estate/gift taxes. The exemption equivalent is basically adjusted each year for inflation. The big changes in the exemption equivalent come after the year 2003. The exemption equivalents are shown in Appendix 1, along with the estate tax rate table. For this example, let's assume you and your spouse die in 1998. The exemption equivalent amount in 1998 is $625,000. The family will actually start paying estate taxes when there is more than the exemption equivalent amount moving to the kids. With a $900,000 estate, tax will actually be paid in

1998 on $275,000 ($900,000 - $625,000 = $275,000). The actual estate tax to be paid will only be $114,000. Such a bargain!

That money is paid to the IRS in cash—green. The IRS doesn't accept payment in kind. They want money! The money will be due in the IRS's hands 9 months after the surviving spouse dies. If the kids have to sell the house cheap when the real estate market is down, the IRS really doesn't care. That's what is called a motivated seller.

Life insurance can help the family in this trap, because it can give the family enough cash to pay the tax and prevent a forced sale of the estate assets. I have seen life insurance policies ransom more than one family caught in the tax trap. Whether they use insurance, sell the house or do something else, the family will get the money to pay the estate tax. It's the law.

Families that have had one spouse die recently (within nine months) and can see the tax trap locking shut can do a quick move to get out of the trap. They will come out scraped-up, but they will come out with their skin. The surviving spouse has to "disclaim" at least part of his or her right to inherit property under the deceased spouse's will. The property that the disclaimer applies to will then go to the kids as part of the deceased spouse's estate. If the estate, after taking the marital deduction for property that isn't disclaimed and passes to the surviving spouse, is less than the exemption equivalent, there won't be any estate tax payable to the IRS. Because the disclaimer was used, the estate has been divided between the surviving spouse and the kids. The kids actually own whatever was disclaimed by the surviving spouse. They can spend it. It is theirs. It isn't available to support the surviving spouse, but it is out of the surviving spouse's estate and the family got the full exemption equivalent amount out to the kids without an estate tax. When the surviving spouse dies, the family can move another amount equal to the exemption equivalent without an estate tax.

The disclaimer can leave the surviving spouse a relatively small estate, and place the family wealth directly in the hands of the kids, who may not use it wisely. Don't use the disclaimer technique unless you are already in the trap. It is expensive, messy, and doesn't always work. Just use a trust before either spouse dies.

Avoiding the Estate Tax With The Two Trust Trick

Would you like to avoid estate taxes for your family? Estate taxes are what are called "voluntary taxes." That means if you do your estate planning correctly, there won't be any tax to pay.

The super wealthy don't lose half of the family wealth when the patriarch and matriarch die. They often don't pay any tax. Why should you lose one dime to taxes when you or someone in your family dies? The same laws that protect the super wealthy estates from estate taxes are available to you to protect your estate from the tax trap.

The law says that if you have a living revocable trust that meets the IRS requirements, a legally married couple can avoid the John Loves Mary trap with the stroke of a pen. Estate tax traps for singles and alternative lifestyle couples will be addressed in the next chapter. Watch how a trust can work for you as a married couple.

Instantly upon the first death, your death or your spouse's death, whichever comes first, your living revocable trust will split into two pieces. Two trusts will actually be created out of the one trust that existed before the first death. Lawyers call one trust "A" and the other trust "B." It is that easy. You may have heard of an "A-B" trust. The A-B trust is simply one where trust A and trust B are created at the first death. Diagram 19.1 (next page) shows a "flow chart" of the creation of trust A and trust B from a couple's joint living revocable trust.

It is important to note that the two trusts are automatically being created by a written document signed by both the husband and wife. The two trusts were "created" prior to either spouse dying. The trusts are not being created at the whim of the surviving spouse. Technically, trust B was created by the deceased spouse prior to his or her death. This technicality is important.

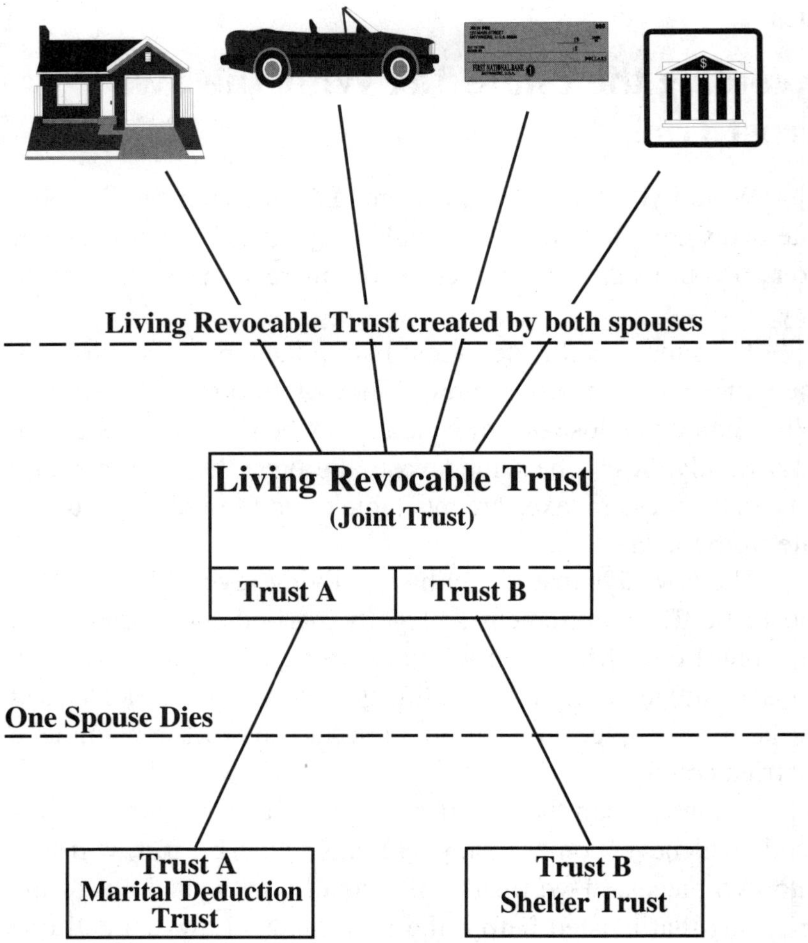

Diagram 19.1—Creation of a living revocable trust while both spouses are alive, and the split of the trust into Trusts A and B following the death of one spouse

The IRS will not give the estate tax benefits trust B enjoys to a trust created by the surviving spouse. Everything for the split of your living revocable trust into trust A and trust B must be in place in writing before either you or your spouse dies.

Saving $202,050 With The Stroke of a Pen

The B trust is known as the "decedent's trust" or the "shelter trust" because it shelters up to the exemption equivalent amount from estate taxes. No, it isn't one of "those" tax shelters that the IRS doesn't like. It is a sanctioned technique the IRS lets you use to control your estate taxes. If the trust is written properly, an amount of a couple's estate equal to the exemption equivalent will escape the tax trap at the time the first spouse dies.

At the first death, the exemption equivalent amount in assets is transferred on paper to trust B, and the remaining family assets, $275,000 in this example case, are transferred on paper to trust A. All of the assets in trust B are subject to estate taxes at the time of the first death. The IRS gets to tax those assets all they want. The assets are moving to trust B, not the surviving spouse, so they do not qualify for the unlimited marital estate tax deduction. The unlimited marital estate tax deduction applies only to property which goes directly to the surviving spouse. So, trust B assets are actually taxed as the estate of the deceased spouse. An estate tax form must be timely prepared and submitted to the IRS. The IRS is dead serious about this tax. Note that trust B is funded with the exemption equivalent amount applicable for the year in which the decedent dies. In the example case of a $900,000 estate and a death in 1998, the exemption equivalent amount is $625,000, and the real tax on that amount is $202,050. It is a real tax, and it is due and payable 9 months after the death.

At this point, you should rightfully be concerned because $202,050 doesn't sound nearly as good as $114,000 (the amount of tax that would be paid with the John Loves Mary setup). But, there is a catch. The federal government gives each person a tax waiver, a "credit" of exactly $202,050 in 1998. Therefore, because trust B is considered the estate of the first spouse to die, the credit of $202,050 applies, and it wipes out the tax owing. No tax is actually paid out of the family's pocket on trust B assets, if there is only $625,000 (the exemption equivalent amount for 1998) in trust B. The tax was "paid," but it came out of Uncle Sam's pocket. You didn't know Uncle was so generous, did you?

In 1998, the $202,050 (the amount of taxes levied against an exemption equivalent value of property) is called the "unified credit amount." It is "unified" because it can be applied to "pay" the estate taxes due on an individual's estate after he dies, or it can be applied to pay the gift taxes a person racks up during his life and at his death. If large gifts (over the annual exclusion amount—$10,000 in 1998) have been given during life, the full exemption equivalent value of property can't be sheltered in trust B at death because part or all of the unified credit will have been used up to "pay" the gift taxes assessed on the gifts.

Wouldn't it be nice to be rich enough to be able to give gifts of over $10,000 to loved ones you wanted to help? Unfortunately, most of us don't face a gift tax problem during our life. The good news is: that leaves the maximum possible amount of unified credit available to shelter property—the maximum exemption equivalent amount—in trust B. If you use trust B and play the IRS game wisely, both the husband and the wife can move the maximum exemption equivalent amount to their heirs without an estate tax. See Appendix 1 for the exemption equivalent values and the corresponding unified credit amounts.

Under the law, the assets controlled under trust B will not be included in the surviving spouse's estate if the trust document is properly written. The property in trust B isn't owned by the surviving spouse, it is owned by trust B. Because the assets held in trust B are not owned by the surviving spouse, they will not be considered part of the surviving spouse's estate when he or she dies. They will not be exposed to the estate tax assessed at the time the surviving spouse dies.

But, wait a minute; you have already been told that all of the living revocable trust assets were subject to estate taxes, even though the trust owned them. Why aren't the trust B assets included in the estate of the surviving spouse? Why are the assets in trust B, the "decedent's trust" or "shelter trust," protected from any exposure to estate taxes when the surviving spouse dies? It's easy. Trust B isn't a living revocable trust. It is a different animal under the law. Trust B is an irrevocable trust, and the tax laws which apply to it are totally different from the tax laws which apply to a living revocable trust. The courts also treat trust B totally different than they treat a living revocable trust. The surviving spouse cannot treat trust B as a living revocable trust. Trust B is not a living revocable trust. It is an irrevocable trust—a very different trust. Yes, I am being very redundant, but the point has to be driven home.

How did trust B get to be this weird irrevocable trust animal? All there was prior to the death of the first spouse to die was a living revocable trust. The words in the living revocable trust simply said that at the death of the first spouse to die there would be a division in the living revocable trust. One part would become an irrevocable trust, and the other part would continue on as a living revocable trust. The law says that if it is written down properly, the irrevocable trust can be created, and the law, IRS, and everyone else will grant it full status as an irrevocable trust.

An irrevocable trust has more rights and privileges under the law than a living revocable trust does. It also has more restrictions and obligations. It cannot be revoked, which is a big difference over a revocable trust. It has to file its own tax returns and have a tax ID number. But, if it is established properly and it follows all of the IRS laws while it is alive, it is outside of the estate tax laws (not the income tax laws). When the trust finally "dies" or terminates, which is usually when the grantors (the people who established the trust) die, the assets of the trust are not subject to an estate tax. Do you realize how powerful this irrevocable trust can be?

There is a catch—a fly in the ointment. Actually, it is more like a little, tiny, itty bitty gnat, because there really isn't a problem. Judge for yourself.

A living revocable trust gives its controller (i.e., trustee) full control to do absolutely anything with the trust property, as long as the property is used for the benefit of the beneficiary(ies). An irrevocable trust has more restrictions placed on it by the law. The way in which assets in trust B can be used is restricted. Assuming the surviving spouse is the trustee of trust B, he or she has full control over the assets. If that control is totally unrestricted and the surviving spouse is also a beneficiary of the trust, then the surviving spouse could use the trust property totally as if the trust didn't even exist. The IRS says that full control of property with no restrictions on how you can use it for yourself is tantamount to ownership. And, the IRS is right.

The problem is, if you own something, it will be included in your estate when you die. The surviving spouse usually wants to control the property in trust B and wants to be able to use the property for his or her benefit. So, in order to keep trust B property out of the surviving spouse's estate when he or she dies, trust B's terms have to restrict the use of the property.

Yes, as far as the IRS is concerned, the surviving spouse can act as the sole trustee of trust B and have full control over all of the trust B assets. Almost all of my couple clients want the surviving spouse to have as much control as possible over the full estate, and that is OK. While he or she is alive, the surviving spouse can even be the sole beneficiary of trust B. However, the main reason for creating trust B is to shelter its property from estate taxes. The IRS says that trust B property can be sheltered from estate taxes and the surviving spouse can be the sole trustee and be a beneficiary, PROVIDED the trust property can be used by the trustee only under an "ascertainable standard."

Is the authorization to purchase a new top-of-the-line, fully loaded BMW each January an ascertainable standard? Yes, we can ascertain whether or not the trust money was used for that purpose and whether or not the car met the proper standard. The trustee could be restricted to only using the trust money (or trust property sold to obtain money) for the purpose of buying food eaten by the surviving spouse and the couple's minor children. Listing all of the do's and don't's in the trust would be ridiculous, but the IRS says that in order to get the benefit and protect trust B from estate taxes, all of the trustee's actions must be restricted to fulfilling ascertainable standards. Courts and the IRS have agreed that if trust B property can only be used for the "health, education, maintenance, and support of the surviving spouse and children," then the trustee is sufficiently restricted. Wait a minute.

What could the spouse or children possibly want which doesn't fall within their needs for "health, education, maintenance, and support"? Well, there are things. A second Rolls Royce is one case I remember. The standard is fluid because it is measured against the standard of living that existed before trust B was created. But, for us common folk, and even most of the not so common folk, we can get everything we need and want.

The surviving spouse can basically use trust B property any way he or she wants, and the trust B property will not be included in his or her estate. The estate tax on all trust B property (up to the exemption equivalent amount) will be totally avoided! Not a bad deal from the IRS. However, the right words have to be written in the trust, or the IRS says "no deal."

You should be aware that trust B can be funded with more or less than the exemption equivalent amount. Of course, the exemption equivalent is the ideal amount because that is the exact value of the property necessary to take full advantage of the unified credit amount the IRS gives each person. Only the deceased spouse's solely owned property and "jointly" owned property can go into trust B. Yes, property owned by your living revocable trust where both you and your spouse are trustees and beneficiaries is considered "joint" property in this case and is available to fund trust B. If trust B is funded with more than the exemption equivalent, there will actually be a federal estate tax paid on the amount above the magic exemption equivalent amount, but all of the appreciation that would occur in the property, if it were to pass unsheltered to the surviving spouse, will be out of the surviving spouse's estate. So, all is not lost. Some people choose to fund trust B with more than the exemption equivalent.

If your goal is purely to avoid estate taxes, you do need to be careful to try and equalize the amount of solely owned property held by you and your spouse. A large amount of wealth (over the exemption equivalent amount) should not be owned by you alone, while your spouse owns nothing. If you own everything when your spouse dies, it could end up being a financial disaster in addition to a personal tragedy. When your spouse dies, the split of your living revocable trust will occur, and trust

A and trust B will be created. No problem! But, if you own everything, there won't be anything in your spouse's estate to fund trust B with, and effectively your family will lose the chance to shelter the exemption equivalent at your spouse's death. Everything will have to go into trust A which will be taxed in your estate when you die.

Providing For the Widowed Spouse

Trust A is called the marital trust, or spousal trust. The surviving spouse, acting as the trustee of trust A, has total, unrestricted control over and use of all trust A property. For estate tax purposes, it is a trust like the living revocable trust. Yes, property in trust A is owned by the trust as far as the probate laws are concerned, so trust A property won't be probated when the surviving spouse dies. Tax laws and probate laws are totally different sets of laws, just like football and golf are totally different sports.

Because trust A is totally controlled by the surviving spouse, as far as the IRS is concerned, property which is moved to trust A qualifies for the unlimited marital tax deduction. Therefore, any property moved to trust A is not exposed to estate taxes when the first spouse dies. However, it will be taxed when the surviving spouse dies.

In the case of a $900,000 estate, look at what happened. At the first death in 1998, trust B was created, funded with $625,000 in assets, and taxed. The tax was Ø, zero, nada, nothing. Trust A was created and funded with everything that didn't go into trust B (in this case $275,000 in assets). Because trust A assets qualified for the marital tax deduction, they were not exposed to the estate tax when trust A was created.

At the death of the surviving spouse, trust B will not be taxed, because the surviving spouse had to use trust B assets according to the ascertainable standards, and trust B has been carefully maintained as an irrevocable trust. Trust A will be taxed at the death of the surviving spouse. It will be considered the surviving spouse's estate. The surviving spouse is entitled to the same unified tax credit everyone else is entitled to, so he or she can pass up to the exemption equivalent amount to his or her heirs without actually losing any of the estate to taxes. (Remember, the unified tax credit is the tax which is "used" to pay the estate/gift taxes on property up to the exemption equivalent amount of property.) Therefore, you can pass at death or during your life an amount equal to the exemption equivalent without actually paying a tax.

Trust A is going to be taxed at the death of the surviving spouse. It has $275,000 in it. What is the tax? Zero!! All $900,000 ($625,000 in trust B and $275,000 in trust A) was moved to your family without losing a dime to estate taxes. You gave your family an additional $104,750 when you trashed your John Loves Mary wills and signed your A-B trust. By the year 2006, you will be giving your family up to $435,000 extra dollars. These are big numbers. Your living revocable trust should be an A-B trust.

Yes, instead of an A-B trust, you could also have a living revocable trust which is a Qualified Terminable Interest Property (QTIP) trust. QTIP trusts will be discussed later, but the tax results are essentially the same as the A-B trust. Actually, there are a number of variations on using trusts to split the estate at the time the first spouse dies. I will give you some of the other variations a little later.

Diagram 19.2 (next page) pictorially shows you what happens with an A-B trust when a final distribution is made. Note that at the death of the surviving spouse, the assets of trust A and trust B merge to be distributed to the family according to your instructions.

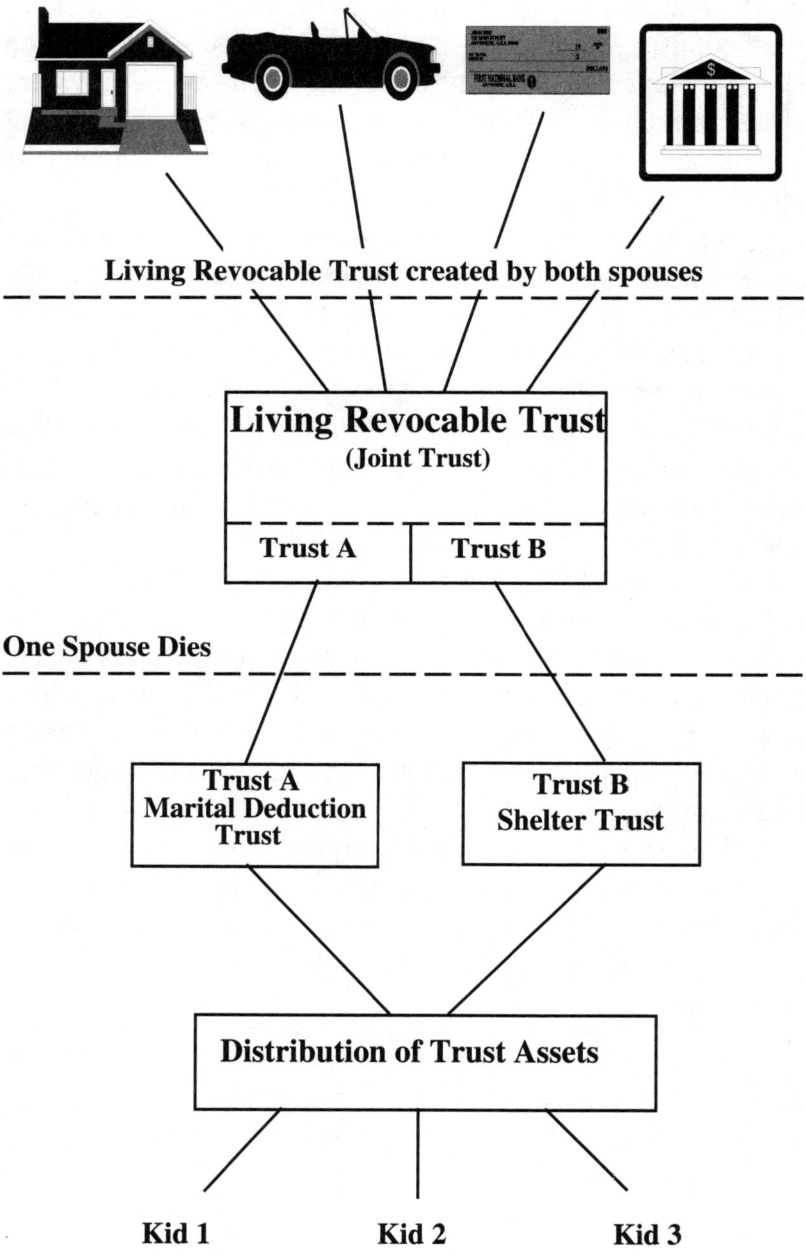

Diagram 19.2—Assets of trusts A and B merge to be distributed to the couple's heirs in the manner described in the trust

How to Eliminate Estate Tax For Most American Families

Hang with me, and let me now explain in detail exactly how trust A, trust B, and a new trust, called the QTIP trust, work. Lawyers have a bad habit of screwing up the A-B trust division and operation, so when it comes down to paying the tax, the IRS says, "Sorry your trust doesn't follow our rules. Pay your estate tax." If a piece of paper is worth $104,750 to you when you only have a $900,000 estate, and a whole lot more if you have a larger estate, isn't it worth a couple more pages of explanation to be sure you get the tax benefit?

Actually, the A-B trust plan effectively protects up to $1.25 million from federal estate taxes in 1998, and that number goes up to $2 million in 2006, if both the husband and the wife are able to pass the exemption equivalent amount (note: $625,000 + $625,000 = $1,250,000). Assuming a $1.25 million estate in 1998, using the living revocable trust instead of the John Loves Mary Will just saved your family over $246,000 in taxes plus the probate and estate fees that could easily reach $50,000. That isn't a bad return, even if you paid several thousand dollars for your living revocable trust. If you have more than $1.25 million in 1998, federal estate taxes can still be eliminated, but you are going to have to use additional legal techniques that support your living revocable trust and go beyond its power. Many middle class families have estates that are above the exemption equivalent amount. Yes, the exemption equivalent steps up slowly to $1 million in 2006, and that sounds like a number that can never be reached, but experts say the tax rates won't keep up with inflation. Whoever is left in the "middle class" by 2006 will be worth over $1 million. Whether it is today or in 2006, the living revocable trust totally solves the federal estate tax problem for most middle class families.

The Survivor Controls

As explained, trust A is called the "marital deduction" trust or the "spousal trust," because assets which are transferred to it qualify for the marital deduction. More or less, whatever goes to trust A from the estate of the first spouse to die is deducted on the estate tax return filed at the first death. Of course, assets owned solely by the surviving spouse are usually put into trust A (if they are put into a trust) and cannot be used to fund trust B.

Trust A is established so that the surviving spouse can do anything he or she wants with the principal (the assets) and the income (the investment increase) of trust A. The surviving spouse can even make out a new will or amend trust A so that the property goes to the new husband or wife, the new kids, or anywhere the surviving spouse directs. If you want to protect your full estate so that the new husband or wife can't get to it, check out the QTIP trust described in Chapter 21.

Trust A is a revocable trust. The surviving spouse can amend or revoke it at will. All of the income from trust A must be reported on the surviving spouse's income tax, just as if it were his or her direct income. The surviving spouse will live with trust A just as he or she lived with the living revocable trust while both spouses were alive. The new house, the new car, any bank accounts that are established, and any other property acquired by the surviving spouse must be owned by trust A, just as property has to be owned by your living revocable trust. In fact, trust A could be considered the private living revocable trust for the surviving spouse.

When property is purchased by the surviving spouse using trust A, it should be purchased in the name of the trust. The name which would be used to purchase property in the name of trust A would be something like the following:

Mary A. Doe, Trustee of Trust A
The John H. and Mary A. Doe Living Revocable Trust
U/A August 1, 1997

The surviving spouse will probably be the trustee of trust A. Of course anyone or any institution, such as a bank, could serve as trust A trustee, just as anyone can serve as the trustee for your living revocable trust.

Considerations the Survivor Must Address

Trust B is an irrevocable trust. In theory, it cannot be changed by the surviving spouse or anyone else. The terms of trust B are set in cement. Although the surviving spouse cannot use trust B assets free from all restrictions (the ascertainable standard restricts his or her use of the assets), the surviving spouse can be the trustee of trust B. That means the surviving spouse can effectively be in total control of trust B assets, even though he or she is restricted to deal with the trust property only within the ascertainable standard.

As a matter of fact, if your living revocable trust is properly established, the surviving spouse can decide what assets go into trust B to make up the exemption equivalent property sheltered there. The assets that are owned solely by the deceased spouse and any jointly owned assets, whether they are owned as joint tenants, tenants in common, or in the living revocable trust you share, can be allocated to trust B or trust A by the surviving spouse. So, the house could be allocated to trust A. The business, stocks, and bonds could be allocated to trust B.

Assets put in trust B should be carefully selected because they are protected in several special ways.

1. Already-appreciated assets. Assets put in trust B are subject to estate taxes as part of the deceased spouse's estate. The government taxes the assets at their fair market value when the first spouse dies and trust B is created. In most cases, no tax will be paid, because trust B is usually only funded with the exemption equivalent amount. When property is subjected to the estate tax, it gets a step-up in basis for income tax calculations. That means if trust B sells the property at the step-up value, trust B will not have any income. This can be a great income tax advantage, because assets that have experienced a large appreciation in value, before trust B was created, can be moved to trust B and later sold by the surviving spouse (acting as trustee) and the new stepped-up basis will be used to figure the income tax. If the same appreciated asset were to be sold by trust A, or the surviving spouse as an individual, the original basis, not the stepped-up basis, would have to be used to calculate the income tax.

2. Assets that are going to appreciate. Assets that could appreciate a lot in value, after the surviving spouse dies, should be carefully considered for inclusion as part of trust B. This is especially true if the total estate is over the exemption equivalent available to both the husband and the wife. Assume, for example, you own a duplex, a stock, or any other asset that is going to double in value during the period the surviving spouse lives after the death of the first spouse. If that asset is allocated to trust A, its full value, including the increase in value, will be subject to estate tax when the surviving spouse dies.

Assume the duplex that was worth $400,000 when Dad dies doubles in value by the time Mom dies. It will be worth $800,000 when Mom dies. By funding trust B with other assets and putting the duplex in trust A at Dad's death, the family is looking at a federal estate tax on $800,000 when Mom dies. That is bad, but imagine the tragedy that would have occurred if there wasn't an A-B split and a full exemption equivalent worth of property hadn't been put in trust B, at Dad's death, which sheltered it from the tax at Mom's death.

Had the $400,000 duplex been put into trust B when Dad died, as part of the exemption equivalent in property allocated to trust B, it would have been out of the IRS's reach when Mom died. This is true even though it doubles in value before Mom dies. When the asset is moved to trust B, its value is "frozen" as far as Mom and Dad's estates are concerned. Its increase in value, after it is placed in trust B, will not be taxed until it is caught up in the next generation's estates or until it is sold.

Do you see how important it is to make sure Mom and Dad, you and your spouse, and the kids with their spouses, all have living revocable trusts? It is worth big bucks in probate and tax savings to make sure your parents, if they are living, put a living revocable trust in place immediately. Maybe this book can help them break the ice and become comfortable with the living revocable trust.

3. Income from assets. Income generated by the assets held in trust B is not automatically the surviving spouse's income, unless the trust says it is. Trust B can direct the trustee to give the income to the beneficiaries in specific proportions, or Trust B can give the trustee the right to decide which beneficiary(ies) will receive the income. However, the surviving spouse can't be a beneficiary of the trust and have the right to send the trust's income to the children without paying personal income taxes on all of the trust's income. The trustee's power to send the trust's income to where it is needed most by the beneficiaries is called a "sprinkling power." A trustee who is also a beneficiary can't have income sprinkling power over trust B income without causing himself or herself tax problems. But, it can save the family a lot of income taxes if the trust's income can be sprinkled on the beneficiaries that are in the lowest income tax brackets. In order to get around the tax problems, an independent trustee (a person who is not a beneficiary or close family member) must be given the sprinkling authority. Banks make great independent trustees. The surviving spouse can hold all of the other powers, but not the sprinkling power. However, if the surviving spouse has enough income from his or her job, retirement, and trust A assets, the independent trustee can move the income of trust B to the daughter who is getting a Ph.D., the son who is sick, or to any other family member for any reason. That income must be claimed by the recipient as his income, but because he needs the money, he is obviously going to be in a lower income tax bracket than the surviving spouse. He won't have to pay as much income tax as the surviving spouse would pay if the "trust income" were given to him or her. Thus, the family gets more real money than they would have had if the surviving spouse had paid the income tax at his or her higher level and then given money to the child that needed help.

If the probability is high that the surviving spouse really will need the income from trust B, just make the trust state that all income goes to the surviving spouse. Without the sprinkling power, there isn't any need for an independent trustee, and the surviving spouse can act as sole trustee.

4. Lawsuits and Creditors. Trust B actually becomes a fairly good asset protection tool, because it is an irrevocable trust.

ASSET PROTECTION TIP #8

Assets moved to trust B are not owned by the surviving spouse, and trust B is irrevocable, so the surviving spouse cannot get the assets back. In fact, the surviving spouse only has restricted control over the trust assets. I have already written that, but do you catch the asset protection value in that set up? When the surviving spouse gets sued, goes bankrupt, gets divorced, or has financial problems of any type that come up after the first spouse dies, the creditors and people suing can take whatever the courts say the surviving spouse owns or has the right to own. The standard living revocable trust is a poor asset protection tool because the grantors, you and your spouse, can revoke the trust and get ownership of the property back at any time. If you can get the property back at anytime, then the courts will give your creditors access to that property. But, trust B is irrevocable, so the surviving spouse can't revoke the trust and get the property back into his or her personal ownership. Therefore, the courts protect trust B. The creditors and litigators don't have much of any claim on property that the courts don't consider "owned" by the surviving spouse.

Someone suing you couldn't take my property away from me, because you don't own or have any interest in my property. The surviving spouse doesn't own trust B as far as the IRS and courts are concerned, and the surviving spouse can't gain ownership of trust B property, so it is not directly subject to his or her lawsuits or tax bills. The property held in trust B is protected, and the creditors won't get anything when they sue the surviving spouse. If the surviving spouse doesn't have any personal assets and is only living off the income and assets of trust B, there probably won't even be a lawsuit filed by the creditor. The creditor can't get anything, so why sue? Trust B just effectively protected the family wealth from attack. Having said all this, I have to point out that the surviving spouse does have some interest in the trust and so everything isn't really cut and dry. Additionally, the lunch theory of justice always has to be taken into consideration. But, the trust will definitely help.

Because trust B is irrevocable and cannot normally be changed, the assets of trust B are almost guaranteed to be distributed to your heirs in the manner you described prior to your death. This is very important if you are worried about black widows. The assets of trust B can be used to support the surviving spouse, but whatever is left in the trust when the surviving spouse dies is protected from the black widow(er), and his or her kids. Trust B gives you the ability to control the distribution of assets long after you die. This ability is important to most people.

Ways to Make An A-B Division

Your living revocable trust will have a section that dictates how trust A and trust B will be established. There are a number of ways to divide the assets between trusts A and B. Diagram 19.3 (next page) shows you schematically one way trusts A and B are divided and funded. Scroll 19.1 (page 286) is an example of language which appears in trust documents and makes the division. Other language could be used.

Basically, all assets that are owned by the surviving spouse and the couple's living revocable trust are moved to trust A. All of the decedent's separate property (all of the property he or she had sole ownership of) will be allocated to trust B. The trust document then directs the trustee to move enough additional property from trust A to trust B, if any is needed, to bring trust B's total value up to the magic value needed to maximize the exemption equivalent. If funding trust B with the deceased spouse's assets puts its value over the exemption equivalent amount, property that belonged to the decedent spouse, which qualifies for the martial deduction, will usually be moved to Trust A, so there isn't an estate tax actually paid on any trust B property. Because

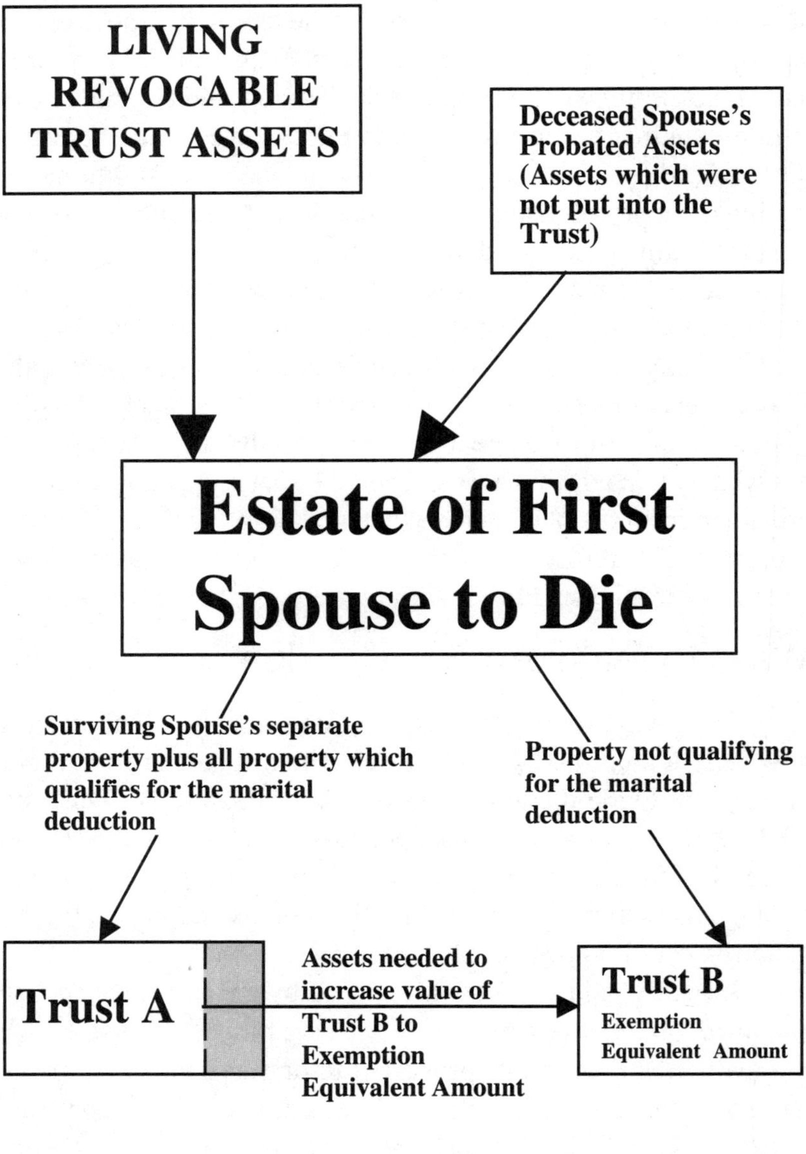

Diagram 19.3—Schematic of the process used to fund trusts A and B

actual amounts are used in dividing money between trust A and trust B, this technique of dividing property between the two trusts is called a pecuniary technique. Another common technique used to divide the living revocable trust into trust A and trust B is called "fractional division."

Assume a family has a $1.5 million estate. By splitting the assets, at the death of the first spouse to die, such that only the exemption equivalent amount (the amount of property needed to take advantage of the full unified credit available) goes in trust B (the shelter trust), there is no estate tax on trust B assets. The remainder of the assets ($875,000 in 1998, i.e., $1,500,00 - $625,000 = $875,000) are placed in trust A, and they will not be exposed to an estate tax until the surviving spouse dies. Thus, the surviving spouse has the opportunity to live off the assets in trust A and "lower" the value of trust A below the available exemption equivalent limit prior to his or her death. Believe me, I know people who could burn the $875,000 in trust A down below the exemption equivalent amount if they live one week longer than their spouse. As long as trust A is under the exemption equivalent amount, there is no tax at either death.

Actually, the full exemption equivalent amount shown in the IRS tables for a specific year may not be available to fund a trust and shelter the value from estate taxes. Large gifts (over the annual exclusion amount) may have reduced the amount of unified credit available to offset estate taxes.

Disposition After the Death of Either John H. Doe or Mary A. Doe

Upon the death of either John or Mary, whichever spouse should die first, and subject to a change in Trustees, this Trust shall continue as then constituted or as it may be increased from any sources, and it shall be administered as follows:

(A) The Trustees shall divide the Trust Estate (which shall include any property which may be added from the deceased spouse's estate) into two (2) separate shares. One share will be designated and referred to as Trust "A" and the other share will be designated and referred to as Trust "B." Trust A shall be composed of cash, securities, the surviving spouse's separate property being held in the Trust Estate, and/or other property of the Trust Estate (undiminished by any estate, inheritance, succession, death or similar taxes). The assets, other than the surviving spouse's separate property, set aside from the Trust Estate in order to establish Trust A shall have a value equal to the maximum marital deduction allowable to the deceased spouse's estate for federal estate tax purposes. However, this value equal to the maximum marital deduction shall be reduced by the sum of (1) the aggregate amount allowed as a marital deduction for interests passing or that have passed to the surviving spouse otherwise than by the terms of this Article and (2) the amount, if any, needed to increase the deceased spouse's taxable estate (for federal estate tax purposes) to the largest amount that will not result in a federal estate tax being imposed on the deceased spouse's estate. This amount needed to increase the deceased spouse's estate should be determined after allowing for the unified federal estate tax credit available to the deceased spouse's estate and the state death tax credit against such tax (but only to the extent that the use of such state death tax credit does not increase the death tax payable to any state).

Scroll 19.1—The text commonly used in living revocable trusts to make the division of property between trusts A and B after the death of the first spouse

A Will Can Give You the Same Tax Protection—But...

The living revocable trust advocates that say your teeth will fall out if you don't have a living revocable trust had better not read this section. As a general rule, a living revocable trust and a specially drafted will should have the same estate tax consequences. Yes, you can establish a shelter trust using a will. Both Mom and Dad can move a full exemption equivalent estate tax free with a will, just as they can using a living revocable trust. However, most wills do not establish shelter trusts. So, don't even begin to think you don't have to worry about estate taxes because you have a will. But, you need to know that you can get as much estate tax relief by using a will as you can by using a living revocable trust. Note that the will can give you estate tax relief, but it cannot give you any probate relief.

In fact, over half of the lawyers will say that you don't ever need a living revocable trust. Obviously, I don't agree with the majority. Could I be wrong? Certainly, over half of all lawyers can't be wrong—can they?

The argument about living revocable trusts is becoming very heated. The argument centers on your use of the trust. The majority of lawyers say that the public is too dumb to use a living revocable trust and that the public wastes their money on living revocable trusts because they don't use the trust, and they end up going through probate anyway. The lawyers argue that there is no need to use a living revocable trust.

I disagree! If you are given the training to use the trust, you are certainly smart enough to use it. If you are going to go to the trouble of setting up a living revocable trust, I think you will be diligent enough to use it. If you don't use your trust, then the majority of lawyers are right; you shouldn't have a trust. But, if you do use a trust, you have the option of avoiding probate and enjoying all of the advantages the trust offers.

The majority of lawyers will give you a will. Then, you don't have any options. You go through probate. If the will sets up a trust, a testamentary trust will be established as the shelter trust. In order to get the double whack at the exemption equivalent allowing a husband and wife to pass the maximum amount of property without estate taxes, a trust must be established. The court will have control over the trust as long as it exists. The lawyers not only make the bigger bucks for setting up the "fancy" will, they also make the even bigger bucks in probate because all of the property has to be probated before the trust is established. Then they get a great income stream for years because the trustee of the shelter trust has to continually report to the court.

If you establish the living revocable trust and don't use it, your property will have to be probated when you die, but testamentary trusts will not have to be created. You don't need to have a testamentary shelter trust created because you already have a living trust. Your living revocable trust just wasn't funded while you were alive. At your death, your property is probated and "pours over" into the trust which is free from further court control. In my opinion, you are still ahead by using the living revocable trust even if you don't fund it prior to your death. But, that is just my opinion. Can you really trust me? After all, I am a "liar"—that's Texan for "attorney."

Can You Overkill?

I have always prepared trusts for my clients that make the split at the death of the first spouse to die. One client got my trust and hauled it down the street to a second attorney. The attorney blew his stack when he saw the trust. Oh, he agreed it was a beautiful sight to behold, but he told the client that it was a total overkill. He informed the client that he had gotten a Rolls Royce when all he needed was a Ford Pinto. The client didn't need the A-B split and all of the bells and whistles because the client only had a small estate.

The attorney was absolutely correct. At the time I prepared the trust, the client didn't need a fancy A-B trust. You may have been told you don't need any trust because you don't have enough assets to reach the exemption equivalent amount and you don't have to worry about estate taxes. In fact, you may not need the living revocable trust to avoid estate taxes, but remember, the trust is also used to avoid probate, and estate taxes have nothing to do with probate. Should you have an A-B trust document even if you have a small estate?

The client came back to my office blowing steam. I was informed in no uncertain terms that I was a crook and had done twice as much legal work as he needed. The obvious conclusion was he had paid me way too much because he didn't need an elaborate trust. After a couple of cold drinks, the client started to settle down a little. I agreed with him. His trust was an overkill. I agreed that all he needed was a simple living revocable trust which didn't set up the A-B split—no split, no tax protection, just avoid probate. That is all this man needed as he sat across the desk from me.

I calmly asked how much the other attorney would charge him to prepare the stripped down version of a living revocable trust. He didn't know. He had forgotten to ask what the charge would be. I had him call and ask what the stripped down version would cost at the other lawyer's shop. When my client found out he would have paid more for a Ford Pinto trust than he actually paid for a Rolls Royce trust, he settled right down. In this day and age of computers, the computer can just as easily put out a Rolls Royce version. A surprisingly few law firms use a computer for anything more than a glorified typewriter, but the computer can do much more.

I want my clients to have the maximum protection. You should get the maximum protection also. No, the man in my office didn't need an A-B trust at that time. If he never needed an A-B split, there still wasn't any harm in his getting the Rolls Royce version. If his ship did come in and he ended up with a million dollars, the trust would protect his family and save them some big estate tax payments. They would have had to pay a couple hundred thousand dollars in estate taxes if he had only had a simple living revocable trust without an A-B split.

However, if it is guaranteed that Mom and Dad are never going to have an estate big enough to have any estate tax problems (i.e., the total estate can almost be guaranteed to be below the exemption equivalent value), go ahead and establish a living revocable trust without an A-B split. Why add more complication to their lives than necessary?

Estimating Your Estate Value

Appendix 3 should be used to estimate the value of your estate. Clients often grossly underestimate the value of their estate. One widowed lady came in to me and wanted a trust. She convinced me she was really very poor, and she even talked me into a discount because she was so poor. Today, I never believe a client who pleads poverty. In her mind she was poor. In the bank's mind she was loaded. She had over $500,000 in the bank plus all of her other assets.

An estate includes the real estate, bank accounts, stocks and bonds, cars, boats, and the personal property including diamonds, silverware, collectibles, horses, dogs, cats—no, not the kids. (The IRS figures the kids are a liability, not an asset, to you.) When clients just add up assets like these to determine what their estate is worth, they are in trouble. They are forgetting things like the life insurance policy death value and cash value; their business, and all of its inventory; the note payable by the kids; the partnership interest they have with Uncle Joe, which doesn't give them any income, but is worth a ton of money on paper; their retirement; IRA; and the list goes on.

Of course, the debts, mortgages, and other financial liabilities you may have are subtracted from the total assets in order to arrive at a value for your taxable estate.

Inflation—Gotcha

Because values don't stay the same, it is hard for you and me to estimate the value of things. Values usually increase due to inflation. The couple that paid $25,000 for their home in San Marino, California in 1960 may not realize that the house is worth about $1.5 million in today's market. My neighbor built a house two years ago. In our town real estate values have been very flat for about 10 years; in fact, values have gone down. The neighbor sold the house last week. The sales sign hadn't been up 24 hours before the "sold" sign went up. Obviously, the neighbor hadn't realized that real estate values have gone up 30% in our town during the past year. Someone in our town that had a nontaxable estate a year ago may now be looking at big time estate tax problems. Can you see why I recommend the full A-B trust even for people who may not technically need it today?

I also recommend funding trust B with the full exemption equivalent amount. Many trusts are written so that there is an equal division of the family estate between trusts A and B. The trust document simply says that the estate will go 1/2 to trust A and 1/2 to trust B. This type of trust division is more common in smaller estates. There are pros and cons to funding the trusts this way. If you fund trust B with less than the exemption equivalent amount, you are wasting part of the tax sheltering capacity of trust B. I hate waste. It is possible to fund trust B with a full exemption equivalent and simply fund trust A with less, but the trust document has to be written to permit such a funding technique.

For example, in 1999, a $900,000 estate could be divided with the exemption equivalent ($650,000) going to trust B and $250,000 going to trust A. That way, the family takes advantage of the full sheltering power of trust B, and trust A can "grow" a lot more with investments or inflation before the family faces an estate tax. Make sure you understand what options your trust gives you when trusts A and B are established.

Chapter

20

Preventing a Lawsuit Disaster

Splitting Your Trust to Safeguard Assets

Whether or not your estate has big time tax problems or is a small estate, psychologically you are very attached to what you "own." Most couples feel that they are in a common enterprise, the family, and that their assets are all in "one pot." The joint trust, where all assets are held in one trust until the death of one of the spouses, works well because it preserves the "one pot" way of life the couple is used to having. The joint trust has been used primarily in community property states. The other states have used a two trust system where he has one trust and she has one trust. The joint trust is becoming more popular in all states. Diagrams 19.1 and 19.2 are diagrams of the joint trust.

The two trust system appears to be cleaner for asset protection planning. In reality the same level of asset protection can be achieved by a joint trust, but it just doesn't "look" as good because the separation of his estate and her estate isn't as visible. In the two trust system, two separate trust documents are actually created—one for each spouse. Both trusts are living revocable trusts. They have to be funded and managed just as the joint living revocable trusts I have been writing about. The property in the trusts avoids probate, and a full exemption equivalent can be sheltered from estate tax at the death of the first spouse to die with no actual tax being paid, just as it can be sheltered in the joint living revocable trust.

The husband creates one trust acting as grantor and is named as trustee and beneficiary. The wife creates the other trust acting as grantor and is named as trustee and beneficiary. The property in each trust is, of course, owned by the trust and controlled by the trustee to be used for the benefit of the beneficiaries named in the trust. The husband is usually named to receive the benefit of the wife's trust after she dies and vice versa. Other than the benefit that arises after the death of the grantor, each spouse has no legal interest in the other's trust.

Upon the death of the husband or wife, the trust he or she created becomes irrevocable, just as trust B became irrevocable after the death of the first spouse to die. The property in the trust will be taxed at the grantor's death—unless the property is transferred to the surviving spouse or the surviving spouse's trust. The trust papers are written to retain up to the exemption equivalent amount in the deceased spouse's trust and transfer the rest of the property to the surviving spouse's trust. Thus, the maximum exemption equivalent amount is protected, just as it is using trust B, and the surviving spouse's trust goes on as a revocable trust, just as trust A remains revocable when the joint trust splits.

The surviving spouse can be the trustee of the decedent's trust and use the sheltered property for his or her benefit under the same ascertainable standard that is used to protect trust B from taxes when the surviving spouse dies. Diagram 20.1 illustrates the two trust system.

As long as the wife is alive, her husband has no legal interest in her trust. That means the property in her trust is, in theory, protected from his legal problems. Can you see the power in what that means?

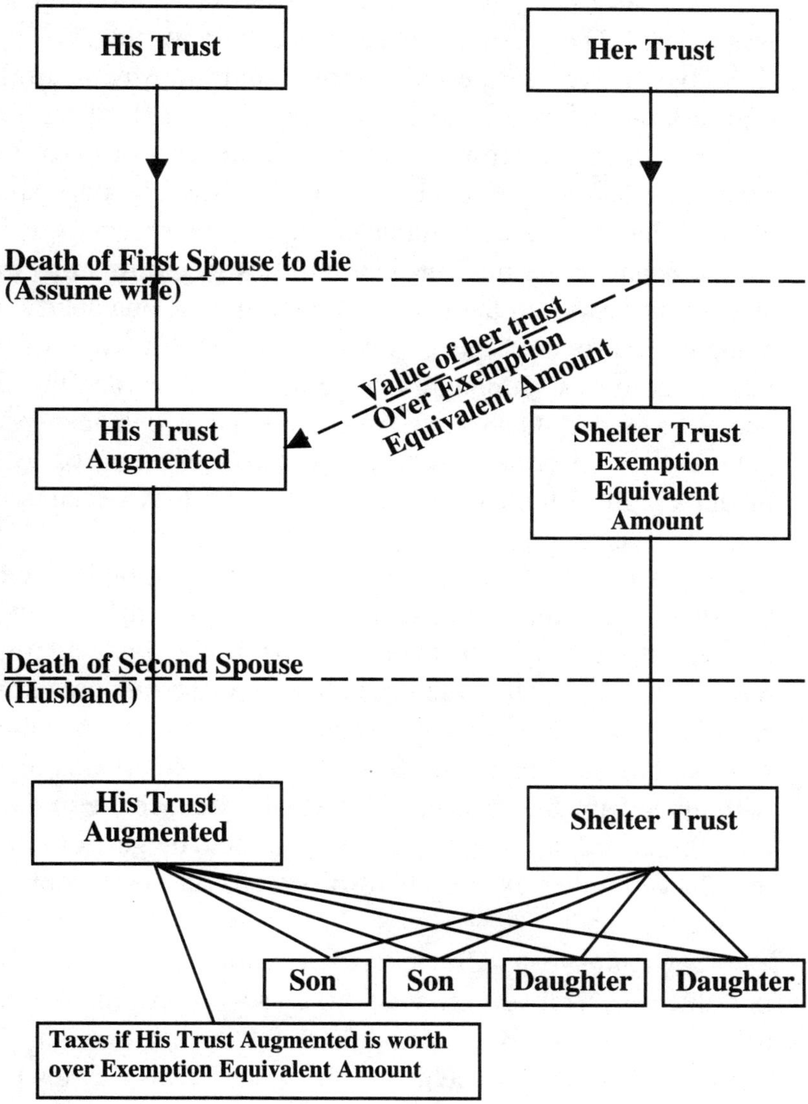

Diagram 20.1—A his-and-her two-trust system

The courtroom was packed. People were standing in the aisles. There was no question; the man was guilty, and the citizens wanted justice. Many millions of dollars had been siphoned out of the little town, and unless the money was recovered, a lot of businesses were going to go under. The state attorney general was poised. The defense counsel was calmly waiting.

Over a five year period, the man on trial, Mr. Smart, had built a large business with a huge cash flow. All of the businesses in town had grown to rely on Mr. Smart's business. Although he had always paid his bills and was a good man, he couldn't handle success; and he changed. His success was big. His company made millions and millions in profits in its third and fourth years. In the fifth year everything came apart. The company was overextended. It went into debt. It hired way too many employees. It bought a huge new building, and the Gulf War hit America. Overnight, Americans changed their spending patterns. For a brief period, they became preoccupied by the media's high tech coverage of the war, and they became very conservative buyers.

Company sales went from $10,000,000 a month to under $1,000,000, but the overhead kept right on coming. All of the businessmen in town who supplied parts for the product, printed the advertising, mailed the products, fixed the computers, and supplied all of the company's needs didn't know how bad things were getting for Smart. Because they knew Smart was loaded with money, the businessmen in town all extended credit for 30, 60, 90, 120 days. Because Smart was their biggest customer, they had to either extend credit or start laying off people and cutting way back.

The company and Smart tried everything they could. They introduced several new products. They advertised, and they sold the new products. But, sales didn't pick up fast enough. The company was too far in debt, and its overhead was way too high. Sales of the new products had actually gone well, but the buyers began to complain to the company and the state agencies. The new products were late in delivery. The new products were never delivered. Smart had done something dumb. He had sold products that never existed. The new products didn't exist—except in the minds of Mr. Smart and his executives.

"All rise!" ordered the bailiff. The judge in his flowing robes entered and took his position behind the bench. Court was in session. After opening statements, the defense attorney stood and asked the judge to dismiss Mrs. Smart from the suit. She had been named in the suit, but as the defense attorney clearly pointed out, there were no allegations in the complaint of her ever doing anything wrong. The attorney general had to agree.

The judge demanded, *Do you have any charges against Mrs. Smart?*

She has all of the money. It's all in her trust, the attorney general stated.

Has the money been illegally transferred to the trust?

No.

Was it transferred when the company owed all of its current bills?

No.

Since the money had been taken out of the company in the third and fourth year, over a year earlier while things were going well, its removal from the company couldn't be considered an attempt to defraud the company's creditors.

Because the money had been removed and gifted by Mr. Smart to his wife years earlier, it was well outside of the bankruptcy statutes of limitation. As soon as she got the money, it was put in her individual trust where Mr. Smart had no interest in it. Even if Mr. Smart declared personal bankruptcy, the money was well beyond the reach of his creditors.

In spite of the attorney general's pleading with the judge, there was no legal reason to maintain the case against Mrs. Smart. Within twenty minutes the case against Mrs. Smart was dismissed with prejudice, meaning it could not be reopened against her. The attorney general was helpless in her fight for the money that was in the trust.

Several years later, I came upon Mr. Smart while I was strolling down the beach on Kauai. We sat on the beach and talked in the shadow of his penthouse condominium. During the conversation, he stated that he had been wiped out. He was flat broke. He was a kept man—a well kept man.

ASSET PROTECTION TIP #9

Use two individual trusts—one trust for you and one for your spouse. The two trusts can be created using the two trust system or using a joint trust which establishes separate trust divisions for you and your spouse. Divide the wealth evenly or stack the wealth with the spouse (the spouse's trust) that is least likely to be exposed to legal attack. A spouse that is a professional or runs a business is especially open to attack, so plan on stacking the wealth in favor of the other spouse.

If one spouse is attacked by someone through a lawsuit, the other spouse's trust is beyond the reach of the suit as long as the other spouse cannot be drawn into the lawsuit.

Dividing the estate into two trusts is not a total protection if one spouse gets sued, but it can certainly help protect half of the estate. It is a step which is easy to take. I have seen it be a futile effort in some cases, but I have also seen it save a family's financial future in many other cases.

Joint Trust Asset Protection Techniques

A joint trust document, a trust document where only one document establishes the trust for a couple, can be used to create separate divisions or "trusts" for each spouse, in addition to the joint trust. The trust document simply needs to state that separate trusts are being created in addition to the joint trust.

Property that is the separate property of one spouse, such as an inheritance, can be placed in his or her trust and segregated as separate property. The property should receive the same legal advantages achieved by using two separate written trusts.

Think! How would you open a checking account that is to be owned by the husband's part of a joint trust. Property to be placed in the husband's trust would be purchased as follows:

The John Doe Trust, a separate division of the John and Mary Doe Living Revocable Trust U/A July 4, 1997, John Doe, Trustee.

or

John Doe, Trustee of the John Doe Trust, a separate division of the John and Mary Doe Living Revocable Trust U/A July 4, 1997.

It is certainly possible to establish a joint trust and also establish a separate husband and separate wife trust using three written trust agreements—one for the joint trust, one for the husband's trust, and one for the wife's trust.

You should now be comfortable recognizing that trusts can be used in many different combinations to accomplish whatever you desire. There isn't any "one right way" to establish a trust or set of trusts for your family. If you have a classic joint trust, that's OK. It's also OK if you have separate his and her trusts.

Joint trusts tend to be a little simpler to manage while both spouses are alive. Separate trusts are actually a little simpler to manage after one spouse dies. There are advantages and disadvantages to every variation of the living revocable trust structure. Use the structure that best fits your needs and circumstances.

If you already have a living revocable trust, did you get what you wanted? Can you determine what you want if you don't already have a living revocable trust?

Whenever you get your trust, the text of the trust should be pretty standard, at least in the parts of the trust which should be standard. You should now be able to actually use your trust or trusts. All living revocable trusts are basically used the same way. The concepts of trusts, property ownership, and beneficiaries are always the same. The advantages of the trust are always the same. Married people use their trust the same way single people use their trust. However, single people do have a tax disadvantage they have to work around.

How Singles Can Use Trusts

It is just as important for a single person to have a trust as it is for a married couple to have a trust. Probate is just as devastating when a single person dies. In fact, because the distribution of a single person's estate is often more complicated, it may be worse. At the death of one spouse, the other spouse usually receives everything. At the death of a single person, the property seldom goes to only one other person. It usually goes to many other people, making distribution much more complicated.

The trust for a single person reads almost exactly the same as the couple's trust. There is only one major difference. There is no possibility of splitting the trust in order to get a double whack at the exemption equivalent in order to save estate taxes. Therefore, all of the provisions addressing the division of the trust into trust A and trust B and the management of the trust by the surviving spouse are not found in a single's trust.

The trust division creating the shelter trust and the marital trust clearly won't work for a single's estate. The whole concept of splitting the estate rests on the unlimited marital deduction. When the unlimited marital deduction can be used, the decedent's entire estate is subject to an estate tax, but all of the property which goes to the spouse is "deducted" from the decedent's estate. The property which doesn't go to the surviving spouse is held in a shelter trust so that it won't be included in the surviving spouse's estate when he or she dies. Thus, a couple can get a double whack at the estate tax exemption.

The John Loves Mary Will gives everything to the surviving spouse. There isn't any estate tax when the first spouse dies. However, in the John Loves Mary Will, nothing is held back to be sheltered, and the surviving spouse ends up with everything, which is then taxed at his or her death. Because everything goes to the surviving spouse under the unlimited marital deduction, there isn't any estate tax when the first spouse dies, but the couple can only pass one exemption equivalent amount to their family tax free.

With the little review you have just had, it should be easy to see how a single estate is limited in its ability to avoid estate taxes. There simply isn't a surviving spouse to pass property to and have the property qualify for the unlimited marital deduction.

The widow or widower comes to me after his or her spouse has died, and wants to use the A-B shelter trick. It can't be done. All of the paperwork has to be properly in place before either spouse dies. I get sick when I have to explain to a family with a taxable estate that they are a year late in getting their paperwork done, and their delay will cost them over several hundred thousand dollars in lost estate tax savings.

If your mom and dad are both alive and you put the trust in place for them, it could easily save their estate and you an extra couple hundred thousand dollars when they die.

Don't even begin to think that a single person shouldn't do his or her estate planning. The opportunities for estate tax planning are far fewer than the opportunities for a married couple's estate, but the single's estate still needs planning. Of course, a living revocable trust can be used, and taxes can be reduced by gifting, establishing irrevocable trusts, family limited partnerships, or a half dozen other techniques.

The single's estate can easily be planned using a living revocable trust so that the transfer of property at his or her death is orderly. Probate can certainly be avoided. The trust can be used to manage the single's property should he or she become incompetent. The trust is just as powerful for a single; however, the double whack at the estate tax exemption equivalent cannot be achieved. Naturally, the single is entitled to one exemption equivalent amount.

A pour-over will must be prepared for a single person, just as one must be prepared for each spouse in a couple. The pour-over will performs the exact same functions and acts as a support for the living revocable trust.

I talk to a lot of single people. I have spoken about living revocable trusts on thousands of occasions in 46 states. I have been from St. John to Guam, and I am saddened by the number of people who are totally alone. They have no family, no children, no parents, no brothers or sisters, no nieces or nephews, no close friends. They have no one. I hurt for them. Being alone is so hard. Many such people I have worked with are very wealthy. I always tell them that I am up for adoption, for a joke. But, who would want to adopt a lawyer? The only thing they can do is leave their wealth, big or small, to a worthy cause. Even in their case, the living revocable trust will avoid court battles in probate and leave much more wealth to whomever is designated to receive the benefit of the estate.

Trusts For Alternative Lifestyle Couples

Alternative lifestyle marriages are simply not recognized by the federal estate tax laws. There is no such thing as an unlimited marital deduction for the couple when one of them dies. That may change, but for now, the couple needs to basically apply single estate planning techniques for each partner.

Probate still needs to be avoided. Tax planning still needs to be done. If each partner has an individual living revocable trust, the trust can be established so that at the death of one partner, the trust property is not "given" to the second partner, but rather held in trust for the benefit of the surviving partner. The full value of the property in each partner's trust will be taxed at his or her death. Because the estate tax exemption equivalent will apply to each partner, there will only be a tax paid on the value of the property in his or her estate that is above the exemption equivalent mark. By using ascertainable standards and carefully maintaining the deceased partner's trust outside of the second partner's estate, the trust property will not be "caught up" in the second partner's estate and taxed at his or her death.

After the second partner dies, both trusts can be distributed in whatever manner the separate trusts designate. Care must be taken to divide the partners' total estate evenly between each trust. This will allow the full estate tax exemption to be claimed by both partners if their combined estate is over the double exemption equivalent amount. Thus, a full double exemption equivalent can be moved estate tax free just as it can be moved by the traditional couple. So, all is not lost for the alternative lifestyle couple. They simply have to do their planning carefully as they go along and not rely on the possibility of dividing things up when one of them dies.

The living revocable trusts will avoid probate, provide for support of the surviving partner, and provide for easy distribution of the assets when both partners are gone. Should one partner become incompetent, the other partner can step in and manage all of the property as the successor trustee.

Each person needs his or her own pour-over will, living will, and durable power of attorney. In fact, the same basic estate planning documents are required for everyone—single, married traditionally or alternatively, old or young. The exact same knowledge is needed by everyone to use the trust and get its benefits. The principles of this book apply to everyone.

Chapter

21

The QTIP Trust

The Trust Clients Want

How to Protect Your Estate From the New Guy or Gal

Black widows bite Congressmen just as they bite normal folks. In 1981, Congress issued an extermination order for black widows. They passed a law which authorized the creation of what is called Qualified Terminable Interest Property or "Q-Tip" property.

You and your spouse should be able to assure that your kids will get all of your property after you both die. You should also be able to have the property available to both of you as long as you live. The property should also be protected from the new guy or new gal that might come into the picture after you die or your spouse dies. Trust B, which is established by the living revocable trust, does a great job for you. However, under the standard A-B trust situation, the A trust property is not protected from the new guy or gal.

The A trust is the marital trust, and all of the property that goes into it qualifies for the unlimited marital deduction. That means the property is fully deductible from estate taxes assessed when the first spouse dies, and no taxes are assessed until the surviving spouse dies. In order to have the property qualify for the unlimited marital deduction, the IRS says that the property has to be "given" to the surviving spouse with no strings attached.

Even though the property is in the A trust, it is considered by the IRS to be the surviving spouse's property. He or she can do anything with the property, including give it all to the new guy or the new gal. With the A trust, there are no strings attached for the surviving spouse. That's great. After Dad dies, Mom uses the A trust property just as though it wasn't even in the trust. There aren't any problems until Mom remarries.

After Mom has been married to the new guy for a while, the conversation will always come to money.

He says, *Don't you love me, sweetie?*

She says, *Why, of course.*

He says, *Then you want me to be taken care of when you die, and I certainly want you to be taken care of when I die. So let's put our name on everything as joint tenants and get rid of those trusts you have. We can make out wills so that you get everything if I die, and I get everything if you die.*

At that point, Mom says, *Well, trust B is irrevocable, and I can't get rid of it. The property in the B trust can only be used to help me and my kids under an ascertainable standard, and whatever is left when I die has to go to my kids the way it says in the trust. I have to treat the property in trust B the way the trust tells me to. But only part of "my" property is in that trust. Trust A is mine, and I can do whatever I want to with trust A property. It has a million dollars in it. I really love you so much, Mr. New Guy. We can take all of the property out of Trust A, put our names on it, and make out new wills. You can have the whole million dollars when I die.*

Mom dies, and the new guy makes off with everything that was in trust A.

Enough Congressmen got burned by trust A on the "Sweetie, don't you love me?" trick that they changed the laws. We pay Congressmen to change their minds and the laws; so they were doing what they were supposed to do. They said, "We need a new trust that will be taxed like trust A. Everything that goes into the new trust must qualify for the unlimited marital deduction, and it can't be exposed to estate taxes until the second spouse dies. Additionally, the trust has to be irrevocable so that the new guy or gal can't get to it." To satisfy all of these requirements, Congress created the QTIP trust. In the QTIP trust, all of the property qualifies for the unlimited marital deduction. No estate taxes are assessed until both spouses are dead, and it can be structured so the new guy can't get to the property!

Attorneys don't count too high, so they named the QTIP trust "Trust C." Now there is a trust A, B, and C. Your estate plan will always establish a trust B, the shelter trust or decedent's trust. You can choose to have either a trust A or C. Or, you can have both trust A and trust C. Some of the property left over after trust B is funded can go to trust C so that it is protected from the new guy or gal. Additionally, some property can go into trust A so that the surviving spouse can give it away or do whatever he or she wants with the property. Of course, all of the property that doesn't go into trust B could go into the QTIP trust, and there wouldn't be any need for a trust A.

To satisfy the IRS, the law sets down some rules that trust C has to follow. The following requirements are necessary to form a QTIP trust:

1. The QTIP property must pass from the decedent spouse to the surviving spouse.
2. The surviving spouse must be entitled to receive, at least annually, all of the income from the QTIP property.
3. The surviving spouse is the only person who can be given the principal (property) in the trust.
4. On the deceased spouse's estate tax return, the personal representative must make the affirmative election to establish the QTIP trust and claim the marital deduction for the QTIP property.

The language used to administer a QTIP trust is shown in Scroll 21.1.

Management of Trust C

Trust C, which is often referred to as the Qualified Terminable Interest Trust, will be established when the first of either John H. Doe or Mary A. Doe dies, whichever spouse should die first. This Trust C shall be held, administered and distributed as follows:

(A) Commencing at the death of John or Mary, whichever should die first, the Trustees shall pay to or apply for the benefit of the surviving spouse, whether John or Mary, during his or her lifetime all of the net income from Trust C. The net income from Trust C may be paid to the surviving spouse in convenient installments, but all of the income must be paid out at least annually. Any accrued and undistributed income which is being held in the Trust at the time of the death of the surviving spouse shall be paid to his or her estate by making payments to the estate's personal representatives or administrators.

(B) In addition to the net income payments, the Trustees may pay to or apply for the benefit of the surviving spouse any amount of the principal of Trust C. The Trustees may use their discretion in determining the timing, necessity, and advisability of these principal payments. The Trustees may take into consideration, to the extent they deem advisable, any other income or resources of the surviving spouse known to the Trustees.

(C) By giving written notice to the Trustees, the surviving spouse may at any time require the Trustees either to make any nonproductive property of this Trust productive or to convert the nonproductive property to productive property within a reasonable time.

(D) Unless the surviving spouse's Will specifically provides that the estate, succession, death or similar taxes assessed with respect to the assets of Trust C be paid otherwise, the Trustees shall pay to the personal representatives and administrators of the estate of the surviving spouse for the purposes of paying such taxes, the amount by which such taxes assessed by reason of his or her death shall be increased as a result of the inclusion of the assets of Trust C in his or her estate for such tax purposes.

(E) Upon the death of the surviving spouse, the entire remaining principal of Trust C shall be paid over, conveyed and distributed to or put in trust as appointed for John's and Mary's children. Trust C shall be divided in the manner appointed in the surviving spouse's Last Will. This appointment power must be specifically referenced and exercised in the Last Will. In disposing of Trust C, the Trustees shall be protected in relying upon an instrument admitted to probate in any jurisdiction as the Last Will of the surviving spouse. TheTrustees may also be protected by acting upon the assumption that the surviving spouse died intestate if the Trustees have no notice of the existence of a Will of the surviving spouse within six (6) months after his or her death.

If this special power of appointment is not specifically exercised in the surviving spouse's Last Will, or insofar as any part of such Trust C shall not be effectively appointed, then upon the death of the surviving spouse, the entire remaining principal of Trust C, or the part of such Trust not effectively appointed shall be added to and become a part of Trust B and shall be held and administered or distributed in whole or in part, as if it had been an original part of Trust B.

Scroll 21.1—Text used in a living revocable trust to manage a Qualified Terminable Interest Property (QTIP) Trust

Don't Be Intimidated—The Surviving Spouse Is Still In Control

The rules may sound a little intimidating. Don't be intimidated. Everything is still under control. Yes, the surviving spouse can be the trustee of a QTIP trust (trust C), so he or she will have full control over the property.

When the surviving spouse is the trustee, the rules are really not too hard to live with. For example, the rule that says only the surviving spouse can be given the trust property is easily worked around. The surviving spouse, acting as trustee, could give himself or herself the property and then turn around and, acting as an independent person, give the property to the kids or even the new guy.

In a vast majority of trusts, trust B and trust A can protect the estate very effectively. The surviving spouse is going to live the same life with a trust A or a trust C. However, if Mom has a C trust instead of an A trust, when the new guy puts the moves on Mom with the "Sweetie, don't you love me?" trick, Mom can say, "Sure, I love you, but both trust B and C are irrevocable. I can't just take the property out and put your name on it. That would be a violation of my fiduciary duty as trustee; and the kids, who are beneficiaries, could sue us if the trusts were violated."

The "sue" word should slow the new guy down. However, you need to be aware that Mom could actually get at all of the trust C property, move it out of the trust, and put the new guy's name on it. If she did it right, the kids wouldn't have anything to say about it. The bottom line is: Trust C is not an absolute protection from the new guy when the surviving spouse is the trustee. But, the QTIP trust gives Mom (or Dad) a good excuse and a legal reason to protect the property, and the excuse works most of the time. (Just make sure the new guy or gal doesn't read this book.) If preventing the new guy from getting a dime is really the absolute goal, trust C can be established with someone other than the surviving spouse as the trustee. When Mom isn't the trustee, she can love the new guy all she wants, but the trust is outside of her control and the new guy isn't going to get at it. He had better marry Mom for love, not an inheritance.

The words used to create a QTIP trust are all there for a reason. For example, the surviving spouse is given a "special power of appointment." This allows the surviving spouse to make out a will and give away the trust C property in his or her will. The catch is, the property can only be given to the "class" of individuals named in the trust. In the wording shown in Scroll 21.1, the class is defined as John and Mary's children.

If John dies first, Mary, the surviving spouse, would have the chance before she died to look at their children and leave them money according to their needs. She could leave it all to their poor son, and none to their rich son; or she could leave it in any proportion she chose. But, whatever is left in trust C when she dies can only be left to their children. If she doesn't exercise the right to write a new will and use the power of appointment, trust C property will be distributed as described in trust B.

Other than the surviving spouse's ability to exercise the special power of appointment among the class established in the trust, his or her "interest" in the property "terminates" when he or she dies. So, the property "qualifies" for the unlimited marital deduction, and the surviving spouse's "interest" in the property is "terminable" because it terminates at his or her death. Thus, the name "Qualified Terminable Interest Property" trust or QTIP.

The QTIP trust is a nice wrinkle in the standard A-B trust setup. Many of my clients want it when it is explained to them.

ASSET PROTECTION TIP #10

The QTIP trust is used to hold property in excess of that required to fund trust B. It is an irrevocable trust. If it is drafted with the right terms, such as a good spendthrift provision, a discretionary power in the trustee to distribute trust money, and the surviving spouse is not named as the sole trustee, the property in the QTIP trust will not be subject to the claims of the surviving spouse's creditors. The surviving spouse can be a co-trustee with someone else, but he or she can't be the sole trustee for the asset protection trick to work.

Avoiding a QTIP Trap

As an irrevocable trust, the property in the QTIP trust is "owned" by the trust, not the surviving spouse. Yes, the property can be used for his or her benefit, and all of the trust's income will be paid to the surviving spouse each year. The surviving spouse will feel like they own the property in trust C, but according to the IRS, all of the trust's property is "owned" by the QTIP trust, because it is an irrevocable trust. (Remember, the IRS treats revocable trusts and irrevocable trusts very differently.) Under the current laws, a problem can occur after the living revocable trust is divided into the two *irrevocable* trusts, trust B and trust C. The problem centers on the house and which trust to put it in after the division.

A couple can sell their personal residence (the home they own and have lived in for two of the past five years), and up to $500,000 of the sale is totally income tax free. That is great! A single person, such as the surviving spouse, can sell his or her house, and up to $250,000 of the sale is income tax free. That is a big tax benefit when Mom wants to sell the house and move into one of those retirement condominiums after Dad dies.

Can you see the trap? When Dad dies and a trust B and a trust C are established, the house has to go into one of the two trusts because it is held in the living revocable trust which directs the trustee to divide all of the trust property between either trust B or trust C. But B and C are both irrevocable trusts. The IRS says that property held in them is actually "owned" by the trust. When Mom sells the house, which is held in either trust B or C, she will not be entitled to $250,000 income tax free, because she is not selling the personal residence she "owns." According to the IRS, when the house is in either trust B or C, Mom doesn't own the house. It is not hers, and when the house is sold, the $250,000 tax free benefit isn't available to Mom. That is going to hurt when Mom sells the house.

When there is a house involved that is going to be sold, your trust plans need to establish a trust A (marital deduction trust) so that the house can be placed in it. Trust A is a revocable trust, and according to the IRS, Mom still owns the house even though it is held in trust A and will avoid probate. Your trust plan can establish all three trusts—trusts A, B, and C. The tax advantages available to home owners can still be obtained by holding the house in trust A. All of the rest of the property can be sheltered from the new guy or gal by holding it in trust B or C. When the house is held in trust A, it won't be protected from the new guy or gal. So, you will have to weigh the $250,000 tax free dollars against your fear of a new guy or gal. The tax savings seem to be pretty important to lots of clients and black widows may not be such a big deal, because I am writing a lot more trusts that don't have a QTIP trust established.

Of course, there is always a little legal trick called a prenuptial agreement, where the real intents of the new guy can be tested and he can give up his interest to Mom's house before they get married. More and more people are using prenuptial agreements in order to ward off the black widow problem and then just using a shelter trust with a marital deduction trust.

Chapter

22

Solving the Rest Home Dilemma

Statistically, up to 75% of the families in America are going to put a family member in a rest home within the next 10 years. When Mom or Dad is put in the rest home, they get a bill each month. The bill will run between $3,000 and $6,000 each month. Mom and Dad have worked all of their lives and paid to support social security, Medicare, Medicaid, and all of the government programs. The family is entitled to have the government help pay part of the rest home bill. But, before government Medicaid will pay one dime on the rest home bill, Mom and Dad have to "spend down" all of their wealth until they are basically broke.

The rest home is a real problem for most families. It attacks your family from every angle. Of course, there is the financial frontal assault. There is also an emotional attack, which can inflict wounds that cause a lot more pain than the financial wounds. Caring for Mom and Dad and making the decision to put them in a rest home can turn the kids' lives upside down. It can be a nightmare.

Vivian is a loving daughter who moved her parents into a house near her so that she could take care of them in their old age. Mom and Dad made her give her most sacred oath that she would never put them in a rest home and would care for them until their death—just like they had done for Dad's parents when they were old and dying. Vivian took the oath and started to care for her parents. Her act of kindness has turned into a nightmare that is not only consuming her time and energy, it may well take her life.

Shortly after she got her parents settled into the house eight years ago, Dad had a massive stroke. He was rushed to the hospital and placed on full life support. He was declared brain dead and the doctors asked if they could remove the life support equipment. Mom and almost all of the kids were at Dad's side. One sister was on the other side of the country on a business trip, and she insisted on being present when the doctors "pulled the plug." She was very vocal about her desires to be there when the plug was pulled. The doctors were afraid to do something against her strongly expressed wishes, and the rest of the family wanted to honor her wishes. In order to avoid any legal problems and keep the family happy, the doctors simply kept Dad on life support for a couple of extra days while the daughter made her way across the country.

The family gathered to say their last good-bye to Dad, and the plug was pulled. Dad, in his total vegetative state, didn't take his final breath and slip away peacefully. He didn't die! He had stabilized while the family waited to pull the plug. Vivian's nightmare was just beginning.

Mom, who was weak but fully competent, demanded that Dad be brought back home. It was over her dead body that he would ever go to a rest home. She made all of the children avow their everlasting love for her and Dad. All of the children's vows of love and support were conditioned on their promise never to put her or Dad in the rest home. After all, if the kids had any love for their parents, they would take care of them and not commit them to a rest home. She had taken care of Dad's parents until their death, and she expected her kids to do the same for her and Dad.

Of course, all of the kids gave their oath, and the ambulance transported Dad to his resting place at home—not in the cemetery. Rest assured, he was dead, just not cold. Vivian's brothers and sisters all said their good-byes, renewed their promises to Mom, and left for their homes in distant cities. Vivian's nightmare had begun in full horror, and Vivian wasn't even asleep. It has been eight years since Dad's stroke, and Vivian has literally never slept.

Every two or three hours Dad needed to be turned to prevent bed sores, maintain his circulation, and preserve his "life." Mom could not do a thing to help. She was as weak as a kitten. For eight years in rain or snow every three hours, twenty-four hours a day, four hundred eighty days a year, Vivian or her husband has gone the three blocks down the hill to turn Dad. Her skills as a nurse have allowed her to feed Dad through his tubes, change his diapers, clean him, and take care of him in every way possible. Every day, Mom has Vivian rehearse the pledge never to commit either of them to a rest home.

She has tried to reason with Mom and has solicited her siblings' support. Mom is immovable, and the siblings think everything is great. Dad is getting good care, Mom is happy, and they have kept their oath. During the eight years, Vivian has been relieved for a day or two so that she could travel to see a new grandchild for the first time or attend a child's funeral, but she has basically been a prisoner and slave.

Mom now has fairly advanced Alzheimer's. She needs full-time care. But, she still remembers the oath. It is literally her last memory. She doesn't remember who Vivian is most of the time, and she certainly doesn't remember who any of the other kids are. But, she remembers the oath, and all of Vivian's brothers and sisters remember the oath. Yes, Vivian also remembers the oath.

Vivian's health is failing faster and faster, but she keeps her loving vigil over her father's body and her mother. She performs her acts with the deepest love. She is a daughter in every sense of the word. She cannot be faulted for her service, and I believe the rewards for her Christlike service will be eternal.

I have counseled her on many occasions, and my last sentence to her is always the same, "Do what you need to do." I do have some observations I can share about Vivian's situation, which isn't all that unique. Many families face Vivian's decisions and challenges.

Mom's and Dad's fear of the rest home is unfounded, but real. When they investigated putting their parents in the rest home 40 years ago, or worse yet, when they investigated putting their grandparents in the "home" 60 years ago, the "homes" were truly hell holes. They saw nothing but filth, abuse, and misery. Most rest homes aren't that way anymore. Yes, there are good ones and bad ones, but the good ones are really nice, and even the bad ones are nothing like they were 50 years ago. Government regulations are very strict. Rest homes are literally the most regulated industry. The government watchdogs and the legal beagles help families police the homes by threatening suit if Mom or Dad is mistreated.

Before Mom and Dad become candidates for a rest home, you need to make sure that they frequently visit their friends in the rest homes. Chances are the friends will tell them that the "home" really isn't that bad. I have many friends in rest homes.

One of the ladies that worked with me for many years died a couple of weeks ago of breast cancer. She chose to go into the rest home so that she wouldn't be a big burden on her children. She stayed there for about 8 months before she died, and she liked it. It was her home. She had a bed, TV, telephone, dresser, her computer, couch, and a day bed for family members who wanted to stay the night.

I often went to visit her. I was lucky when I could catch her alone and just talk when one of her daughters or another visitor wasn't there. We would talk, and the nurses would give her pain medication, feed her, change her bed, or do dozens of other things for her. The family would come and go many times each day. They were there for her emotional support. They would oversee her physical support, but they were not burdened with it. Their love and support for their 63 year old mother was just as strong as Vivian's love and support for her parents, but somehow life was better for them. They weren't frantically meeting a schedule of support. Their own health and family relationships were not threatened by their mother's illness and pending death.

Parents, you need to know that you do not have to challenge your children's love when they suggest that you need continuous help in a long term care facility. It is not a disgrace. The kids have not abandoned you. If they will take care of you at home, they will take care of you in the rest home, and your relationship will be much nicer. Whether it is at home or in the care facility, realize that you are losing some of your independence, and surrender it gracefully with dignity.

Don't fight it. It is hard to be totally dependent. I have been there, and I know. But, loss of your dependency can foster a deep relationship with your family, if it is handled well. People who have a bitter attitude when they give up their independence hurt everyone who tries to help them, and people don't want to help if they get their nose bruised every time they try to do something.

Kids, don't fall into the guilt trap. Because you help a parent get into a rest home doesn't mean you don't love them. But, don't put them "away" in the rest home too early. Care for them as long as possible and preserve their independence as long as possible. Joel C. Dobris, author of *An Aging World*, points out that Mom and Dad want three things: (1) independence from the nursing home, (2) possession of their home, and (3) to pass an inheritance on to their children and grandchildren. Yet, the number of parents that will go in the rest homes in the next few years is staggering.

When Mom or Dad do have to give up their independence and go into the rest home, don't put them there to be forgotten. Just because their physical needs are met by the home, that doesn't mean that they don't need your love and emotional support. You don't need to do the physical tasks to help them, so spend more time just getting to know them better. Actually sit down and talk to them. They took care of you when you were an infant and totally dependent. Whether they like it or not, they will be totally dependent before they die. They will need help. Learn to fulfill their needs and return all they gave to you and more. You will be the better person, and there will be a warmth and beauty you have never experienced.

How to Finance the Rest Home

Putting Mom and Dad in the rest home is emotional, and it is expensive. Long term care isn't cheap for the provider or the recipient. Middle income American families are the ones that are the hardest hit by the rest home problem. The common scenario repeats itself over and over again.

In the scenario, Mom and Dad aren't broke, but they certainly aren't rich. They have a little pension, social security and some savings. Their house is paid for, so they can get by on the little bit they get each month. If they need more, they can take a little out of savings for special things and to help the kids or grandkids now and then. When Dad gets to the point where he needs constant care and Mom can't give all the care he needs, it is time to look for a rest home, i.e., a "continuous care facility" or "long term care facility."

The cost will be expensive. The family is faced with $3,000 to $6,000 per month bills, and that is something you don't take lightly. Mom is only getting $2,800 per month from the retirement and social security. What does she do? On kind of a practical level, there are a lot of "practical" things that she can do to work within the "system" of state and government regulations. And, on a different level, there are a few things the family can do in the form of legal "planning" that might help.

In addition to what Mom can do, the kids can help a lot if they emotionally let go of their "inheritance." Unless the kids are willing to go to the lengths that Vivian is going to, their inheritance may well be spent taking care of Mom and/or Dad in the care facility. (Believe me, Vivian isn't worried about her inheritance. In fact, the type of service she is giving is something no person in their right mind would do for money.) Mom and Dad don't have a responsibility to leave the kids a dime. Of course, that isn't the way they feel about it, because they want to leave the kids all they can. Unfortunately, a lot of kids feel like their parents owe it to them to leave a big inheritance, and when the rest home takes some of "their" inheritance they go berserk.

Parents of the baby boomers are in a position to leave their kids over $12 trillion. The transfer of this wealth will be the largest transfer of wealth in history. How the parents and kids handle that transfer could mean a lot more money for the kids. Handling the "inheritance" will probably be the largest monetary transaction the kids will ever handle. It is worth planning for. This book has already helped families put millions of extra dollars in their pockets, but that is another story.

"What is going to happen to the inheritance?" is not the question to ask when the rest home decision is made. Mom and Dad have the responsibility to provide for themselves—not to leave an inheritance. Of course, an inheritance is nice and Mom and Dad want desperately to leave one, but if they can pay their own way all of their life, they are doing great, and they have done everything the kids can expect. Everyone needs to keep a proper perspective when the rest home planning is made.

State and federal laws combine to form the set of rules that have to be followed in order to get government aid to help pay for long term care. The whole dynamic set of rules and regulations is a real can of worms. Your best bet is to go rest home shopping early. The better facilities have a specialist that will help you sort out the can of worms and walk through the maze of regulations. There are lots of tricks. For example, if a person who has already been accepted by Medicare is moved directly from a hospital where they have stayed for at least three nights and four days, the Medicare program will pick up the first 20 days at 100% and the next 21-100 days is split, so that Medicare will pick up all but $95.50 each day in the long term care facility and the family pays the rest.

Note that Medicare is the insurance program that everybody pays into all of their life, so they will supposedly be taken care of when they are old. A couple of months before retirement (or two years after becoming disabled), everyone should apply for Medicare. Medicare has two programs, "Medicare A" and "Medicare B." Medicare A covers hospital expenses and Medicare B covers medical and doctor expenses. You should always apply for both Medicare A and Medicare B. Medicaid is the "poor people's" aid program that only works when the family can prove that they are basically indigent.

Often, one of the goals in planning for the rest home is to structure the plan so Dad can qualify for Medicaid. It isn't easy to get Dad qualified. If Dad is single with no expectation of ever returning home, all of his assets have to be sold and the money has to be "spent down" to the point where he has less that $2,000 in total worth.

If Dad has an expectation of being able to return home within six months, the family won't have to sell his house to qualify for aid. Keeping the house helps Dad emotionally, because he still "has" his house, even though he may not be living there. A lot of the "Medicaid game" is dependent upon how well the facility specialist coaches you and how willing Dad's doctor is to play along. That doesn't mean that the specialist or the doctor has to do anything illegal or even shady, but they need to say the right things and give you the right cues at the right time. Everything is above board, but the procedure is delicate, and if you trip walking through the maze, it can be a big setback or you can be out of the game. Unfortunately, even the specialist usually won't tell you what you need to know.

It is real easy to get caught in the maze. When my Grandpa Elmer went into the facility, he was largely paralyzed with a stroke. His mind was good, and he was otherwise healthy—too healthy. He lived for over ten years in the facility. I went to see him often, and his kids saw him almost daily. He was on the patients' grievance board, and made real improvements in the care facility for the patients. He lead a group of thousands and thousands of men before his stroke, and he continued to be a leader in the facility. He was middle class and all of his sources of income in retirement just about paid for the rest home. Several years after his death, I discovered he had been cheated for seven years. The family had lost over $200,000! The law says that a person automatically qualifies for full coverage of the rest home expenses by Medicaid after they have paid for the facility care for three years. They don't have to spend all of their money.

When I discovered that we had been duped, I demanded, "Why didn't anyone ever tell us?" The answer was, "Nobody will ever tell you." The facility wants your check, not the government's hassle to get money. If Grandpa Elmer was still alive, we could have gone back and claimed an overpayment, but he was dead. Don't you love the whole system?

Shop for the best care facility. Don't just look at the price. Ask lots of questions. Find out all you can before you start filling out forms and handing over financial information. Last week I worked with a lady who lost a full month of eligibility and stacked up a lot of medical bills during the month. She really is indigent and should qualify for Medicaid assistance, but she got a check for a workers compensation claim and deposited it in her checking account. When it posted at the bank, it brought her checking account balance to $2,004. For one day she was just over the $2,000 limit. She didn't qualify for Medicaid that month and the nearly $50,000 in medical bills she racked up was ineligible for government payment. The hospital and doctors aren't happy, because they lapped up the $2,000 in ten seconds flat, and there is no other source of income if they can't turn to the government. In her case, it is in everyone's best interest to help the patient qualify for as much government aid as possible.

In case you haven't figured it out, the government only helps poor people. Unless Dad is in for the long haul, the inheritance has to be gone before the government will kick in anything—no matter how long or how much Dad has paid into the system.

When I was sick, I couldn't work for a long time. When you are a 28 year old man, 5'9", and weigh 85 pounds with no hair or eye lashes, it is really hard to convince a law firm you are the man for the job. Even McDonalds questions your ability to flip burgers. Before I got sick, we had done everything right. Even as students we only had a house payment to worry about. We had equity in the house. We owned the cars and furniture outright. We even had a little money in the bank. When the hospital bills hit, everything was gone in a flash. I needed government help to keep my family from being homeless. We never got a dime. In fact, our last savings went to pay income taxes for the little analytical chemistry company I had started and which we lost because I got cancer. The government was a big help—not! We didn't actually lose everything, because our parents were in a position where they could step in and save us. But, I can see how a family of five can be put literally on the street, through no fault of their own.

You can tell I have a warm spot in my heart for government aid programs. You will too, by the time you get Mom or Dad settled in the long term care facility. (Note that the government doesn't call the place a "rest home." The government calls it a "long term care facility," so I had better refer to it properly from here on out.)

If the government programs won't help until all of the inheritance is spent, isn't there anything the family can do to save their inheritance and still take care of Dad when he goes in the facility? Yes, maybe.

Everyone wants to sell the house as soon as Dad hits the care facility. When my other grandpa, Levi, went in the care facility, there was always a chance he would make it out and return home. He actually rallied quite a bit under the care of the facility. He gained weight, got more mobile, went to physical therapy, and showed improvement in lots of ways. When he first went in the care facility, he fought like a mad man, and even though we went to see him almost every day for the almost 2 years he was there, he never forgave us for putting him in that place. He was mad at us, but the fact was, he was a lot happier and healthier there than he was at home—his home. He did his own gardening until he was 93 years old, and he didn't want to give up his independence. He called my father (his son) every name in the book for putting him in the facility. I was in trouble too, because I had taken the oath on my sacred honor never to put him in the "home." When it was truly in Grandpa's best interest, we violated the oath. We did hold off until his mind was very confused, and he fell in his backyard. He would have frozen to death had a friend not found him and helped him back into the house. Even after he went in the care facility, we always held out some hope that he might get well enough to go home again.

I am making a point of this "possibility of returning home" because as long as there is a possibility of going home, the family doesn't have to sell the house. The government is going to hold out every possibility of hope also, because it is in everyone's best interest to have Grandpa get better, leave the facility and have a place to go home to. In Grandpa Levi's case, we would not have had to sell the house in order to qualify for government assistance. Before the decision to sell the house is made, take a good hard look at the situation. The house can be a lifesaver if it isn't sold immediately.

If the spouse is still living at home, he or she doesn't have to sell the house. The spouse that is at home doesn't have to spend down his or her half of the wealth before the other spouse will qualify for Medicaid. Good news! But, the spouse in the care facility has to spend down his or her half of the wealth in order to qualify. Bad news!

In Grandpa Levi's case, he never got any government Medicaid assistance. He did go from the hospital to the care facility, and so Medicare picked up the first 20 days and then paid all but the $95.50 a day for the next 80 days. After that, he paid the bills for over a year and a half. He had his house and twenty or thirty thousand dollars in savings when he went into the long term care facility. He also had a little pension from the post office (imagine a postal supervisor today living to be 95 years old without getting killed on the job), and he had a little social security.

The facility's bill was about $3,000 per month. With the social security and the pension, he had about $1,800 per month. Rather than selling the house, we rented it furnished for $1,000 per month. With the pension, social security, and rent he had a total income of about $2,800 per month. We took $200 from his savings to supplement the income and pay the $3,000 long term care facility bill. Actually, the $200 was from the interest on his savings. He didn't have to worry about income taxes anymore, because everything went to medical expenses which were tax deductible and offset his entire income. His estate didn't grow any while he was in the facility, in fact it shrank some. But, most of my father's inheritance was maintained. It wasn't a lot, but my father, his only child, was happy Grandpa could take care of himself financially and there was a little left over. Grandpa was never rich, but he had played his cards perfectly, and he won the game.

Don't forget to look at the possibilities of using Mom's and Dad's assets as money generators rather than just liquidating them. Rally all of their sources of income, and go through the maze of regulations to try and get government assistance. If you can't get the government assistance, don't become bitter. Be grateful that Mom and Dad saved and can take care of themselves financially. You may not get an inheritance, but at least Mom and Dad are independent financially. Knowing they kept their financial independence should make them feel good and make you feel good. May we all do as well!

There are long range planning opportunities that a family can use to protect assets from being eaten up in paying for the rest home. However, the new laws and emotional struggle required to do the planning and get the government aid makes the opportunities almost worthless for most families.

Long Term Care Planning

Frankly, the Clinton administration put long term care planning out of business. Before the new laws, Mom and Dad could create trusts for themselves, move property into the trusts and keep it out of the reach of the government when one of them went in the long term care facility. With their property safely in the trust they created for themselves, they could qualify for government assistance, and they got it. The family could keep their wealth and Medicaid would still pay for the long term care. Today, basically any trust that Mom or

Dad creates within 5 years of applying for government assistance *will not* remove the trust's assets from the government's reach.

The Omnibus Budget Reconciliation Act of 1993 almost totally wiped out any trust planning for older and disabled Americans, so that they can qualify for Medicaid. Just to make sure planning for long term care in rest homes was dead, the Balanced Budget Act of 1997 did some fine tuning on previous laws. As the law stands now, planning for long term care using Medicaid is dead in the water for most families. In fact, the new legislation makes it a criminal offense for an advisor, like a lawyer or financial planner, to even discuss ways to structure a family's assets so that they will qualify for Medicaid when Mom or Dad needs government help. Is that constitutional? That is like saying the government is going to jail anyone who helps you do tax planning. Lawyers and financial planners are scared to death to even mention planning for the "M" word.

Even if you can get someone to discuss Medicaid with you, few families looking at putting Mom or Dad in the long term care facility can wait five years after making a gift, setting up a special trust, or taking any other planning action. Yes, it takes five years after a plan is set in place before the government loses its right to come in and unwind your plan. If the plan is put in place and then Mom or Dad applies for Medicaid, the government can potentially disqualify them from getting Medicaid forever. They take the amount of money (property value) that is gifted, put in the trust or otherwise "disposed of" within five years of the application date and divide that amount by the monthly cost of the rest home. The resulting number is the number of months Mom and Dad are disqualified for Medicaid help. For example, if $250,000 is moved (the summer house is given to the kids) and the cost of the rest home is $3,000 per month, then if Mom and Dad apply for Medicaid within five years of the date of the gift, they will be disqualified for 83 months ($250,000 divided by $3,000 is 83). That is almost 7 years.

Don't be mistaken. The living revocable trust is neutral in all of this Medicaid stuff. It doesn't disqualify you for Medicaid, but it doesn't help you plan and move property outside of the government's consideration when you apply for Medicaid. Remember, when you use the living revocable trust, the government says you are not giving the property away. For income taxes, estate taxes, Medicaid qualification, etc., the government says it is still yours, even when it is in the revocable trust. In order to "give" the property away you have to use an irrevocable trust of some type.

The government always says it is watching out for older Americans, but under all of the rhetoric, it is obvious that the government is hell bent on reducing its obligation to take care of the old or sick in our country. The new laws devastate the lower middle class—basically the elderly in America.

For most people, rest home planning is history. However, there are still some special circumstances where a person can create a trust for long term care planning and even get a benefit out of the trust during their lifetime. Having said that, I don't hold out much hope for your family actually being able to use any of the techniques. For example, it is possible for parents to set up trusts for a disabled child and still have themselves (the parents) qualify for Medicaid within the five year period. But, most families don't have a disabled child they have to plan for. Because a living revocable trust is powerless against the Medicaid laws, the trust that the family will have to establish for their disabled child is a special trust which carefully has to follow the Omnibus Budget Reconciliation Act of 1993 Sections 1396p(d)(4)(A) and (C). Even with all of the planning, when the disabled person dies, the trust has to be liquidated to reimburse the government for all of the expenses it has paid on behalf of the disabled person during his or her life.

"Income only trusts," "charitable disability trusts," "Miller trusts," and others with weird names can be established and Mom and Dad can still qualify for Medicaid, but they are all so specific that they are useless for most families. They must each follow very specific rules, and the government gets its pound of flesh when the beneficiaries die, because the government gets all of the money remaining in the trust to reimburse it for all of the money it has put out on behalf of the beneficiaries. Basically, any trust that is created by Mom or Dad that gives them any continuing benefit, such as supporting a child, will not help them protect their property and qualify for Medicaid assistance.

Trusts Created By Third Parties

If Mom and Dad cannot create a trust for themselves that will protect property from being consumed by the rest home, the logical next question is, "Can someone other than Mom or Dad create a trust which can benefit Mom and Dad and still not be considered when they apply for Medicaid?" The answer is yes, if you follow the rules. For example, a parent can create the trust for a disabled adult child, who they have no legal responsibility to support, and the disabled person can still qualify for Medicaid. (This is different than the scenario above where the object was to qualify Mom and Dad for Medicaid.) A child can create the trust for Mom and Dad, and because the trust is not a "self created trust," Mom and Dad can apply for Medicaid, and the trust property will not be considered as their "wealth" in the government's calculations made to see if they qualify for Medicaid. No, Dad cannot create a trust for Mom. The person creating the trust (the grantor or settlor) has to be a person who doesn't have any "support obligation" for the beneficiaries of the trust, i.e., the settlor must not have a relationship with a beneficiary where the settlor is legally obligated to provide food, shelter, clothing and other necessities of life for the beneficiary.

The trust has to specifically state that the trustees can only use the income and principal of the trust to supply special nonsupport needs of the beneficiary. As soon as the trust says that the trust property can be used for the "health, education, maintenance and support" of the beneficiary, the whole trust is available to be consumed by the government to pay for the rest home. In order to make the trust protect the trust property from being sucked in by the rest home, the income and principal of the trust cannot be "actually available" to the beneficiary. These special trusts are called either "discretionary spendthrift trusts" or "supplemental care trusts."

It is worth summarizing the rules for these special trusts. In order to effectively shield the trust assets from government inclusion in Medicaid qualifications, the trust has to be created by a third party. For example, the parents must create the trust for the children, or the children have to create the trust for the parents. The person creating the trust cannot have a relationship where there is a duty of support owing the beneficiary. The intent and the stated purpose of the trust must be for nonsupport of the beneficiary. And, the trust must be funded with the assets of the person creating the trust, not with the assets of the beneficiary. The trusts should each have a spendthrift provision in them.

The laws allow these special nonsupport trusts for a good reason. If the individual setting up the trust doesn't have a legal obligation to give anything to the beneficiary who is disabled or is in the long term care facility, it is in the government's best interests and in the public's best interests to have the individual give all of the support possible to the beneficiary. People would be a lot less likely to give to a disabled or elderly person who qualifies for Medicaid if they knew that their gift would disqualify the individual for Medicaid funding. Therefore, it is in everyone's best interests to permit such trusts and continue the beneficiary's Medicaid funding.

The law says that the trust must be funded with the assets of the grantor of the trust. Stated another way, if the son sets up one of the trusts for his parents, his property has to be used to fund the trust. But, if Mom and Dad happened to have made a gift to the son before the trust was established or even happen to make a gift to the son after the trust is established, the law says that the trust cannot be used to disqualify them from getting Medicaid assistance. Of course there cannot be a contract or even an agreement between the son and Mom and Dad about gifts, trusts, support, and the like, otherwise the creation of the trust based on giving of gifts would be fraud.

If all the t's are crossed and the i's are dotted, then the trust established by the gift receiver will probably not disqualify the beneficiaries (donors of the gift) from receiving Medicaid support. In order to get it just right, there cannot be any implied agreement to use the gifted funds for the subsequent funding of a trust. An attorney needs to represent the gift givers (donors) and make it clear to them that once they make the gift it is the receiver's, and the receiver can do whatever he or she wants with the gift. When everything is done properly, the government cannot legally presume that the gift was used to fund the trust, but it would be best if, in fact, the gifted funds were not put into the trust created for the donor/beneficiary.

This sounds great. Mom and Dad give a big gift to the son, wink at him, and he happens to establish a discretionary spendthrift trust for them. Remember, there are bad tax consequences associated with gifting. The gift tax raises its ugly head, and the step-up in basis rules associated with gifted property come back to haunt the son. Additionally, the Medicaid rules have that really ugly five year rule which applies to gifts. Everything adds up, and you have to admit Congress has been real busy figuring out how to squeeze every last dime out of Mom and Dad when misfortune falls upon them and they need long term care.

Playing with trusts and trying to qualify for Medicaid is something you shouldn't try at home. An attorney specializing in "elder law" or trusts should walk the family through the maze, because the government is gunning for people who try to receive Medicaid benefits. It doesn't matter whether or not they should be entitled to the benefits because they have paid into the system all of their lives.

Even after all of the discouraging laws, playing the long term care game early and with skill can mean a lot of money to the family. Start investigating before the time comes to make the "rest home decision." Asset protection isn't something that is slopped together when the tragedy is bearing down on the family. It is important to have Mom and Dad plan early for the possibility of going to a rest home. How you approach the planning with them may set the tone for your relationship for years to come. Maybe after reading this chapter everyone will have a better perspective.

Conclusion

Take The Path Around The Traps

Your plans for life, your estate plans, and your asset protection plans all meld together and give order to the way you live your life. Some people never have any plans. They move from financial disaster to financial disaster. Physical disasters often cannot be prevented, but financial disasters can almost always be prevented. Families and individuals who ignore what this book teaches will never have a significant accumulation of wealth. If you want to be wealthy, you must use the tools of wealth that the law has available for you. The will, living revocable trust, living will, durable power of attorney, and durable power of attorney for health care are five of the most basic tools. Use them!

The Asset Protection Tips given in this book are easy to implement. Just taking the few steps outlined in them could be the most important thing you ever do to protect your family from a life of poverty. The steps have to be taken now. If you already have a problem, such as a lawsuit or a bankruptcy, it is obviously too late to plan on avoiding that problem. But, your planning can certainly help you avoid future problems that stand in your path to success.

You are unique. The path to success you must follow and the plan you develop for yourself will be unique to you. The same plan won't work for every person. The tools of wealth are always the same, but how they are used to build a fortune is unique to every person. The strategies we have gone over are always the same, even though they are uniquely woven together to form each plan. Sometimes it is difficult to know exactly how to construct a plan for life, estate plan, or asset protection plan.

Kristy and I had a problem designing our asset protection plan. Because I am a lawyer, I have a fairly high exposure to lawsuits and activities that could threaten our family wealth. If one spouse is a professional with a high liability exposure, most couples will try to protect property by dividing it, using a his trust and a her trust, so that the other spouse owns and controls the family property. In response to her experiences while I was down with cancer, Kristy took some actions which make it difficult to use a his and her trust system and protect the majority of our assets in her trust.

When I was sick, the legal system took us to the cleaners, even though I was a lawyer. Kristy learned that she couldn't blindly trust doctors, lawyers, or any other professionals. She also came face to face with the reality that she might have to support herself and our three children. What could she do?

Kristy overreacted. Nearly 10 years to the day after I graduated from the Brigham Young University Law School, Kristy graduated from the same law school. When we married each other, as youngsters, we never imagined that we would both be lawyers.

I know, it is hard to believe that we could both stoop so low as to become lawyers, but life takes strange turns. In all seriousness, we find great satisfaction in helping people avoid the financial tragedies and legal disasters that we struggled so hard to get through. Yes, we do understand you, and we are different than most lawyers. We make our living helping our clients prevent legal problems, not laying legal traps and capitalizing on someone's legal misfortunes. I have flown millions of miles and given thousands of speeches in an attempt to help people reach their financial potential. If you have a group that should hear our message, please call our office in Provo, Utah, and I will be happy to schedule a speech. I am ranked among the top of the nationally recognized speakers. We want our message to be disseminated as far and as wide as possible. It is important.

We hope that this book has taught you to recognize a few legal traps and that you will have the courage to take the path around the traps—the path to peace of mind, greater wealth, more success, and a happier life.

Appendices

Appendix 1

Exemption Equivalent, Unified Credit and Estate Tax Rate Tables

Year of Death	Exemption Equivalent Amount	Unified Credit Amount
1997	$600,000	$192,800
1998	$625,000	$202,050
1999	$650,000	$211,300
2000-2001	$675,000	$220,550
2002-2003	$700,000	$229,800
2004	$850,000	$287,300
2005	$950,000	$326,300
2006	$1,000,000	$345,800

Unified Transfer (Gift and Estate) Tax Rate Table

Column A	Column B	Column C	Column D
If the Taxable Amount is: Over	But not over	Then the tax on the amount in Column A is:	And the % rate of tax on the excess over the amount in Column A is:
0	$10,000	0	18%
$10,000	20,000	$1,800	20%
20,000	40,000	3,800	22%
40,000	60,000	8,200	24%
60,000	80,000	13,000	26%
80,000	100,000	18,200	28%
100,000	150,000	23,800	30%
150,000	250,000	38,800	32%
250,000	500,000	70,800	34%
500,000	750,000	155,800	37%
750,000	1,000,000	248,300	39%
1,000,000	1,250,000	345,800	41%
1,250,000	1,500,000	448,300	43%
1,500,000	2,000,000	555,800	45%
2,000,000	2,500,000	780,800	49%
2,500,000	3,000,000	1,025,800	53%
3,000,000	---	1,290,800	55%

Appendix 2

Trust Planning Information

Client Personal Data

Full Name ____

Name as commonly used ____________________________________

Other names you have used _________________________________

Date of Birth______________ Social Security # ________________

Home Address ____

City______________County__________State____Zip____________

Home Phone (____)_____________Work Phone (____)___________

Employer ____

Business Address ____

Occupation/Duties ____

Country of Citizenship _____________________________________

Marital Status: Single___ Divorced___ Widowed___ Married _______

Date of Current Marriage ___________________________________

List all previous marriages, if any, by spouse and year. Indicate whether the marriage ended by death or divorce and the year it ended.

Spouse	Marriage Date	Death/Divorce	Date
____________________	________________	____________	__________
____________________	________________	____________	__________

Children (Include Children Who Have Died)

1. Child's Full Name_________________________Date of Birth _______

Living: Yes___No___ Adopted: Yes___No___ Married: Yes___No___

Child's Spouse's Full Name if married ___________________________

Address ____

City__________________________________State_____Zip ________

Business Ability: Excellent <--->Poor

Number of Children________Approximate ages _________________

2. Child's Full Name______________________________Date of Birth ________

Living: Yes___No___ Adopted: Yes___No___ Married: Yes____No____

Child's Spouse's Full Name if married __________________________________

Address ____

City____State________Zip ________

Business Ability: Excellent <-->Poor

Number of Children__________Approximate ages ______________________

3. Child's Full Name______________________________Date of Birth ________

Living: Yes___No___ Adopted: Yes___No___ Married: Yes____No____

Child's Spouse's Full Name if married __________________________________

Address ____

City____State_______Zip _________

Business Ability: Excellent <-->Poor

Number of Children__________Approximate ages ______________________

Your Parents:

	Father	Mother
Alive:	Yes/No	Yes/No

Name ____

Address (if alive): ____

City____State_______Zip _________

Approximate Ages ____

Do you expect an inheritance from your parents or someone else?

Yes_______ No ______ Approximate Amount __________________________

From Whom______________________

Your Brothers and Sisters:

Number of Siblings: Living_______ Dead__________

Sibling to be contacted if necessary:

Name____________________________________ Phone (_____) ____________

Address ____

City_________________________________State________Zip ______________

Spouse Personal Data

Full Name ____

Name as commonly used ________________________________

Other names used _____________________________________

Date of Birth_______________Social Security #_________________

Employer____________________________ Phone (_____) __________

Business Address _____________________________________

Occupation/Duties_____________________________________

List all previous marriages, if any, by spouse and year. Indicate whether the marriage ended by death or divorce and the year it ended.

Spouse	Marriage Date	Death/Divorce	Date
________________	__________________	______________	___________
________________	__________________	______________	___________

Spouse's Parents:

	Father	Mother
Alive:	Yes/No	Yes/No

Name ____

Address (if alive) _____________________________________

City________________________________State_______Zip __________

Approximate Ages _____________________________________

Do you expect an inheritance from your parents or someone else?

Yes______No______ Approximate Amount _______________________

From Whom ____

Spouse's Brothers and Sisters:

Number of Siblings: Living________Dead__________________________

Sibling to be contacted if necessary:

Name__________________________________Telephone ___________

Address ____

City___________________________________State________Zip _______

Trust and Will Information

Personal Representatives:

Who do you (and your spouse, if applicable) wish to have serve as your Personal Representatives? (The person who administers your will.) Please name at least three persons in the order you wish them to serve. The spouse will usually be the first choice.

Client	Spouse
1. ____________________	1. ____________________
2. ____________________	2. ____________________
3. ____________________	3. ____________________
4. ____________________	4. ____________________

Trustees:

Who do you (and your spouse, if applicable) wish to have serve as Trustees for your Trust when you (and your spouse, if applicable) can no longer serve? Name at least three persons and/or institutions such as banks. No institution need be named. The same person can serve as Personal Representative and Trustee. The surviving spouse can be the sole Trustee as long as he or she can serve. You may require two or more of the Trustees to act jointly.

1. Name(s) ____

   Address(es) ____

2. Name(s) ____

   Address(es) ____

3. Name(s) ____

   Address(es) ____

Special instructions: (act singly, act jointly, other)

____

____

____

Guardians:

In the event that both you and your spouse, if applicable, die, a guardian must be named for each of your minor children. The same guardian does not need to be named for all of the children, i.e., a different guardian could be named for each child, but usually one guardian is named for all the children. You may place restrictions on the guardians, such as the guardian must raise the children in your home, the guardian must have a certain marital status, or the guardian must be in good health. Name three guardians in the order you want them to serve.

1. Name(s) ______________________________

   Address(es)______________________________

   Restrictions______________________________

2. Names(s) ______________________________

   Address(es)______________________________

   Restrictions______________________________

3. Names(s) ______________________________

   Address(es)______________________________

   Restrictions______________________________

Distribution of estate after both you and your spouse are dead. (It is assumed that the entire estate will be held for the surviving spouse during his or her life.) For example: I/We wish all of our assets to be distributed equally among the children. If one child predeceases us, his or her share should go to his or her children (or spouse). (Designate who, what, how much, and the time and manner of each division, i.e., all or part, immediately or at specific ages, equal among children, 1/3 at age 25, 1/3 at age 30, remainder at age 35, etc.)

____

____

____

____

Additional distribution considerations: If all of your issue predecease you and your spouse, then what? For example: If all of our issue predecease us, then hold the estate in trust for my parents and my spouse's parents. When they are dead, divide the trust equally among my and my spouse's brothers and sisters or their issue. Because our families are small, there is a chance that all of our "heirs" may predecease us. If there are no heirs, we want to give all of our property to the XYZ Church.

____

____

____

____

Dollies and Doilies:

Most personal effects can be disposed of in a personal letter authorized in the will or as a listing as part of the trust, but there might be some very special personal effects such as family heirlooms that should be specifically mentioned in the will and/or trust. Please list such special items.

Item Description	Current Owner	To Whom	Contingent Person
____________	____________	________	____________
____________	____________	________	____________
____________	____________	________	____________
____________	____________	________	____________

If you wish to make a bequest to a charity after your death, please write the circumstances under which such a gift should be made. (After my wife and I are dead, 10% of our estate should be given to the XYZ Foundation to be used for breast cancer research.)

____

____

____

____

____

General Information

A. Accountant

Firm Name____

Contact Name ____

Address ____

City ___________________________ State _____ Zip Code _____

Phone Number (_____)_____________________________________

B. Bank

Bank ____

Contact Name ____

Address ____

City ______________________________ State _____ Zip Code _____

Phone Number (_____) ____________________________________

C. Broker

Firm Name ____

Contact Name ____

Address ____

City _________________________ State _____ Zip Code ___________

Phone Number (_____) ____________________________________

D. Casualty Insurance Agent

Company Name ____

Contact Name ____

Address ____

City _________________________ State _____ Zip Code ___________

Phone Number (_____) ____________________________________

E. Financial Planner

Firm Name ____

Contact Name ____

Address ____

City _________________________ State _____ Zip Code ___________

Phone Number (_____) ____________________________________

F. Life Insurance Agent

Company Name ____

Contact Name ____

Address ____

City _________________________ State _____ Zip Code ___________

Phone Number (_____) ____________________________________

G. Other

Company Name ____

Contact Name ____

Address ____

City _________________________ State _____ Zip Code ___________

Phone Number (____) _____________________________________

Appendix 3

Estimate of Estate Value

Instructions:

Estimate the value of each asset and the amount of each liability. You shouldn't have to look up exact amounts. Remember, this is only an estimate. Estimate assets at a high value, because inflation must be taken into account.

Assets	Estimated Value
Personal Residence	$ ______________
Investment Real Estate	______________
Vehicles/Boats, etc.	______________
Savings/CDs/Cash	______________
Stocks/Bonds	______________
Life Insurance (death benefits)	______________
IRAs	______________
Retirement that will go to heirs	______________
Annuities	______________
Small Business (value of portion you "own")	______________
Personal Property/Household/Jewelry	______________
Collectibles/Art	______________
Other	______________
Total Assets	$ ______________

Liabilities	
Home Mortgage	______________
Other Real Estate Mortgages	______________
Vehicle Debts	______________
Business Debts (if business is in your estate)	______________
Other Debts	______________
Amount you plan to leave to a charity	______________
Total Liabilities	$ ______________

Total Estate Value (Assets minus Liabilities) $ ______________

Glossary

Glossary

A/B Trust - A type of living revocable trust used by married couples. In this type of living trust, two trusts (trust A and trust B) are created at the time the first spouse dies. By dividing the couple's estate into two trusts at the first death, each spouse can pass the maximum amount of property allowed to avoid federal estate taxes. One trust, usually trust A, is often referred to as the marital deduction trust and the other trust, usually trust B, is often referred to as the shelter trust.

Accumulation Trust - A type of trust which retains and accumulates income for longer than a year, instead of paying all of the income out to the beneficiaries at least annually. These types of trusts are also known as complex trusts.

Administrator - The person designated by the court to manage and distribute a probate estate when there isn't a will. If there is a will, the person so designated is called the executor (male), executrix (female), or personal representative.

Adult - Any person over the age of 18 or 21 years. The age of an adult depends on specific state laws.

Affidavit - A sworn, written statement executed under oath in front of a witness or witnesses.

Affidavit of Domicile - A sworn, written statement verifying city, county and state of residence.

Affidavit of Survivorship - A sworn, written statement verifying the identity of the survivor in a joint tenancy or other property ownership relationship.

Ancillary probate - A probate proceeding conducted in a state other than the state where the decedent lived and the primary probate occurs.

Annual Exclusion - The amount of property the IRS allows a person to gift to another person during a calendar year before a gift tax is assessed and/or a gift tax return must be filed. The current amount is $10,000 per year. There is no limit to the number of people to whom such $10,000 gifts can be made. To qualify for the annual exclusion, the gift must be one that a recipient can enjoy immediately and have full control over.

Ante-nuptial Agreement - A contract between two potential marriage partners specifying how the property owned by each prior to marriage and owned individually or jointly during marriage will be divided should the couple divorce.

Ascertainable Standard - The IRS defined standard which governs the use of trust B property and prevents the property from being considered part of the trustee's property for estate tax purposes. The standard is defined as "health, education, maintenance and support" of the surviving spouse and children.

Asset Protection - Protecting your property from legal problems and taxes during your life and after your death.

Basis - A tax term, which refers to the original or acquisition value of a property, used to determine the amount of tax that will be assessed. The basis is deducted from the sales price of the property when it is sold to determine the profit or loss.

Beneficiary - The person(s) or organization(s) who receive(s) the benefits of trust property held under the terms of a trust.

Bequest - An old legal term meaning to give a gift or leave property under the terms of a will.

Bond - An insurance policy used to ensure a legal representative will do his job and not misuse or steal funds he is controlling. The bond guarantees that a certain amount of money will be paid if a party is injured due to acts of the legal representative.

By Right of Representation - Common terminology for the Latin term, Per Stirpes. This is the most common way of distributing an estate such that if one of the children is dead, his children share equally in his share of the estate distribution. This term is often summarized by the phrase, "if the parent is dead his children stand in his shoes."

Charitable Remainder Trust - A trust used to make large donations of property or money to a charity so the person making the gift or donation can obtain a tax advantage. In a charitable remainder trust, the donor reserves the right to use the trust property during his life or some other specified time period, and when the agreed period is over the property goes to the charity.

Codicil - A written change or amendment to a will.

Community Property - Some state laws require that all assets acquired during a marriage belong equally to both spouses, except for gifts and inheritances given specifically to one spouse. The eight states with such laws are known as community property states. The eight states are Arizona, California, Idaho, Louisiana, Nevada, New Mexico, Texas and Washington. Puerto Rico also uses the community property system, and Wisconsin has a modified community property system.

Complex Trust - See Accumulation Trust

Conservator - A person appointed to be legally responsible for the management of property and money belonging to a minor or incompetent person. The conservator may act as the guardian or the guardian may be a separate person and the conservator will just work with the guardian.

Conservatorship - A court controlled program where a conservator is appointed by the court to manage the monetary affairs of a person(s) who is unable to manage his/her own affairs.

Contract - An agreement between two or more parties. It may be oral, but generally it is written.

Creditor - A person or institution to whom money is owed.

Custodial Parent - The parent given custody and responsibility by the divorce court for the children of the divorced couple.

Decedent - The person who has died.

Death taxes - Taxes levied on the property of a deceased person. Federal death taxes are usually referred to as estate taxes. Local and state death taxes are often referred to as inheritance taxes, or simply death taxes.

Deed - A written document used to evidence ownership and/or transfer title to real estate.

Debtor - A person who owes money.

Devise - A legal term referring to real estate which passes through a will.

Disclaimer - The refusal of a beneficiary to accept property willed to him. When a disclaimer is made, the property is generally transferred to the person next in line under the will. A disclaimer is also called a renunciation.

Dispositive Provision - A clause in a will or trust that gives away property.

Disposition - The parting with or giving away of property.

Disinherit - Cutting a person off from his or her inheritance in an estate where he or she would have been a natural heir.

Doctrine of Independent Significance - The legal power to make reference in one document to an independent document that stands alone. By making reference to the independent document, the law will allow the independent document to be incorporated into the document making reference to it.

Domicile - The state or county which is the primary residence of a person.

Donee - A person who receives a gift.

Donor - A person who makes a gift.

Durable Power of Attorney - A document established by an individual (the principal) granting another person (the agent) the right and authority to handle the financial and other affairs of the principal. The Durable Power of Attorney survives through the period of incompetency of the principal.

Durable Power of Attorney for Health Care - A document established by an individual (the principal) granting another person (the agent) the right and authority to handle matters related to the health care of the principal.

Due-on-sale Clause - A clause in a mortgage document which requires that the mortgage be paid in full if the encumbered property is transferred.

Escheat - A legal word that describes the situation where property transfers to the ownership of the state government because there are no legal inheritors to claim it.

Estate - The aggregate of all assets and debts held (owned) by an individual during his or her life or at the time of his or her death.

Estate Taxes - Taxes imposed on the "privilege" of transferring property by reason of death. Estate tax is most commonly used in reference to the tax imposed by the Federal Government rather than the state government. Estate taxes are intended to raise revenue for the government and break up a family's wealth, so that the nation's wealth doesn't concentrate in the hands of a few families.

Executor/ Executrix - The person (male/female) named in a will to manage a decedent's estate. The more modern term is a "personal representative," which removes any reference to the sex of the person.

Exemption Equivalent - When property is given as a gift or passed to heirs as part of an estate, it is subject to federal estate and gift tax laws. Each person is given a tax credit (the "unified credit") that can be used to offset the tax assessed against a specific amount of property. The amount of property that results in a tax exactly equal to the unified credit is known as the "exemption equivalent" (see Appendix 1 for exemption equivalent values). Technically, no property is exempt from federal estate and gift taxes, but the term exemption equivalent is commonly used. Stated another way, the unified credit is equal to the amount of tax due on a gift or estate transfer of property that has a value equal to the exemption equivalent amount.

Family Trust - Another name for a living trust.

Fiduciary - A person with the legal duty to act primarily for another's benefit in a position of trust, good faith, candor and responsibility. "Fiduciary" is often used as an alternative term for "trustee."

Fiduciary Duty - The duty of a fiduciary to act in a position of trust, good faith, candor and responsibility, on behalf of another. The duty is one of the best defined responsibilities under the law and is very strictly enforced by the courts.

Fraud - The use of deception for unlawful gain.

General Power of Attorney - A legal document that, when properly executed, gives one person (the agent) full legal authority to act on behalf of another (the principal). The scope of the document can be as broad or narrow as you desire as defined in the document. A general power of attorney becomes invalid when the principal dies or becomes incompetent.

Gift - A transfer of property without receiving some benefit in return. The person making the transfer cannot be obligated in any way to make the transfer.

Gift Taxes - Taxes levied by the Federal Government on gifts. Gift taxes and estate taxes have been "merged" into a single tax called the "unified tax."

Grantor - The person who establishes a trust and transfers assets into it. Other terms for the "grantor" include "trustor" and "settlor."

Grantor Trust - A trust in which the person establishing the trust retains enough "ownership rights" or "incidents of ownership" that the person is treated by the IRS as the owner of the trust assets for tax purposes. The right to revoke the trust is sufficient to make the trust a grantor trust.

Gross Estate - The total value of an estate at the date of the decedent's death. The value is determined before debts and other "deductions" are subtracted from the estate value.

Guarantor - A party who guarantees repayment of a loan, using their own assets if necessary.

Guardian - A person designated by court appointment and given the responsibility of managing the personal affairs of a minor child or a person that is legally incompetent to manage his or her own affairs.

Heir - A person who, by law, inherits property from a deceased relative who didn't leave any type of will or trust which distributes his or her property after death. The term is more "loosely" used to refer to a person who receives property from a decedent through any means.

Heir Head - A person who inherits property, other than brains, from his or her parents.

Heirloom - A personal possession that usually has a sentimental value which exceeds its monetary value.

Holographic Will - A do-it-yourself handwritten will. To be valid this will must be totally in your own handwriting, signed and dated. About 20 states allow holographic wills, but it is best to have a more formal will.

Homestead Laws - State laws which protect your house, clothing, and personal property, up to a specific dollar amount, from being taken away by most types of lawsuits or bankruptcies.

Household Items - The phrase in a will which indicates everything which may be used for the convenience of the house such as tables, chairs, bedding, etc. Apparel, books, weapons, and the like are not included.

Incapacitated - A person who is legally incapable of managing his or her own business affairs. A person may be permanently or temporarily incapacitated. A probate court usually decides if a person is incapacitated or not. "Incapacitated" is often used interchangeably with "incompetent."

Incidents of Ownership - All or any management control over a trust or an insurance policy. In relation to an insurance policy, incidents of ownership include the right to change the beneficiaries, borrow cash value, and change the ownership, among other rights.

Income Tax - A tax assessed on gain made by an individual or entity.

Incompetent - A person who is legally incapable of managing his or her own business affairs. A person may be permanently or temporarily incompetent. A probate court usually decides if a person is incompetent or not. "Incompetent" is often used interchangeably with "incapacitated."

Independent Trustee - A trustee who is unrelated to the person who establishes a trust (the grantor) and the beneficiaries of the trust. Unrelated attorneys, banks, corporations, etc., are usually chosen to act as independent trustees. The IRS requires a trust to have an independent trustee if the trust is to achieve certain estate tax and income tax benefits available to irrevocable trusts (not living trusts).

Inherit - To take or receive property by legal right from a deceased person.

Inheritance Tax - A tax imposed upon the transfer of property from a deceased person's estate. "Inheritance Tax" is a term which is usually applied to the taxes charged by a state, where as the taxes imposed by the Federal Government are usually referred to as estate taxes.

Inter Vivos Revocable Trust - One name for a living trust. "Inter vivos" is Latin for "between the living."

Intestate - To die without a will or other valid estate transfer devise.

Intestate Succession - The order of persons entitled to received property distributed by a state court when the deceased failed to write a will or trust, or the will or trust has failed to legally distribute the deceased person's property.

Irrevocable Trust - A trust that cannot be changed, canceled, or "revoked" once it is set up. A "living trust" is not an example of an irrevocable trust. Insurance trusts and "Children's Trusts," or "2503 Trusts," are examples of irrevocable trusts. Irrevocable trusts are treated by the IRS very differently than revocable trusts.

Insurance Trust - An irrevocable trust used to hold insurance and pass it on to your heirs without any estate taxes on the death benefits of the policy.

Issue - A legal term used in wills and trusts meaning one's children, grandchildren, etc., either through birth or adoption.

Joint Ownership - The situation where two or more people own the same piece of property together. The property can be "owned" by the people as joint tenants, tenants in common, tenants by the entirety and other legally defined relationships.

Joint Tenancy - When two or more people take title to the same property and simultaneously each owns 100% of the property, or has full rights to the property. At the death of one joint tenant, his or her share immediately transfers to the ownership of the survivor(s).

Jurisdiction - The location where a person has access to the court system. The place where a person lives usually determines which court has the legal right to adjudicate his or her claims, probate proceedings, or other matters. The location of real property can also determine the "jurisdiction" of legal matters related to that property.

Kristy - One of the authors of this book, and she really wanted a "K" word in the glossary.

Letters Testamentary - A formal court order (document) issued by a probate judge giving the personal representative authority to conduct business, contract, sell estate property, pay bills, distribute estate property, and otherwise act on behalf of the estate.

Life Estate - The right to have all of the benefit from a property during one's lifetime. The person with the right doesn't own the property, and when he or she dies, the property is not included in his or her estate.

Life Insurance Trust - A type of irrevocable trust used to hold life insurance. When a life insurance policy is held in an insurance trust, it is protected from estate taxes when the insured dies; provided the trust is established properly, managed properly, and the insured does not retain any "incidents of ownership."

Living Trust - A type of revocable trust used in estate planning to avoid probate, help in situations of incompetency, and allow "smooth" management of assets after the death of the grantor or person who established the trust. The trust can be effective in eliminating or reducing estate taxes for married couples. Living revocable trusts are established during the life of the grantor, who retains the right to the income and principal and the right to amend or revoke the trust. When the grantor dies, the trust becomes irrevocable and acts as a substitute for a traditional will.

Living Will - A document defining your "right to die." It usually states that you do not want to have your life artificially prolonged by modern medical technologies. You can specifically define the means which you do not want used or do want used.

Lunch Theory of Justice - Lee's theory concerning the way courts dispense justice, i.e., the outcome of a case depends on what the judge or jury ate for lunch. We don't really believe that, because we have a deep respect for the jury system, but the outcome of some cases can't be explained any other way.

Loving Trust - Another name for a living trust. The term "loving trust" was popularized in the 1980's by a group selling living trusts.

Marital Deduction - The unlimited deduction allowed under federal estate tax law for all qualifying property passing from the estate of the deceased spouse to the surviving spouse. The value of the property passing to the surviving spouse under the marital deduction is "deducted" from the deceased spouse's estate before federal estate taxes are calculated on the estate. Proper planning and use of the deduction allows more property to pass estate tax free to the family.

Marital Deduction Trust - The trust which "receives" the property passed under the marital deduction laws, from the deceased spouse's estate to the surviving spouse. Property in the marital deduction trust will be included as part of the surviving spouse's estate (for estate tax purposes) when he or she dies.

Minor - A child who is not old enough to have the legal capacity to govern his or her own affairs. Depending upon the specific state and the specific laws being applied, a minor is usually either under 21 years old or 18 years old.

Net Taxable Estate - The value of an estate upon which the federal estate tax is levied. The net taxable estate or "net value" is the total or "gross value" of the estate less liabilities, expenses and other deductions allowed by the tax laws.

Notice - The legally prescribed process of making someone aware of a legal proceeding or matter.

Notarized - The affirmation of an agent (the notary) of the state affirming that the signature on the document being "notarized" is in fact the signature of the person purportedly signing the document.

Notary - A person who has state granted authority to certify the validity or authenticity of the signature being made on a document.

Pay on Death Account - See POD Account.

Per Capita - A method of distributing an estate such that all of the surviving descendants share equally in the property. Also know as Pro Rata.

Per Stirpes - The most common way of distributing an estate such that if one of the children is dead, his or her children share equally in his or her share. Also know as By Right of Representation.

Perpetuities Savings Clause - A "safety net" clause included in most trusts, which automatically terminates the trust at the last possible moment to prevent any possible violation of trust law caused because the general terms of the trust did not properly provide for a termination of the trust as required by law. Under most state laws a trust must have a finite "life" and end prior to the time required by law.

Personal Letter - A letter directing the distribution of personal items. This letter is referenced in a person's will and is recognized by the courts upon the death of the person making the will and letter.

Personal Property - Property other than real estate (land and permanent structures on the land). Cars, furniture, securities, bank accounts, and animals are examples of personal property.

Personal Representative - The "modern" term for the executor or executrix, who is the court appointed individual that probates the will and carries out the will's instructions under court supervision.

POD Account - A bank account that is designed to avoid probate. It is a contract between the bank and the account holder guaranteeing that, upon the account holder's death, the bank will pay the balance of the account to whomever is designated to receive the account.

Pour-over Trust - A trust designed to receive property that is "poured over" into it. The property is usually "poured over" or received from a pour-over will through the probate process.

Pour-over Will - A will which contains a clause that transfers some or all of the assets that pass through the will into a trust for final distribution from the trust. The will's assets are said to "pour over" into the trust.

Power of Appointment - The power given to a person, by appointment in a will or a trust, to distribute the property that passes through the will or trust at the discretion of the person appointed. Other than to give the appointed person the authority to make the distribution, the will or trust doesn't make distribution of the property.

Power of Attorney - A document established by an individual (the principal) granting another person (the agent) the right and authority to handle the financial affairs for the principal. A power of attorney becomes invalid at the death or incompetency of the principal, unless the power of attorney is a "durable power of attorney" which remains in effect after the principal becomes incompetent.

Prenuptial Agreement - A contract between two potential marriage partners specifying how the property owned by each prior to marriage and owned individually or jointly during marriage will be divided should the couple divorce.

Primary Beneficiary - The person or persons for whose benefit a trust is originally established. When conditions change and the primary beneficiaries are no longer in a position to receive the benefit of the trust, the benefit goes to the "secondary beneficiaries."

Probate - The legal process which facilitates the transfer of a deceased person's property whether they leave a will or don't leave any will. The court establishes the authenticity of the will (if any), appoints a personal representative or administrator, identifies heirs and creditors, directs payment of debts and taxes, and oversees distributions of the assets according to the will or state law in the absence of a will.

Probate Court - The part of the judicial system dedicated to handling probate matters which includes settlement of intestate and testate estates, adoptions, appointment of guardians, name changes, and other matters.

Probate Estate - A deceased person's property which is subject to the probate process. Property held in a living trust is usually not considered part of the probate estate.

Probate Fees - The fees, often a percentage of the estate, paid to the attorney and others who handle the probate proceeding.

Proving a Will - The process of establishing the validity of a will before the probate court. (See Self Proving Will)

QTIP Trust - A Qualified Terminable Interest Trust (Q-Tip) is a type of trust which provides an unlimited marital deduction for qualified property put into the trust. However, rather than permitting the surviving spouse to have full power to distribute the property to anyone he or she wishes, the trust restricts the ability of the surviving spouse to distribute the property in the trust to a select group of individuals, such as the children, as agreed when both spouses were alive. Without the new QTIP laws, any attempt to "tie down" the property and restrict the surviving spouse's rights to transfer the trust property would have resulted in the property not qualifying for the marital deduction tax benefit.

Quitclaim Deed - A document (a deed) that transfers a person's interest in a piece of real estate, without the warranties or guarantees that are made in a warranty deed.

Revocable Trust - A trust which can be amended or revoked by the person(s) who established the trust.

Real Property - Land and attachments to the land, such as buildings, fences, etc.

Right to Die - The right to decide not to have life prolonged by extraordinary, artificial means.

Rule Against Perpetuities - A rule of law limiting the duration of a trust. Some trusts can go on in perpetuity (forever), but most types of trusts have a maximum duration or life established by law.

Section 2053 Trusts - A type of irrevocable trust, authorized by section 2503 of the IRS code, often established for children. Section 2503 allows annual gifts up to $10,000 to be made to the trust, rather than directly to the child, and still have the gift qualify for the $10,000 annual gift tax exclusion.

Self Proving Will - A will which has been properly witnessed (by either two or three witnesses depending on state laws) and the witnesses have signed an affidavit before a notary public stating that all of the proper formalities of the will's execution have been complied with. This usually makes it very easy for the court to "prove" the will.

Separate Property - In community property states, all property which is not held commonly by a married couple is considered separate property. In general, it is property owned by one spouse in which the other spouse does not own an interest.

Settlor - A person who establishes a trust. The term settlor is used interchangeably with the terms "trustor" and "grantor."

Simple Trust - Trusts that are established with terms that require the trust to "pay" all of its income out, so that it does not accumulate income on which income taxes would have to be paid.

Spendthrift - An individual who cannot handle money wisely and spends it wastefully.

Split Gift - Each spouse is entitled to give any individual $10,000 in a calendar year and, provided it is given properly, there is no tax consequence to the giver or receiver according to the "annual exclusion" laws. However, if a married couple tries to give more than $10,000 to an individual, they must file a gift tax form declaring that the gift is split between them. If the form is not filed, the IRS cannot determine who gave the gift or gifts, and one member of the couple may be allocated the entire gift amount. Thus, he or she would actually owe a gift tax because his or her gift was over $10,000.

Springing Power - A power to act on the occurrence of some certain criteria, such as an illness or incompetency. The power is said to spring into existence upon the occurrence of the event. The agent's power to act for the principal under a durable power of attorney is usually a springing power.

Sprinkle or Sprinkling Power - The power given a trustee to decide how, when and why to distribute trust income to the trust's different beneficiaries. The sprinkling power allows the trustee to "sprinkle" the trust's income over the beneficiaries. It is a valuable power to give the trustee in irrevocable trusts because is allows the trustee to distribute income to the beneficiaries who will pay the smallest amount of income tax on the distribution.

Sprinkling Trust - A trust that grants the trustee a sprinkling power which allows the trustee to decide how, when and why to distribute the trust income among the trust's beneficiaries.

Spouse - Legal term for husband or wife.

Stepped-up Basis - The new basis established for a property after the property has been evaluated and taxed as part of an estate. The new basis or "stepped-up basis" is the value of the property used to assess the estate tax.

Successor Trustee - The trustee who takes over when the initial trustee can no longer function.

Surviving Spouse - The husband or wife that lives after the death of his or her spouse.

Taxable Estate - The portion of an estate that is subject to federal estate taxes or state death taxes. Technically, all of an estate is subject to federal estate taxes, but because of the unified credit, only estates with a value over the exemption equivalent amount actually have to pay any estate taxes (see Appendix 1). Therefore, it is common to refer to an estate with a value over the exemption equivalent amount as a taxable estate and an estate with a value under the exemption equivalent amount as a nontaxable estate.

Tenants by the Entirety - A way of owning property which, for almost all practical purposes, is the same as joint tenants. Tenancies by the entirety are creations of state law and are used only between husbands and wives, whereas joint tenancies can be used by anyone, not just by husbands and wives, who wants to own property jointly.

Tenants in Common - A way of owning property in which two or more owners all "share" ownership of the property. The owners can own various percentages of the whole property, unlike joint tenants which each own an equal share. When one owner dies, his or her share does not "automatically" go to the other owner(s), because tenancies in common do not have a survivorship provision like joint tenancies.

Testamentary Trust - A trust created by a will.

Testate - One who dies leaving a will.

Title - Document proving ownership of property.

Totten Trust - A bank account that is designed to get around probate. The account is created by a person in his or her own name as the trustee for another person. It is a type of revocable trust until the creator dies, then it is paid out to the designated beneficiary(ies).

Trust - A legal document in which property is held and managed by a trustee for the benefit of another known as a beneficiary. A trust is a relationship in which property is held by one person for the benefit of another. The trust can be created verbally, but will most often be in writing.

Trust Certificate - A summary of the trust's terms prepared by an attorney that evidences the trust exists.

Trust Corpus or Res - The property of a trust.

Trustee - The person or institution that manages the trust property under the terms of the trust.

Trustor - A person who establishes a trust. The term trustor is used interchangeably with the terms "settlor" and "grantor."

Unified Credit - A tax credit is given to each person by the IRS to be used during his or her life or after his or her death. The tax credit equals the amount of tax (gift or estate) which is assessed on the exemption equivalent value of property. It is considered the "unified" credit because it applies to both gift taxes and estate taxes and results from the IRS's effort to unify these two taxes or make them consistent. It is often thought that the total value of taxed gifts and estate transfers can equal the exemption equivalent before any tax is assessed. This thought is wrong because a tax is actually assessed on the first dollar of taxable gift or estate property. Note: Some property gifted is not exposed to the unified tax; for example, gifts that qualify for the annual gift tax exclusion ($10,000). Some property transferred in an estate is not exposed to the unified tax, such as property which goes to a spouse and qualifies for the unlimited marital deduction. Although a tax is assessed, the individual doesn't actually pay the tax on amounts up to the exemption equivalent maximum because the unified credit is applied against the tax.

Uniform Gift to Minors Act - A series of state statutes that provides a method for transferring property by gift to minors who cannot legally manage the property for themselves. The laws allow an adult to manage the property and yet not have it owned by the adult.

Uniform Probate Code - A standardized code designed by the American Law Institute to streamline the probate process. Many states have not adopted the code as part of their laws.

Unlimited Marital Deduction - The tax law that allows a person to give an unlimited value of property as a gift, or leave an estate of unlimited value to his or her spouse without a gift or estate tax being assessed.

Warranty Deed - A deed which warrants that certain contracts will "run" (continue) with your property.

Will - A legal document stating the intentions of a deceased person concerning the distribution of his or her property, and management of his or her affairs following his or her death. State law dictates the legality of a will.

Index

Index

Symbols

A

B

C

D

E

F

G

H

I

U

W

Y

Additional Resources

Additional Financial Protection and Profit-Making Resources for Families and Businesses by Lee and Kristy Phillips

Protecting Your Financial Future: The Inside Story on Wills, Living Trusts, Probate, Estate Taxes, and Asset Protection: Protect your loved ones and your money from taxes, probate, lawsuits and other threats. With this book, you'll understand how to sidestep financial pitfalls that are inevitable without preparation.

Speaking: Lee Phillips is an internationally sought-after speaker. His asset protection lectures have been given to groups of doctors, lawyers, CPA's, insurance professionals, millionaires, real estate agents, clubs, national associations of all sorts, company meetings, retirement groups and almost every other type of group you can imagine. His lectures range from two hour overviews to five day luxury retreats and cruises for the superwealthy. If your group needs to book a speaker, his humor and practical advice mix to make an event the attendees will never forget. He motivates people to change their lives. Call well in advance to book Lee as a speaker.

Continuing Education Credit: Protecting Your Financial Future and several of the other courses developed by Lee and Kristy are qualified for CE credit by many organizations. Lee's lectures can almost always be qualified as a CE course for an organization. For example, *Protecting Your Financial Future* is now accepted by the National Certified Financial Planners' Board, Certified Life Underwriters, and PACE for five hours of CE credit, and it meets the requirements for many state insurance, CPA, and other organizations. Lee and Kristy's Internet training materials also qualify for CE credit with teachers, dietitians, CPA's and other groups.

Accumulation and Preservation of Wealth: For the person serious about protecting themselves, an eight-hour audio tape lecture course by Lee Phillips loaded with proven strategies on effective tax planning, estate planning, and asset protection. Step-by-step instructions allow you to save thousands in legal fees and fully protect yourself and your business using wills, living trusts, durable powers of attorney, general partnerships, limited partnerships, irrevocable children's trusts, life insurance trusts, corporations, and leases. Includes a 361-page manual with an example of each document discussed and a computer disk with each sample document in electronic format. No legal expertise necessary. *Call 1-800-806-1997 for free introductory audio tape, "Asset Protection Strategies."*

Flexible Benefit Plan/Retirement Savings Plan: Four-hour audio tape lecture course by Lee Phillips which shows you and your company how to maximize your retirement and employee benefits by using the legal system to your advantage. Easy-to-follow instructions teach you to use and self-administer Section 125 benefit plans (self-directed tax advantaged benefit plans) and 401K retirement plans. Course includes a 249-page manual with samples of the legal documents required by the law for both plans; including the plan documents, plan summaries, administrative trusts and compliance forms. All documents are in printed form and on disk. No legal expertise necessary.

Business Success Source: 169-page primer to help you start a profitable, legally sound business. This guide covers the essentials for every entrepreneur. Discusses partnerships, LLCs, corporations, limited partnerships, and more; how to comply with laws; how to finance your business; and how to pick a business that suits your personality.

How to Approach a Venture Capital Firm: 81-page book that demonstrates how to successfully present your business ideas to a venture capitalist. You'll learn how to pick the right firm for your idea, present your business plan, use the law to protect your idea, and structure a profitable agreement.

Capital Source Course: A 90-minute audio tape lecture by Lee Phillips introducing you to one of the hottest new business opportunities: the venture capital industry. Includes a 64-page manual that walks you through the use of Capital Source, Inc.'s computerized database of venture capital firms. The database lets you make a profitable match with your business needs and venture capital companies interested in filling those needs. Also loaded with tips on how to make money helping others fund their projects. *Call 1-800-806-1997 for free introductory audio tape.*

Superhighway to Wealth: Making Money on the Internet: 241 pages packed with everything you need to know to make money on the Internet. Discusses each of the Internet tools and how they can be used in business applications. Discover how you can market your product or service using the Internet (not just the World Wide Web) to gain advantage over your competition. Easy-to-understand format — no prior Internet knowledge necessary. *Call 1-800-WANT NET (1-800-926-8638) for a free business opportunity audio tape.*

WorldWalk Internet Power: A comprehensive training course which shows you how to maximize the benefits of the Internet. Includes two 60-minute video tapes and six workbooks. Using it is just like having an Internet expert sitting next to you teaching you all about this century's most powerful business and personal tool. The course includes up-to-date information about the World Wide Web, E-mail, chat, FTP, searching methods, and even the logistics of getting on the net if you are a beginner. Courses are designed for the beginning or the advanced Net user. *Call 1-800-WANT NET (1-800-926-8638) for free informational brochure.*

NetProfits: This 120-page manual is designed to boost your bottom line by showing you how to advertise with some of the best shopping malls on the Internet. It includes step-by-step instructions on submitting ads ranging from simple classified ads to the most elaborate on-line catalogs. Discover how the Internet advertising industry can be a profitable new business opportunity. *Call 1-800-WANT NET (1-800-926-8638) for free introductory audio tape.*

TO ORDER, CONTACT:
LegaLees Corporation
P.O. Box 1275
Provo, UT 84603-1275
801-377-5952
800-806-1997
30-DAY MONEY-BACK GUARANTEE ON ALL PRODUCTS.
VISA/MASTERCARD ACCEPTED.